"At once simple but profound, humble but sophisticated, unassuming but gently compelling, and subtle but absolutely riveting, this volume offers finely honed pearls of wisdom for implementing growth-promoting and loving connection. … A magnificent piece that will most certainly prove to be an invaluable resource for anyone with a heart and the desire to forge more meaningful connectedness with others."

– **Martha Stark, M.D.**, *faculty at Harvard Medical School and award-winning author of nine books on psychoanalytic theory and practice*

"If you thought you knew what listening is and does, get ready for a mind- and heart-opening journey of discovery. This remarkable tour through the universe of listeners' responses comes alive with the visceral impacts of attuned versus misattuned listening. *The Listening Book* is a potent, unique, and inspiring guide for enriching and deepening your experience of human connection."

– **Diane Poole Heller, Ph.D.**, *psychotherapist and author of* The Power of Attachment: How to Create Deep and Lasting Intimate Relationships

"With charming stories, practical suggestions, and deep insights, this beautiful book shows us how to truly listen – with profound benefits for others, and oneself. It's really a gem, a delightful and comprehensive guide to one of the most important human skills."

– **Rick Hanson, Ph.D.**, *author of* Hardwiring Happiness: The New Brain Science of Contentment, Calm, and Confidence *and* Making Great Relationships: Simple Practices for Solving Conflicts, Building Cooperation, and Fostering Love

"When I was training counselors my repeated advice was 'stop and listen.' If the professional listeners needed reminding, how much more the rest of us! Ticic, Kushner, and Ecker have given us the essential and pragmatic guide to listening for a world that has, to a large degree, stopped listening. But with active listening and empathic responding we can change the world, and *The Listening Book* will equip you to do just that."

– **Matthew Dahlitz, MC**, *editor-in-chief of* The Science of Psychotherapy *and co-author of* The Practitioner's Guide to The Science of Psychotherapy

T0351663

"*The Listening Book* is a great way to unpack what listening is all about. Whether you are a good listener who wants to get better, or a not-so-good listener who is perplexed about why your conversations invariably hit walls, this book is for you. This book is also a dream book for therapy students and therapists, especially for those early in their path. Regardless of the model you are practicing, this book will show you, step by accessible step, what to do and also very importantly, what not to do so that your clients feel heard and understood – because once they do, then you can use all the other fancy techniques you are learning, and they will work. Finally, this book is for your inner nerd who wants to have the science behind listening and its transformative powers.

All this is accomplished through ordinary and relatable stories of people in different interpersonal situations: The dialogue is broken down, line by line, into *connecters* and *disconnectors*: The reader gets to see so clearly how certain comments help people feel understood, while other seemingly innocuous responses alienate and distance. We get a kind of x-ray of people's inner thoughts and inner experience where the protagonists tell us their experience of the comments they receive in such a way that we know exactly why they felt understood and 'gotten' or, alternatively, painfully misunderstood, dismissed and turned off to that relationship.

Add to this the cutting-edge neuroscience of *memory reconsolidation* that explains how feeling heard can be a life-changing, transformative experience, particularly for those who have not felt heard in this way, and you've got yourself a gem of a book: super accessible, easy to read, easy to understand and most important of all, easy to apply. *The Listening Book* is a how-to guide for being a good listener and making those around you, be they family, friends, lovers or clients, feel heard, gotten and understood."

– **Diana Fosha, Ph.D.**, *developer of AEDP, founder of the AEDP Institute, and editor of* Undoing Aloneness and the Transformation of Suffering into Flourishing: AEDP 2.0

The Listening Book

Satisfying, secure connection with others depends heavily on how well we listen to each other and respond to what we've heard. *The Listening Book* lays bare the key elements of both deeply attuned and badly misattuned listening in vivid scenes of real-life interactions that capture the emotional impact and give the reader an illuminating "aha" experience. Added to that is a mind-opening account of psychological processes and principles that normally operate from outside of awareness, showing how skillful listening can reveal those dynamics. Beyond even that, such listening can produce interactions that unlock lifelong emotional conditioning to yield liberating change through one of the brain's most remarkable processes, which neuroscientists call memory reconsolidation. Whether read solo, with a partner, or in a reading group, *The Listening Book* is for everyone who yearns for deeper emotional connection and closeness, everyone who is at a loss to understand what is interfering, and everyone who is fascinated by the subtle and manifold factors involved in interpersonal communication.

Robin Ticic, B.A., HP Psychotherapy (Germany) is director of training for the Coherence Psychology Institute and co-author of *Unlocking the Emotional Brain: Memory Reconsolidation and the Psychotherapy of Transformational Change*.

Elise Kushner, B.A., HP Psychotherapy (Germany) is therapist, coach, and supervisor, as well as trainer of coherence therapy and coherence coaching for the Coherence Psychology Institute.

Bruce Ecker, M.A., L.M.F.T., is co-director of the Coherence Psychology Institute, co-originator of coherence therapy, and co-author of *Unlocking the Emotional Brain: Memory Reconsolidation and the Psychotherapy of Transformational Change*.

The Listening Book

How to Create a World of Rich Connections and Surprising Growth by Actually Hearing Each Other

Robin Ticic, Elise Kushner, and Bruce Ecker

Routledge
Taylor & Francis Group

NEW YORK AND LONDON

Designed cover image by Elise Kushner

First published 2023
by Routledge
605 Third Avenue, New York, NY 10158

and by Routledge
4 Park Square, Milton Park, Abingdon, Oxon, OX14 4RN

Routledge is an imprint of the Taylor & Francis Group, an informa business

ISBN: 978-1-032-25646-7 (hbk)
ISBN: 978-1-032-25645-0 (pbk)
ISBN: 978-1-003-28858-9 (ebk)

DOI: 10.4324/9781003288589

Typeset in Bembo
by Deanta Global Publishing Services, Chennai, India

Access the Support Material: https://resourcecentre.routledge.com/
books/9781032256450

Dedicated to
meeting the need of the entire human family
for living together with kindness and mutual understanding

Contents

Contents

Foreword

Co-authored by longtime friends and close collaborators Robin Ticic, Elise Kushner, and Bruce Ecker and specially designed for easy access by growth-minded laypeople, *The Listening Book* is a gently nuanced and deeply humane book about the power of compassionate listening to create authentic connection and even emotional healing. It is an unpretentious and understated gem of a book that explores the wondrously satisfying impact of listening to others with open-minded acceptance, open-hearted compassion, and loving kindness.

Although written by three highly esteemed, neuroscientifically informed psycho-therapists at the forefront of the rapidly evolving field of memory reconsolidation, the book is down-to-earth and eminently readable. At once simple but profound, humble but sophisticated, unassuming but gently compelling, and subtle but absolutely rivet-ing, this volume offers finely honed pearls of wisdom for implementing growth-pro-moting and loving connection. A treasure trove of invaluable "secrets" gleaned from the magical synergy of the three authors' clinical practices, immersions in theory, and personal experiences, the net result is a magnificent piece that will most certainly prove to be an enduring resource for anyone with a heart and the desire to forge more meaningful connectedness with others.

The format of the book is ingenious, engaging, and evocative. It first features a series of brief interpersonal encounters; then proposes alternative, connection-pro-moting scenarios; then segues into a highlighting of the underlying neuroscientific processes at play. Throughout, it encourages readers to discover their own voice and their own capacity for empathic attunement – always reminding the reader that finely tuned listening is a precious skill that can be cultivated and a joy both to offer and to receive. In truth, the creative and intimate way in which Robin, Elise, and Bruce have masterfully structured the material invites the reader to join alongside them as they tease out the elements of misattuned listening that disrupt and make for painful disconnection between people and, by way of contrast, the elements of quality listening that foster exhilarating connection and "moments of meeting" that give meaning, purpose, and direction to lives that might otherwise have remained disengaged, isolated, and lonely.

But there's more. Not only are the authors deeply spiritual in their sensibilities and extraordinarily gifted as clinicians, but they also have made it their business to do a deep dive into the literature on memory reconsolidation research in order to understand the conditions required by the brain so that deep, liberating change is the result. They can therefore speak with authority when they put forth their claim that conscious, intentional listening and empathic understanding not only foster meaningful interpersonal relatedness but also hold the uplifting and hope-infused potential to effect profound and lasting change by targeting the deepest levels of emotional conditioning. This felicitous impact is possible because of the adaptive capacity of the brain and the dynamic nature of memory.

Indeed, the book's short but vivid vignettes seamlessly, subtly, and subliminally interlace theory and practice. It becomes clear that people do not always need to be in therapy to transform their original, distress-based narratives that were constructed in an urgent yet adaptive attempt to make sense of things but that no longer serve. Such constructions of reality can be unlearned – even eradicated! – and replaced by fresh, updated, more empowering, and more reality-based emotional learnings. One door closes and another door opens.

I myself, as a dyed-in-the-wool psychoanalyst (by training and decades of practice and numerous published books), had always assumed that profound and sustained in-depth change was possible only within the context of a long-term therapy relationship. It was therefore quite an eye-opening and humbling experience for me when, some years ago, I had the privilege of stumbling upon the brilliantly inspired and pioneering therapeutic work of Bruce Ecker and his colleagues, which demonstrated to me the reality of profound change produced by a much shorter and very different kind of therapeutic process. I certainly owe Bruce and his collaborators a debt of gratitude for opening my eyes and my heart to the much more hopeful, optimistic, and enlivening realm of transformational change through memory reconsolidation. This led me to a major expansion of the psychotherapeutic framework I had long been developing, in order to go beyond the limiting conceptualizations of psychoanalytically informed models and incorporate fully the memory reconsolidation revolution.

I am sure that all readers of *The Listening Book*, whether they are laypeople or clinicians, will find themselves similarly captivated by the gently persuasive power of the heartwarmingly uplifting approach to life that Robin, Elise, and Bruce are espousing

– a refreshingly non-pathologizing perspective that offers the opportunity to embrace new, more gratifying, and mutually rewarding relationships.

And underlying the richly textured tapestry that they weave for the reader is their shared passion and desire to make our world, someday, a much better place. Their contribution to this worthy endeavor is in the form of this love-infused and inspirational volume, in which they are able to demonstrate repeatedly the transformational power – for both giver and receiver – of mutual respect, authentic presence, radical acceptance, nonjudgmental listening, open-heartedness, and loving kindness.

The Listening Book is so beautifully and sensitively drawn and explores with such finesse the fine points and subtleties of empathic attunement and listening presence that it should probably be required reading not only for all therapists, but for all people. And as for myself, since I have already read it twice, I know that I will be placing this lovingly rendered work of outstanding artistry within easy reach on one of the bookshelves in my library – right next to my treasured tomes by Freud, Kohut, Winnicott, Guntrip, and Frankl.

Martha Stark, M.D.
Cambridge, Massachusetts, July 2022
Faculty, Harvard Medical School
Creator of the Psychodynamic Synergy Paradigm
Award-winning author with nine books on the integration of psychoanalytic theory and practice, including Modes of Therapeutic Action: Enhancement of Knowledge, Provision of Experience, and Engagement in Relationship

Preface

Each time one of our psychotherapy clients tells us, "You're the first person who has ever really listened and tried to *understand* me!" we are struck yet again by how many people go through life without ever feeling really listened to, really heard, and really understood on a deep level by their closest people. Can those among us who haven't had the good fortune to receive such listening, understanding, and connection possibly provide that to *their* most important people? In living without feeling heard, one soldiers on, enduring a nameless despair and desolation of disconnection and aloneness, even when others are physically present, and without necessarily recognizing what's missing because it just seems to be the nature of human life. Depression is in many cases the mood of feeling hopelessly stranded in that disconnection and aloneness.

What explains the rarity of high-quality listening? Perhaps the cause of its rarity can be found in the very essence of such listening: You park yourself in silence, you forget about time, you forget about yourself, and you give the entire attention of your mind and heart to the other person. In other words, such listening is done from a state of mind that is relatively egoless. Could the unfamiliarity of that stance be why it's rare? If so, then cultivating not only the skills but also, more fundamentally, the *capacity* for that stance of true listening will be a major gain for the listener, a gain that could be viewed as spiritual growth.

This book pays attention, very closely, to listening. You might even say that in this book we are listening to listening. And both highly skilled listening and very unskilled listening get our full, sustained attention. See whether you agree that what becomes apparent in the course of reading this book is this: Giving high-quality listening to someone is an act of remarkable loving-kindness that actually connects two selves internally. You'll be privy to many instances of that happening on the pages that follow.

What can emerge from attuned listening and the connection it creates, beyond how good it feels in the moment to both receiver and giver, is also remarkable. People's behaviors, emotions, and thoughts that sometimes seem senseless or irrational when viewed from an external perspective prove to make complete sense. That coherent sense exists and operates in a person's *interior* world of meaning, which actually becomes apparent when deep listening goes there. Recognizing the coherence of one's own inner world is an illumination that can be freeing and life-changing. It can in turn engage the brain's innate capability to unlock the emotional conditioning of a lifetime through the process of *memory reconsolidation*, which we now understand thanks to neuroscience research since 2000 and extensive use of that process in psychotherapy. It is a natural process that occurs and creates liberating change also in daily life outside of psychotherapy. Each of us is equipped with this capability for change, and we can greatly help each other make use of it through ... listening.

~ ~ ~ ~ ~

This book is designed for a wide range of possible usages and situations, from individual to group, from text to workbook, and from personal reading to counseling and other professional settings. Of course, it is not a replacement for professional therapeutic help, if needed.

A note about pronouns: Our intent is for our writing to be gender-neutral and to make *all* readers feel respected, recognized, and included, but the pronoun problem is a conundrum that seems to require a compromise between the goal of a smooth reading and the goal of explicit recognition. We have used composite binary pronouns such as "he or she" and "his or her" as our way of referring to the entire spectrum of gender and genderless possibilities. We ask that you mentally adjust the pronouns to fit for you and your situation, because this body of knowledge is for everyone.

Acknowledgments

Our big, deep, heartfelt appreciation goes to Els Das, Jackie Dering, Mary Jo Keating, Juliana Kushner, Melissa Reading, Patrick Roost, and John Ticic for their feedback on the developing manuscript, including much patient discussion of many details. We climbed further up our own learning curves for writing about listening, thanks to your pointing out where we needed to say more and where we needed to say less.

Special thanks go to Michał Jasiński for the strong support generated for this book in the course of his international work as a trainer and Associate Instructor of the Coherence Psychology Institute.

Routledge Publisher Anna Moore once again has our gratitude for being the ideal publishing companion and guide, supportively responding to our questions and needs without delay and with creativity and patience.

Of course, we are standing on the shoulders of many major contributors of invaluable knowledge in the fields of psychology, psychotherapy, and memory reconsolidation research – far too many to name here, but we know who they are, and we honor them.

And it's not an exaggeration to say that all people we've ever crossed paths with have contributed to what understanding we have of listening. Family, friends, colleagues, clients, teachers and students, physicians and nurses, shopkeepers, and people with whom we've had chance encounters on the street: All of you are here somewhere.

Lastly, each of the three authors gratefully wants to acknowledge the other two for making possible this complexly rewarding journey together – a journey fueled by a shared passion for understanding and fostering deep well-being, and infused with mutual respect, the spirit of cooperation, and much listening to one another.

About the authors

Robin Ticic, B.A., HP Psychotherapy (Germany), is in private practice near Cologne, Germany, specializing in trauma therapy, and for many years served as a psychologist for the Psychotraumatology Institute of the University of Cologne. She is the director of development and training for the Coherence Psychology Institute and a certified trainer of coherence therapy. She is coauthor of *Unlocking the Emotional Brain: Eliminating Symptoms at Their Roots Using Memory Reconsolidation* and author of the parenting guide *How to Connect with Your Child*. She has extensive experience in counseling parents and conducting courses and presentations, and has been honored for community service.

Elise Kushner, B.A., HP Psychotherapy (Germany), lives and works in Cologne, Germany as a practitioner of coherence therapy, a certified trainer of coherence coaching, a systemic coach, and as a trainer in the areas of interpersonal communication, coaching competencies for leaders, and gender awareness. She has been a guest lecturer at Furtwangen University. She has served as consultant for multiple authors in her areas of expertise. She is also a composer and choral director, with an academic degree in music.

Bruce Ecker, M.A., L.M.F.T., is co-director of the Coherence Psychology Institute, co-originator of coherence therapy, and co-author of *Unlocking the Emotional Brain: Eliminating Symptoms at Their Roots Using Memory Reconsolidation*, the *Coherence Therapy Practice Manual and Training Guide*, and *Depth Oriented Brief Therapy: How to Be Brief When You Were Trained to Be Deep and Vice Versa*. Clarifying how transformational therapeutic change takes place is the central theme of his clinical career, and he has contributed many innovations in concepts and methods of experiential psychotherapy. Since 2006 he has led the development of the clinical application of the neuroscience of memory reconsolidation, driving major advancements in the effectiveness and unification of psychotherapy and identifying its most potent underlying mechanism of change. He lives in New York City, is a frequent presenter at conferences and workshops internationally, and leads the institute's team of researchers.

Contact us here:

www.thelisteningbook.com

Prologue

Have you ever felt not heard, to a quite surprising degree? That's happened to all of us, all through the ages – young and old, rich and poor, real and fictional …

~ ~ ~ ~ ~

Cinderella made it to the ball, just barely, and out of breath. She spotted a group of girls from her neighborhood, who were, thankfully, in a different corner of the room from her evil stepsisters, so she headed toward her friends.

"Hey, you made it!" said Basilea. "I was starting to wonder what happened to you."

"What took you so long?" asked Philippa.

"Well, since you're asking," Cinderella explained, "I had to sweep the hearth, make the beds, wash the pots and pans, harvest the vegetables, and clean the stables. And then I had to wait for my Fairy Godmother to come, since I didn't have a dress or wheels."

Beatrice shot back, "You'll never guess what *I* had to do today. I had to iron my own dress! That was *such* a drag, and it completely *ruined* my mood!"

Cinderella was grateful that Prince Herlewin chose that moment to approach the group and ask her to dance. He was, as we know, entranced with her natural charm and beauty and spent the entire evening at her side. At midnight the great bell in the church tower began tolling, and Cinderella knew she had to flee before the twelfth stroke. "I must leave you now!" she whispered urgently in Prince Herlewin's ear.

"No need to panic, Cinderella. I can escort you home later if you want to stay longer," replied the prince.

"No, you don't understand. My entire world is about to fall apart! I have to go! Now!"

"Aren't you being overly dramatic?" he asked.

On that jarring note, Cinderella, wincing, raced to her waiting coach. When she arrived home, she summoned her Fairy Godmother and told her all about the ball: the fancy dresses, the handsome prince, the lively dancing, and the painful struggle to be heard and understood by other people.

Fairy Godmother said, "Ah, yes. Yes, indeed. Cinderella, my dear, there *is* something that could be done about that. It's a quite magical power that all people can learn to wield, *if* they are open and actually *want* to learn it. It's called ... *listening*."

Introduction

We change our world by listening

It's literally true: You can change the world by listening. In fact, you already do! We all do. Every choice we make about how to interact with others has ripple effects, making people's lives different from how they would have been without us.

By honing our listening skills, all of us have the opportunity to enrich our interpersonal relationships dramatically, minimize conflicts, and maximize peaceful, respectful interactions with partners, children, relatives, friends, neighbors, coworkers, and colleagues. Each of us again and again has the possibility to change the world into a place of more caring, kindness, understanding, and acceptance of one another.

Have you experienced relationships in which you feel free to express what you're really feeling, free to be your authentic self, being heard and seen and accepted as you are? If you can easily think of such a relationship, then you are truly fortunate. If you can't think of such a relationship at this moment and you long to be heard – really *listened to* and *understood* – then please know that you share that longing with the vast majority of people around the world.

Just imagine feeling free to share any problem with a friend, knowing you'll simply be deeply understood … and not told what you should or shouldn't be feeling, believing, or doing. Imagine parents giving their children sensitive understanding of what they're feeling, experiencing, and needing, rather than failing to register or even disregarding all that, as though how they're feeling doesn't matter.

We humans have an innate need for deep, rich connections of these kinds. We need to feel accepted and validated by others who are close to us. And in fact, such connection with *ourselves* is just as necessary as with others – though this is a novel idea to many people. Giving ourselves kindness and understanding dispels much inner conflict and distress, and makes room for inner shifts toward greater well-being.

All this is *true* wealth in life – a major source of happiness and stability. There's so much that we tend to strive for that we don't really need, and that therefore doesn't fulfill us even when attained. And all along, we can give and receive more of what we really *do* need for mental and emotional well-being.

The art of listening is the path to fulfilling those needs. We're talking about *conscious, intentional* listening for deep and empathic understanding of a person – a capability that is fascinating to cultivate and a joy to use! You'll discover that learning about people by listening to them – yourself included – is generally the path of greatest satisfaction as well as least resistance, because virtually everyone wants to feel heard and understood. Listening is what connects us and brings to life the feeling that we are in one big human family.

Perhaps you're wondering why our focus is on the "listening" part of interpersonal communication – which consists of both listening *and* speaking. In our experience, it's listening that's more difficult and less developed for most people. Insufficient listening is most often the cause when an interaction leaves one or more participants feeling alone and hurt – such as the "ouches" felt by Cinderella in our version of her story above, and as many real-life stories below will continue to demonstrate.

In this book you'll find many scenarios of how listening, and the lack of it, happen between people. Our aim is for some of these scenarios to feel very familiar to you from your own interactions with people at home, at work, and from distant or recent memories. We want this book to connect strongly with your own experiences and to inspire you to look for opportunities to apply what you learn here to your relationships: listening to, hearing, and understanding the people in your life, allowing you to respond to them in new ways and at new levels, making your interactions with them more alive, more authentic, and more satisfying for you and for them.

We three authors have spent much of our lives listening to people as practitioners of psychotherapy – specifically Coherence Therapy – and systemic coaching, all along working on ourselves to become better and better at listening to our clients, hearing all that they are telling us verbally and nonverbally, and guiding them to pay attention and listen to themselves at new levels that produce deep, lasting change.

And yet, what's different about high-quality listening is how simple it is, not how complex it is. There's nothing mysteriously intricate or inscrutable about the skills and stances of such listening, as you'll see on this book's pages. They are readily learnable by almost everyone – and are simple because such listening requires "simply" that we stop doing many things we might normally do in reaction to what another person communicates. Instead, we stay closely with what was said or otherwise communicated, without giving advice or making any attempts to change anything about the person. We just meet that person right where he or she is. Of course, two individuals in a relationship may be at quite different points on the listening learning curve. That can entail a mutual adjustment having various delicate aspects, which might be made smoother by enlisting the help of an experienced couple or family counselor. Although *simple* isn't necessarily *easy*, we think you'll find the rewards well worth the investment!

~ ~ ~ ~ ~

In Part 1 we present dozens of short, real-life stories that illustrate the most important principles of effective listening. We begin with these stories because we believe that's the best way for you to witness, feel, and *experience* the inspiring potential of skillful listening. The later explanations will make a lot more sense after you've moved through these vivid examples and have felt how they resonate with your own life experience.

The stories cover a wide range of situations, relationships, and emotions, and you may find them at times entertaining, at times painful, at times moving, and often familiar. They represent a large collection of our observations of communication between people over many years. The stories have been written to be self-explanatory and to elicit an "aha" effect. Each story is followed by several questions to engage you – perhaps together with other people – in actively considering what has been illustrated.

Part 2 goes into more detail and a deeper discussion of the listening principles that were illustrated by the stories, with particular attention to how and why certain ways of interacting forge connection, while others do the opposite.

Part 3 follows up on some of the people who told their stories in Part 1, showing how high-quality listening can open up a world of possibilities to bring about deep, enduring enhancements to well-being. Most people seek greater well-being in some area of their life from time to time. Talking to empathic friends and family members is one of the best ways to sort out feelings and issues to find the needed, freeing shift. In a completely natural manner, the safety and emotional honesty of such conversations tend to open up new awareness and understanding of one's own issues, needs, and limiting assumptions and core beliefs. That, in turn, can precipitate a remarkable process of fundamental change through the brain's innate mechanism that neuroscience researchers have named *memory reconsolidation*.

You will learn about these inner processes and principles that normally operate from outside of awareness to drive behaviors, thoughts, and emotions – but which now become understandable and can be implemented intentionally to bring about a richer existence for oneself and others.

The appendix offers you a series of exercises that are carefully constructed to develop your own listening skills systematically, starting at your individual position on this fascinating learning curve.

Are you ready to discover how listening can change the world?

Listening in: 52 revealing experiences of attunement and non-attunement

DOI: 10.4324/9781003288589-1

Directory of personal stories

The accounts begin

The stories here in Part 1 of the book come from real life and real interactions between people. They are presented in a special format, with every story offering you a unique learning experience.

The speaker in each story tells about a meaningful experience with some other person – the listener. Sometimes it goes well, but more often than not there's an "ouch" moment for the speaker when the listener's response is significantly misattuned. You'll be invited into the emotional world of the speaker, who will explain how that experience feels.

We then rewrite the stories of misattunement with responses from the listener that make the speaker feel satisfyingly heard and understood. (In those altered replays, the portions of text that are repeated appear a shade lighter.)

It's the speaker's experience of the listener that is the overt focus of each story – because that's the best way for you, the reader, to advance your listening skills. That way, you'll be vicariously experiencing both roles, the speaker and the listener. In the position of the speaker, you'll be sampling how it feels to receive either the needed good listening or the "ouch" of poor listening. In the position of the listener, you will recognize some of your own skillful and less-than-skillful listening responses to others, and of course you'll expand your repertoire of skillful responses. What could be more effective for vividly understanding how to be a good listener?

What about the *speaker's* ability to listen and really hear and receive the responses of a good listener? The speaker in each story is the person who happens to be having an emotional experience, whether troubling or joyous, and wants or needs to tell the other person about that experience, often to help clarify it. So a good listener doesn't expect the speaker, who is in the midst of an emotional experience, to be able to use his or her best listening skills at the same time. High-quality listening responses are ones that an emotional speaker can most fully hear and let in. The invaluable effects of better listening to *oneself* also become apparent.

Some of the stories relate entire conversations, while others are snippets of communication that illustrate something very specific. In Part 3 we'll continue a few of the stories to show how a process of lasting, freeing change can unfold from really good listening.

The stories highlight patterns that people often use in everyday communication – patterns that are interpersonal "connectors" as well as many that are interpersonal "disconnectors." Every time a connector is used and the speaker feels heard and understood, you'll see a "heart-and-ear" icon. And when the speaker feels especially pained by not being heard and understood, you'll find an "ouch" icon.

For example, one type of connector is "showing warmth and generosity of spirit." One type of disconnector is "shifting the focus onto oneself." Labels of that type are given with each story in bold font, and Part 2 provides general descriptions of each such category of connector and disconnector.

You don't have to read all 52 personal stories before digging in to Part 2, which distills the essence of the many particular forms of well-attuned and poorly attuned listening demonstrated in Part 1. In fact, for some readers it could be particularly illuminating to alternate between taking in the concrete examples of Part 1 and reading the generalized concepts in Part 2.

Each story is followed by questions for you to consider, either on your own or in discussion with a reading partner, to explore further how the stories relate to your own life experiences of communicating with other people.

Story 1: Olivia

Background

Hey, I'm Olivia, 17 years old. You won't believe what's been going on! My boyfriend, Tony, dumped me for another girl! After we were together for six whole months. That's a really long time, and I was sure it would last forever. I didn't see this coming. I've had other boyfriends, but they were so superficial compared to Tony, the great love of my life.

I cry all day. I wake up in the middle of the night and realize I was crying in my sleep. It hurts so much. I spent the first day – it's been six days now – trying to make it not be true, but it kept being true. I spent the second and third days realizing that I couldn't change reality and there was nothing more I wanted to live for. I thought about killing myself. Fortunately for me, my mom kept a close eye on me and helped me through that. Then I fell into a deep depression, where I've been stuck for the last few days. Will the pain ever end?

I don't really want to talk to anyone, because I'm convinced no one can understand how deep my pain goes. My cousin Mia called – she's 18 – and my mom told her I didn't want to talk to anyone, but Mia knew I was really, really down and she wouldn't take no for an answer, so she came over anyway earlier today.

What happened

Me (Olivia) *(joyless, flat, not wanting to talk to Mia)*: Hey, Mia, what's up.

Mia: What's up with you? How're you doing? I've been worried sick about you.

Me (Olivia) *(totally flat)*: I'm okay.

Mia: Oh, I'm sooo glad to hear you're okay! That means sooo much to me!

DISCONNECTOR – *disregarding signals* of distress or need

What I'm feeling

How come Mia heard my words "I'm okay" but didn't notice that I didn't *look* or *sound* okay? I haven't washed my hair in a week, and I'm obviously depressed. But she seems to be ignoring clear signs that I'm in a bad state. It's as if she's listening for what she *wants* to hear, rather than actually tuning in to *me*.

Mia: I've been beside myself with worry.

Me (Olivia) *(not knowing what to say)*: Yeah …

Mia: You've given us all a scare! I could hardly sleep I was so worried about you.

DISCONNECTOR – **shifting the focus onto oneself,** *specifically:*
burdening the sufferer with one's own worries

It feels as if she's pressuring *me* to make *her* feel better, when *I'm* the one in huge pain right now. It feels weird that she's dumping *her* worries on *my* shoulders.

I wish people could notice my obvious condition, not just the words I say. When I said "I'm okay," it was just to fill the silence and get her off my back, but I definitely didn't look or sound okay in any way!

I'm the one who was dumped by the love of my life, and I'm the one who's in this intense pain *all the time*. It feels like an unfair and impossible burden for me to deal with not only my feelings but also Mia's feelings about *my* issue. Mia really let me down in a big way by being so blind to that and pulling at me to make *her* feel better. She isn't the friend I thought she was – and that's yet *another* loss at the same time!

What I needed instead

Me (Olivia) *(joyless, flat, not wanting to talk to Mia)*: Hey, Mia, what's up?

Mia: I just came to check up on you – I've been thinking about you.

Me (Olivia) *(totally flat)*: I'm okay.

Mia: Hmm, I don't think so. I'm not *that* easy to fool! And I know how bad it hurts to be dropped by a boyfriend. Look, I'm here for you, okay? If you want to talk or maybe need a shoulder to cry on, just let me know, okay?

CONNECTOR – **noticing incongruence among words, emotions, and behaviors**

CONNECTOR – **acknowledging what you're noticing**, *specifically:*
  expressing caring recognition of visible distress rather than going along with disregarding it

CONNECTOR – **offering an expression of interest and caring understanding**

Me (Olivia): Yeah … okay.

Mia *(giving Olivia a hug)*: Okay, sweetie, is it alright if I drop by tomorrow for a couple of minutes?

CONNECTOR – **showing warmth and generosity of spirit**, *specifically:*
  offering ongoing contact and accompaniment through the distress

Me (Olivia): I guess so.

Questions for discussion

1) Can you describe a time when you spoke words that were very different from how you were really feeling? What motivated you to handle it that way?
2) Have you been visibly in distress and experienced people responding to you by telling you about *their* distress about *your* issue, while largely disregarding *your* crisis?
3) Can you describe a situation in which you were talking to someone who was in the midst of an intensely distressing situation? Try to describe how you were feeling during that interaction.
4) How did you interact with the person who was in intense distress? If you could do it over again, what might you do differently?

Story 2: Manuela

Background

Dear reader,

   I'm Manuela, and I'm an animal lover. I really, really love them! I grew up with cats, dogs, rabbits, hamsters, and turtles. My father even brought home a monkey once for a few days until he found out we weren't allowed to keep it.

   I was at the animal shelter today to see about possibly adopting a cat, but I couldn't make a decision. Later I was telling my boyfriend Robert about how hard it was to decide.

What happened

Me (Manuela): There were so many adorable cats that –

Robert: you wanted to take all of them. I know you!

Me (Manuela): No, it's that I couldn't imagine how they could all be homeless, because they're so adorable. I originally thought I would try to get a kitten –

Robert: because they're cuter, right?

Me (Manuela): No, that's not why. I was going to say that a kitten has an easier time adjusting to a new home. With an older cat, you don't know how it's been treated and what kinds of habits it has –

Robert: like scratching up the furniture.

Me (Manuela): Well, that isn't what concerns me. I've had cats that –

Robert: that peed in your shoes. I know – you told me.

ouch!

DISCONNECTOR – **interrupting** *to complete the other's sentence*

What I'm feeling

I'm feeling cut off, blocked, and frustrated. I can't even get to the end of a thought in my own way. I feel like a stream where the water wants to flow, but someone keeps putting up barriers. It's also upsetting that Robert keeps thinking he knows what I want to say, as though he knows me better than I know myself, so he interrupts to finish my sentence and show that he knows how I think. And he's wrong most of the time! I don't feel listened to and I don't feel respected.

When I start sharing a thought, I really want to finish it uninterrupted. Sometimes it's so irritating when Robert interrupts me that I have trouble remembering what I initially wanted to say. Or I spend my energy correcting the wrong direction he just took, and then I have to try to reconstruct what I first wanted to tell him.

Adopting a cat involves many factors that are clamoring for attention in my thoughts and feelings. I need time and space to sort through all of them and come to a decision I feel good about. I was hoping that talking about it would help me sort through these things.

What I needed instead

Me (Manuela): There were so many adorable cats that I couldn't imagine how they could all be homeless. Why aren't there a million people wanting to take care of them?

Robert: They're all so irresistible, right?

*CONNECTOR – **active listening**, accurately and empathically reflected, specifically: showing that the message is received and the sentiment is shared*

Me (Manuela): That's for sure. I originally thought I would try to get a kitten, because it would probably have an easier time adjusting to a new environment. With an older cat, you don't know how it's been treated and what kinds of habits it has.

Robert: I guess you have a lot of experience with some cats having bad habits.

Me (Manuela): Right, I do! I think I'll sleep on it for a night and then see if I can make a decision.

Robert: Good idea.

*CONNECTOR – **allowing time and space for one's individual process to unfold**, specifically: respecting the time needed for decision-making*

Questions for discussion

1) Have you had the experience of someone interrupting you and even finishing your sentences for you? How do you feel when that happens? Are your reactions similar to Manuela's, or different?

2) Are there people in your life who seem to assume they know you better than you know yourself?

3) Are there times when you feel the need to jump in with your own thoughts while someone else is still speaking? Does this come up more with certain people? Or on certain topics?

4) When you have that urge to interrupt, what's behind it? What would be the downside for you if you held back from interrupting?

Story 3: Glenn

Background

Hi to all you readers! My name is Glenn, and I'm a gay man – that's relevant to my story. While I was working at an I.T. firm down south in the U.S.A., my boss quit and moved up north to start his own consulting company. He and I thought highly of each other. He was quickly very successful with his new firm, and one day he called to ask whether I'd like to make a change and come work for him. I discussed it with my husband, Jeremy, and we decided to take the opportunity.

It's a big undertaking to uproot your home and move to a new city in a new region. It was especially challenging for us because Jeremy has special needs. He was in a serious accident a long time ago, and he needs his wheelchair to get around.

My ex-boss was very kind and connected us with one of his employees, Brianna, a woman who "knows people who know people," and she told him she could find an apartment for us at a decent price. So I gave her a call …

What happened

Me (Glenn): It's so nice of you to agree to help us.

Brianna: Oh, my pleasure. What kind of a place are you looking for?

Me (Glenn): Well, we need a three-bedroom place … but the most important thing is accessibility. My husband uses a wheelchair, and he needs –

Brianna: Your *husband*? Wow, you don't *sound* gay!

ouch!

DISCONNECTOR – **interrupting** *mid-sentence*

DISCONNECTOR – **not registering or responding to what was just said**, *specifically: switching to one's own agenda without responding to the speaker's topic*

DISCONNECTOR – **believing and asserting stereotypes**

I was in the middle of saying something important about our needs, and it was jarring to be interrupted like that, with no sign that she had even registered what I said. Instead she was completely on her own wavelength.

What I'm feeling

I feel stereotyped and very annoyed about that. She seems to think that a certain speech mannerism is intrinsic to being gay. That tells me she's had very little contact with LGBTQ people. And with a sinking feeling, I'm suddenly also feeling disappointed and doubtful that this person is capable of tuning in to our needs well enough to provide any actual help, even if her intentions are good.

I really wish Brianna had been capable of putting her assumptions and prejudices aside in order to simply listen to the specific needs of an actual person – *me*. After all, *she* offered to help *us*.

What I needed instead

Me (Glenn): It's so nice of you to agree to help us.

Brianna: Oh, my pleasure. What kind of a place are you looking for?

Me (Glenn): Well, we need a three-bedroom place ... but the most important thing is accessibility. My husband uses a wheelchair, and he needs **ground-level access.**

Brianna: Gee, that does sound really important! Let's make that a top priority.

*CONNECTOR – **active listening**, accurately and empathically reflected, specifically:*
showing that the message is received and the sentiment is shared

Questions for discussion

1) Have you had the experience of someone interrupting you and changing the subject when you had begun to express something specific and important? How did you feel when that happened?
2) Have you ever felt mischaracterized by being stereotyped when someone responded to you based on a personal characteristic (size, age, gender, appearance, race, etc.)? If you have, how did you experience that, and if you have not, can you imagine how that would feel?
3) Can you remember a time when you were distracted by some particular characteristic of another person and had difficulty concentrating on what the person was saying? What can you see about why that particular aspect of the person was preoccupying for you?
4) Are there certain groups of people whom you have difficulties in approaching open-mindedly? What happens inside if you try to think of these people as individuals having many other dimensions than the ones that are uncomfortable or aversive for you?

Story 4: Annie

Background

Esteemed reader,

I have reached the ripe old age of 94, and I still feel pretty good once I get out of bed and get myself moving in the morning – the late morning, I have to admit.

I have the honor of being grandmother to eight grandchildren and great-grand-mother to three great-grandchildren. Well, I think it's three. I get confused some-times about which children belong to which generation. They all call me Granny Annie, and they are my pride and joy, every one of them.

Some of the kids keep in touch better than others. The best way to reach me is by telephone. I do have a computer, but I find the use of email a bit confusing, so I prefer telephoning. Every time one of the kids moves, which young people do frequently, I have to find out their new street address, new email address, and new telephone num-ber. And some of them have multiple telephones! I can't for the life of me imagine why you would need more than one, but if it makes them happy …

I was talking to Daniel on the phone this morning. (He's Paul's boy, I think, but I'm not totally sure right now …)

What happened

Daniel: I'm really excited, Granny! I'm all moved into my new apartment right in the center of the city, and I'm starting my new job on Monday!

Me (Annie): That's wonderful, dear. Now please tell me your new address. Wait … Let me get my notebook and a pen … Okay, what's your address? Okay … And your phone number?

Daniel: It's the same cell phone I've had for the last two years.

Me (Annie): Well, tell me the number, please, just so I have all the information in one place. *(Daniel recites the number.)* And what is your new email address?

Daniel: I've explained to you before, Granny. When you move, you don't get a new email address. You can keep the old one forever.

Me (Annie): Isn't that clever! And while I have you, could you please tell me the phone numbers of Natalie, Julian, Debbie, Archie … have I forgotten anyone?

Daniel *(exasperated)*: Granny, you ask me for the phone numbers every time we talk! I must have given them to you at least ten times!

DISCONNECTOR – implying "you shouldn't need what you need"

What I'm feeling

I'm sad that Daniel feels I'm such a burden. When I write down the phone numbers of my near and dear, it helps me feel connected to them. Then I know that I can call them at any time and hear their voices. Family is the most important thing to me, and the young people are scattered all across the globe.

I need the reassurance and comfort of knowing that I know how to contact my beloved family members. That gives me a sense of connection and the security I need now, living alone at my age. When Daniel became impatient with me, I felt he was telling me it's wrong for me to need this reassurance and security.

In asking for the phone numbers, I thought it would be obvious that I was needing to feel connected to my family. Maybe Daniel is too young to understand that …

What I needed instead

Daniel: I'm really excited, Granny! I'm all moved into my new apartment right in the center of the city, and I'm starting my new job on Monday!

Me (Annie): That's wonderful, dear. Now please tell me your new address. Wait … Let me get my notebook and a pen … Okay, what's your address? Okay … And your phone number?

Daniel: It's the same cell phone I've had for the last two years.

Me (Annie): Well, tell me the number, please, just so I have all the information in one place. *(Daniel recites the number.)* And what is your new email address?

Daniel: I've explained to you before, Granny. When you move, you don't get a new email address. You can keep the old one forever.

Me (Annie): Isn't that clever! And while I have you, could you please tell me the phone numbers of Natalie, Julian, Debbie, Archie … have I forgotten anyone?

Daniel: I have an idea, Granny. I have to leave for an appointment in a few minutes, but how about I send you a post card with all the phone numbers on it? Then you could hang it up right next to the telephone, and you can call me any time you want. What do you think of that idea?

*CONNECTOR – **showing warmth and generosity of spirit**, specifically:*
> *honoring the other's needs even when they don't match one's own personal standards*

Me (Annie): That would be lovely! I'll be checking my mailbox for that post card.

Questions for discussion

1) Can you describe a situation in which a behavior of yours was criticized by another person as annoying, unnecessary, or even irrational, even though the behavior felt emotionally sensible and necessary to you?

2) Do you know someone who has become forgetful with age or hasn't kept up with modern technology? How do you interact with that person? How do you think Daniel felt when Annie didn't ask anything about his new apartment?

3) Can you describe someone's behavior that you have found annoying for years and that never seems to change? What do you imagine might be the unstated emotional needs making that behavior necessary for that person? With this view of the behavior, what new ideas do you have for alleviating your own negative reactions?

4) What patterns do you rely on for creating a feeling of connection with other people?

Story 5: Emily

Background

Hey, it's Emily here. My best friend from college, Janice, is a dear, dear person, and we have so much shared history that nothing can separate us, even though we live hundreds of miles apart. We stay in touch by email, but we're both so busy with our families and jobs that we talk on the phone only two or three times a year, usually on birthdays or holidays.

Now, this isn't really a big deal, but on the phone Janice just keeps on talking and I hardly get any chance to tell her what's been going on in *my* life. I listen to *her*, but she doesn't listen to *me*. I mean, I know she cares, and she's interested in my life, and I'm interested in hers, which certainly comes through in our emails. But on the phone it's like turning on a firehose with no way to turn it off.

During our last phone call I tried to analyze what happens, and I noticed for the first time that she uses a particular technique for "holding the floor" so that I can't get a word in edgewise, and she's probably not even aware of doing it. And I realize that over the years I've developed a kind of coping mechanism of deadening my thoughts and daydreaming and just letting her talk, because otherwise I'd get frustrated at not getting to say any of the many thoughts that pass through my head while she's talking. That's just the way it is with my good friend Janice.

What happened

Me (Emily): Hi, it's me! Happy birthday!

Janice: Hi, Ems!!! I'm so happy you called! Danny's been a sweetheart today, doing the shopping for the party tonight. – um – We invited more people than can possibly fit in the house, but the weather's good, so we can spill out onto the terrace. – um – Remember my 40th two years ago? – um – It was so great that you could make the trip. – um – So … let's see, I think I wrote to you about Janey's graduation. We were so proud of her. – um – She looked so grown up in her cap and gown. – um – How quickly the time flies, don't you think? – um –

DISCONNECTOR – *talking instead of ever listening*

What I'm feeling

Well, I'm not actually feeling much of anything, because I'm used to that from Janice and, as I said, I just deaden myself to get through it. I suppose I still have some low-level feeling of frustration at finding no opportunity to share in the conversation, but I've largely suppressed it. But it's just occurring to me that maybe that's why I don't call her very often on the phone. She expects endless listening capacity from me. It's not a satisfying way to interact as friends.

I'm not the kind of person who likes to interrupt people when they're talking, or even when they're apparently thinking. In my family, interrupting was considered impolite, so I tend to wait for what sounds like the end of a sentence or the end of a thought before jumping in with questions or comments, not to mention a change of topic to something about *me*. I guess I need some indication from Janice that it's okay for me to have some time and space to say what *I'd* like to share. When Janice ends each sentence by quickly tacking on an "um −" I take that to mean that she still has more to say and is about to say it. I end up suppressing my natural desire for give-and-take, and I sort of glaze over, pretending to be interested in the endless run-on of words and ums.

What I needed instead

Me (Emily): Hi, it's me! Happy birthday!

Janice: Hi, Ems!!! I'm so happy you called! Danny's been a sweetheart today, doing the shopping for the party tonight.

Me (Emily): He's such a good helper.

Janice: That's for sure. Remember my 40th two years ago? It was so great that you could make the trip.

Me (Emily): I know! I remember! It was a party I'll never forget. And the weather was perfect. I hope you're as lucky today.

Janice: I hope so, too. We invited too many people, as usual, but somehow it'll all work out.

Me (Emily): Hey, how was Janey's graduation?

(Etc. …)

The next time Janice and I were able to get together in person without the husbands and kids, I decided to try to talk to her about my low-level frustration at not getting a word in edgewise when we talk by phone. I said something like this: "You're my dear friend, you know that! And I'm so grateful that we've maintained our friendship all these years. I have to admit, though, that I sometimes hesitate to call you even though I'm thinking about you. I thought about it and figured out why: When we talk in person it's *great*, but on the phone I can't find a gap or a space in the conversation to start talking ..."

The discussion went really well. I think she heard what I was trying to tell her. I was communicating with her about our pattern of communication, and that helped her become aware of how it feels to me when we talk on the phone. Also I expressed all that as "I-messages," and that made it easier for her to hear what I wanted to say, without her feeling criticized by me. She really got that I love her as a friend and want the best for our relationship.

CONNECTOR – ***using meta-level communication*** *about their phone conversations*

CONNECTOR – ***using I-messages***

CONNECTOR – ***allowing time and space for one's individual process to unfold***, *specifically: giving the other person a chance to speak*

Questions for discussion

1) Do you have a relationship in which you feel as if you have trouble getting a word in edgewise? Describe your feelings and coping strategies.
2) What do you imagine might be the deeper reasons that a person talks non-stop? Try to put yourself in that person's shoes.
3) Can you identify and describe a relationship in which you feel the conversational styles are well balanced between you and the other person? To what do you attribute the balanced nature of the relationship?
4) In your view, when is it appropriate and justifiable for a conversation to be more one-sided, meaning that one person does nearly all of the talking? Describe such a case you've experienced.

Story 6: Emma

Background

Dear reader,

I'm Emma. I'm an adult now, and I'm beginning to understand that a lot of things I experienced as a child continue to affect my current life. Last year I married the most wonderful man in the world, and we want to start a family soon. But I'm troubled by seeing that my insecurities in life are showing up in my moods and behaviors, and I want to make sure I don't unwittingly pass those on to my children.

I've been reflecting on some childhood memories that have haunted me for all these years. One that keeps popping into my thoughts is the time when I was 6 years old and I was helping my father in the garden. It was a balmy late summer afternoon, Mommy was in the house preparing dinner, and I felt so proud that Daddy wanted me to help him. I was full of fervor and the feeling that I mattered.

What happened

Daddy: Now I want you to take that pail, fill it with just the right amount of water so you can still carry it, and then come here and pour it over the seedlings.

Me (Emma) *(proudly carrying the heavy, slurping pail of water)*: Watch me, Daddy!

(When I start pouring, the entire pailful spills out on the first seedling, completely washing it away.)

Daddy *(angrily grabbing the pail from my hands)*: Gimme that! Unbelievable, how you could mess up even such a simple thing? And you're standing right on the plants! Brilliant. Go help your mother in the kitchen.

DISCONNECTOR – ***criticizing, judging, shaming, or blaming***, *specifically: reacting with annoyed impatience, anger, and denigration to mistakes*

DISCONNECTOR – ***demanding or ordering***

What I'm feeling

I'm so stupid that I can't do anything right. I must have been very, very bad for Daddy to be that angry at me. I'm scared that he doesn't love me anymore! I feel guilty, too. I was trying really hard to do it right, and it's a shock to find out that trying hard doesn't count. I have to do it perfectly right at the start, or else I'm too stupid to be loved and I get sent away, with no second chance to get it right. But I don't know how to be perfect, and now I'm really scared to try to do anything new for fear I'll be yelled at and sent away.

I was only 6, and needed time to practice new skills and become competent. But Daddy gave me angry messages of stupidity and incompetence for making a normal mistake.

What I needed instead

Daddy: Now I want you to take that pail, fill it with just the right amount of water so you can still carry it, and then come here and pour it over the seedlings.

Me (Emma) *(proudly carrying the heavy, slopping pail of water)*: Watch me, Daddy!

(When I start pouring, the entire pailful spills out on the first seedling, completely washing it away.)

Daddy: Oops, a seedling swam away in all that water. Can you pick it up and help me put it back in its hole? Thanks. You carried such a lot of water all the way from there to here. And now we know that each seedling needs just a little bit. How about going back and getting more water for the next seedling?

CONNECTOR – **showing warmth and generosity of spirit**, *specifically:*
patience and kind helpfulness with mistakes

Questions for discussion

1) Do you remember childhood experiences that you feel set up patterns that have affected your life in later years?

2) Can you describe a situation in which someone has passed judgment on you for a normal mistake, and you felt it was unfair?

3) Can you describe a situation in which you felt impatient, judgmental, or angry toward someone for doing something unskillfully? If you step back and look at that response, can you see anything of where that comes from in you?

4) Of course, it's natural to feel frustration over other people's slower pace or errors at times. In such moments, what would help you maintain an attitude of patience and kindness toward others?

Story 7: Paul

Background

I'm Paul. Thanks for listening to my story. It wasn't easy for me, a 30-year-old guy, to agree to start psychotherapy. My girlfriend suggested it a couple of times over the last year, but for a long time I couldn't imagine it and felt very resistant. That's for weaklings, I've always believed, and my problems will solve themselves, as they always have in the past.

My issue is about hunting for a new job. I've been out of work for a while, and money is getting tight. I have excellent qualifications, but I get nervous and unfocused when I have to try to sell myself.

At some point last month, I overcame my resistance to starting therapy, because my anxiety has been building and taking over more of my life. I made an appointment with Kathy, a new therapist in town, thinking that she probably doesn't know anyone in my circle of family and friends, so it won't slip out by accident that I'm seeing a therapist. I know therapists aren't supposed to talk about their clients, but I tend not to trust people until they've proven themselves.

Things got off to a surprisingly good start, and the first three sessions went better than I had expected. I was starting to trust Kathy.

Then yesterday, on the fourth visit, she started off by telling me that we needed to discuss a small administrative matter.

What happened

Kathy: As you described, your insurance plan does cover your therapy sessions. But there is a $15 co-payment per session that you'll have to cover on your own. I'll be sending you a bill for the $60 you owe so far from these first four sessions. Just so you know.

Me (Paul): What? How come I'm finding out about this now, after doing three sessions?

Kathy: Sorry, I forgot to tell you at our first appointment.

Me (Paul): You should have told me about this cost *before* our first appointment! I can't believe you didn't think to tell me! You can't just spring it on me, retroactively, after three sessions, and expect that I'll be fine with it. That's something I should have known up front. That's really careless of you, and I don't know how I can ever trust you again. In fact, I don't know how I can continue doing therapy with you.

Kathy: I see that you're surprised. Yes, I forgot to tell you – but that's not a reason to stop therapy. I mean, we can talk about this issue as part of our session today.

DISCONNECTOR – **saying "yes, but"** in hopes of shifting the other person's strongly emotional position

DISCONNECTOR – **counteracting others' feelings, views, or actions**, specifically: using logic to invalidate and dispel negative views and feelings

DISCONNECTOR – **disregarding the deeper message, especially if it involves distress or need**

What I'm feeling

We're quickly going from bad to worse. Kathy isn't getting how bad this feels to me, and her saying "yes, but" right away showed me that she isn't even *trying* to get it. Even though she said, "I can see that you're surprised," offering me a token bit of understanding, I don't believe for a minute that she really understood. She, of all people, should have known that I'm in financial stress, and that trusting a therapist is a totally new thing for me. And who is she to tell me what's a valid reason for stopping therapy? On top of that, she expects *me* to pay for a session spent on cleaning up *her* mistake! Forget it! I can't believe what a train wreck she's creating moment by moment.

If I'm telling her that I'm pretty peeved by something she's said or done, I just want her to *get* it and at least acknowledge that she can see why I'd be upset – not brush aside my feelings with some pseudo-logical "yes, but" excuse. She should fully acknowledge the distress I'm feeling because of her misstep. And then *she* should take responsibility for fixing the situation she caused, not put the burden on *me*.

What I needed instead

Kathy: As you described, your insurance plan does cover your therapy sessions. But there is a $15 co-payment per session that you'll have to cover on your own. I'll be sending you a bill for the $60 you owe so far from the first four sessions. Just so you know.

Me (Paul): What? How come I'm finding out about this now, after doing three sessions?

Kathy: Sorry, I forgot to tell you at our first appointment.

Me (Paul): You should have told me about this cost *before* our first appointment! I can't believe you didn't think to tell me! You can't just spring it on me, retroactively, after three sessions, and expect that I'll be fine with it. That's something I should have known up front. You've been really careless with me, and I don't know how I can ever trust you again. In fact, I don't know how I can continue doing therapy with you.

Kathy: Oh my – I hear what a nasty surprise this is for you. I'm really sorry about forgetting to tell you – totally my responsibility, and I apologize for that. You needed to incorporate that into your decision-making at the start. This reminds me of a sign I've seen in some stores: "If you break it, you buy it." Well, I broke this, so I'll buy it. I *won't* bill you for the co-pay for these four sessions. I realize that can only partially set things right. What do you think about us setting up a time to talk by phone about this between sessions, so we don't use any more of this session's time on it?

CONNECTOR – **repairing rifts**, *specifically:*
> *taking responsibility for missteps, acknowledging the validity of a grievance, and apologizing sincerely for any harm caused*

Questions for discussion

1) Have you been on the receiving end of a "yes, but"? A few examples:
   a. I see your point, but …
   b. I know you'd prefer that, but …
   c. Sounds difficult, but look at it this way …
2) When you feel wronged or hurt by another person, does a quick "sorry" set things right for you? What do you personally need to genuinely dispel your feeling of being wronged or hurt? Describe a concrete example.
3) Can you remember a situation in which you handled something poorly, and someone was upset about it and let you know it? How did you feel? How did you react?
4) What do you imagine was motivating Kathy to respond with a "yes, but"? (She said, "Yes, I forgot to tell you, but that's not a reason to stop therapy.")

Story 8: Megan

Background

Hi. I'm Megan, and I'm furious at my mother right now!

What happened

In gym class this morning we were changing into our bathing suits for swimming, and Alison, who's a friend, but not my best friend by any means, says to me, "I guess you don't have your period anymore if you're going swimming. Ha ha, I heard you just got it last week!" How did she know I had my period for the first time last week? There's only one possible explanation: My mother must have told Alison's mother. They're friends and they gossip a lot. And what really kills me is that I *told* my mother she's not allowed to tell anyone!

*DISCONNECTOR – **disregarding signals**, specifically:*
ignoring an expressed need for boundaries and privacy

What I'm feeling

How could my mother betray a personal confidence like that, especially when I asked her not to? I feel so embarrassed! And I don't know how I can ever trust her again. I don't want people knowing what's going on with my body unless I decide to tell them myself. Didn't my mother even think about that?

This is my private life! It's my body, and I have the right to decide what intimate details I share with which people. My mother had no right to share that information.

What I needed instead

My mother should have kept her mouth shut. Or at the very least, she should have asked me for permission if she had such a need to share the news with her friend. I probably would have said no, but she should have discussed it with me.

After school today I told my mother that I was furious at her, because I was totally embarrassed in gym class when Alison said that about my period, and Mom was obviously the one who had blabbed. She answered with, "Oh, I'm so sorry, sweetie, for causing you that embarrassment! You're so right. That was wrong of me to tell Alison's mother without asking you first. I'll really try to be more aware of your privacy in the future!" (Hey, don't I have a great mother? I'm not angry at her anymore. Not only can I tell her that I'm mad at her, but she thinks about what I have to say, and she apologizes if she's made a mistake! And she doesn't even make excuses or try to explain away what happened. Most of my friends' mothers aren't like that.)

CONNECTOR – *repairing rifts*, *specifically:*
> *taking responsibility for missteps, acknowledging the validity of a grievance, and apologizing sincerely for any harm caused*

Questions for discussion

1) Can you describe a situation in which someone shared personal information about you with a third party without your knowledge or permission? How did you find out about it? How did you feel? How did you react?

2) Where do you feel the borderline is between, on the one hand, someone else's issues that are too personal for you to share with third parties, and, on the other hand, someone else's issues that strike you as shareable? Identify some examples.

3) Have you ever shared someone else's personal news or information with a third party and then felt uncomfortable about it?

4) Can you describe a time when someone told you a story and started with, "I'll tell you, but don't dare tell anyone else!" Have you ever done that? In what situations might that be appropriate? In what situations might that be inappropriate?

Story 9: Tiffany

Background

Hi, everybody! My name is Tiffany, and I'm just about to graduate from college. Lucky me – I have a great job offer in Atlanta as well as an opportunity to continue my studies in London. It's a difficult choice!

I met up with my good buddy Aaron at the Student Union to have cinnamon buns and coffee and catch up on things.

What happened

Aaron: So, what's going on? You sound as if you have some news.

Me (Tiffany): I do! You already know I was accepted into the Master's program in London. And today I got a letter from that company in Atlanta where I applied, and they're offering me a position with a good starting salary.

Aaron: Wow, when it rains, it pours!

Me (Tiffany): You can say that again. And now I'm totally torn. Both options are so great.

Aaron: Oh, you should definitely take the job! It's the kind of thing that spices up your résumé.

*DISCONNECTOR – **giving unsolicited advice or giving advice prematurely***

What I'm feeling

Aaron totally disregarding what I'm going through on the inside over this big decision was a bit of a jolt, and his quick advice didn't help me at all. I'm not terribly upset with him because he doesn't usually do that, but I do wish he had held back with his opinion for at least a few minutes and instead been a sounding board for me, helping me to sort through my feelings about the two options. I'm one of those people who can process complicated feelings best in conversation with a trusted friend, rather than just ruminating alone.

I might have gotten around to asking Aaron which one he would choose. Or maybe I wouldn't have wanted to do that. I'm not sure. He really should have waited until I asked for his advice. Or at the least, he should have asked me whether I wanted his opinion before he offered it.

What I needed instead

Aaron: So, what's going on? You sound as if you have some news.

Me (Tiffany): I do! You already know I was accepted into the Master's program in London. And today I got a letter from that company in Atlanta where I applied, and they're offering me a position with a good starting salary.

Aaron: Wow, when it rains, it pours!

Me (Tiffany): You can say that again. And now I'm totally torn. Both options are so great.

Aaron: What do you like about each option? ... What's your gut feeling about this? ... Any other thoughts?

CONNECTOR – **asking interestedly**, *specifically:*
inviting expression of thoughts and feelings

Me (Tiffany): *(I'm thinking to myself ... This is helping me get clearer about my feelings, needs, and plans.)*

Aaron: I know you pretty well, and I know what I would do if I were you. Would you like to hear my opinion?

Questions for discussion

1) Can you describe a situation in which someone gave you unsolicited advice? How was that for you?
2) Are you more of a sit-alone-and-think or a talk-and-share kind of person when you're trying to make a decision or get clear about your feelings on an issue?
3) When you want someone's advice, do you request that explicitly, or do you imply it by the way you talk about the topic? Give some examples.
4) What do you imagine might have driven Aaron, internally, to give Tiffany his advice so quickly and forcefully?

Story 10: Christopher

Background

Hi. I'm Christopher. Everybody calls me Chris. I'm 14 years old, and soccer is my life. I mean, my *whole* life! I love the training because it feels great to move in a million different directions. I love the games because the energy is so great. And the other guys on the team are my guys, my buds, my entire social life.

I guess I have a special talent for soccer. The coaches told my parents that from very early on. It's my dream to become a professional soccer player. And my parents even like the idea, so I have it much better than some of my friends.

Now maybe you'll understand why I'm so freaked out by having knee pains. They started about three months ago, and at first I didn't tell anybody. I've just been toughing it out through the games so no one notices that I'm in pain. But it's been getting worse, so I finally figured I had to talk to my mother about it.

What happened

Me (Chris): Mom, do you have a minute? I need to talk to you about something.

Mom: Sure, honey, what's up?

Me (Chris): My knees have been hurting me during games.

Mom: Oh, is this something new?

Me (Chris): Yeah, the last couple of months. It's not so bad in training, but when I push myself during a game it's sometimes really painful.

Mom: But you seem to be managing. I'm sure it's from your recent growth spurt. You'll grow out of it.

DISCONNECTOR – **minimizing or trivializing** *distress by offering positive thinking*

What I'm feeling

I suddenly feel panicky! Mom isn't taking this problem seriously, and it's threatening my whole life! Doesn't she understand how important soccer is to me? She's telling me that I'm overreacting by taking the pain seriously, and that it can't possibly be as bad as I imagine, so I should stop complaining. I guess I'm just a wimp.

It also feels awful that Mom seems to think that her unconcerned view of the situation is more accurate than my view, and that I shouldn't trust my own instincts about this, and maybe also that my future in soccer isn't as important to her as I thought.

What I needed instead

Me (Chris): Mom, do you have a minute? I need to talk to you about something.

Mom: Sure, honey, what's up?

Me (Chris): My knees have been hurting me during games.

Mom: Oh, is this something new?

Me (Chris): Yeah, the last couple of months. It's not so bad in training, but when I push myself during a game, it's sometimes really painful.

Mom: Wow, sounds rough. Does it feel serious enough that you want me to make a doctor's appointment for you?

Me (Chris): Yeah, I think that's a good idea. I'm starting to get a little scared, because I don't know what's causing the pain.

Mom: Okay, I'll do that today. I can see why you're worried by not knowing what's going on.

CONNECTOR – **active listening**, *accurately reflected, specifically: acknowledging emotional distress*

Questions for discussion

1) Can you describe a situation in which you were worried or scared about something and told someone else about it, and the other person tried to be helpful by expressing a positive, hopeful view that disregarded your sense of vulnerability? How did you feel? How did you react?
2) Have you experienced a deep worry that you expressed in such a watered-down form to someone else that the person didn't detect your distress? What was your motivation for keeping your worry largely hidden?
3) What do you imagine was Mom's motivation for trying to assure Chris that he would "grow out of it"?
4) Can you describe a situation in which you felt it was important to reassure another person who was in pain or worry? How did you do it? How did that person react?

Story 11: Deborah

Background

Dear reader,

I'm Deborah, 40 years old. I was a chubby kid and a voluptuous teenager, and as an adult I've always battled with my body over those extra pounds. I have what one could call a highly efficient metabolism that stores much of what I eat as fat. Every diet I've ever tried has helped me lose three or four pounds pretty fast, and then, like magic, I find I've gained it all back.

So maybe you can imagine my concern when I noticed a few weeks ago that I've been losing weight without even trying to. In the last month I've lost eight pounds. It's really weird. I've heard of people wasting away due to some dread disease. I think it's time to go see a doctor, but I'm afraid and nervous.

I decided to get together with my friend Connie for dinner and look for an opportunity to talk about it.

What happened

Connie: Hey, Deb, you're looking slim and trim!

Me (Deborah): Well, actually, I'm puzzled at how that's happening. In fact, I'm a bit worried.

Connie: Worried? Why? You look great.

Me (Deborah): The thing is, I haven't been dieting intentionally, and something's going on that I can't explain.

Connie: I wish *I* could lose weight without dieting! I *hate* dieting!

Me (Deborah): But what if it's because of some terrible disease, like cancer or tuberculosis, and I'm wasting away?

Connie: Be happy you're losing weight! You've always wanted to be thin, right?

ouch!

DISCONNECTOR – **disregarding signals** *of distress or need*

DISCONNECTOR – **minimizing or trivializing** *distress by offering positive thinking*

What I'm feeling

I've given Connie enough signals that I'm starting to feel worried and scared, but she's not picking up on them, in fact she brushed them aside. I needed her emotional support and understanding more than I knew, because now I feel almost panicky with how alone I feel facing a possible health crisis. Am I being paranoid or ridiculous for worrying? Even if I am, I certainly don't feel any sympathetic comforting from her. "Be happy you're losing weight!" is a clear message from Connie that I'm foolish to worry, in her view, so that's the end of telling her anything more about it. But where can I turn, if not to my good friend? Sure, I can go to the doctor, but that's for the physical side of things. Where can I get emotional support?

What I needed instead

Connie: Hey, Deb, you're looking slim and trim!

Me (Deborah): Well, actually, I'm puzzled at how that's happening. In fact, I'm a bit worried.

Connie: Worried? **What about?**

Me (Deborah): The thing is, I haven't been dieting intentionally, and something's going on that I can't explain.

Connie: Do you think something's wrong? How are you feeling otherwise?

*CONNECTOR – **offering an expression of interest and caring understanding***

*CONNECTOR – **opening the door to supportive conversation***

Me (Deborah): Well, I don't feel sick, but for me this just can't be normal. What if it's because of some terrible disease, like cancer or tuberculosis, and I'm wasting away?

Connie: Oh, now I see why you're worrying. I know how it is to start fearing the worst when you don't know what's going on. Are you thinking about seeing your doctor?

Me (Deborah): I guess I should go, but I'm kind of nervous about what I might find out.

Connie: Of course. I know how that feels too. If you want some emotional support, just let me know. I'd be happy to go with you.

CONNECTOR – ***showing warmth and generosity of spirit***, *specifically:*
        expressing empathic understanding and offering ongoing supportive accompaniment

Questions for discussion

1) Have you ever been worried about a health issue and not known where to turn for emotional support?

2) Can you describe a situation in which you've seen someone after a gap in contact and the person looked physically changed? What assumptions did you make? What did you say to the person?

3) What do you imagine Connie was feeling that led her to focus only on how great it must be to lose weight without even trying?

4) How could Connie have addressed her own feelings openly without causing Deborah to feel unheard?

Story 12: Veronica

Background

Hi, you guys. I'm Veronica, and I'm an IT analyst in a large corporation. I recently gave a technical presentation at a meeting of our entire division. Overall it went well, but there was one man in the audience whose behavior bordered on what I would call heckling. He interrupted me several times with questions that weren't really for information, but rather seemed designed to show off his own knowledge. I largely kept my cool, but I have to admit I was distracted and I wasn't always sure how to respond.

At lunch, I was reflecting on the experience with my colleague, David.

What happened

Me (Veronica): Yeah, that guy was really annoying. He was already interrupting before I had even finished presenting the agenda.

David: Don't you see that's because you didn't inform the audience that they should save their questions for the end?

DISCONNECTOR – *criticizing, judging, shaming, or blaming, specifically:*
   blame for not foreseeing and preventing problems

DISCONNECTOR – *diagnosing or labeling, specifically:*
   uninvited critique of performance

DISCONNECTOR – *asking closed (yes or no) questions, specifically:*
   asking a pseudo-question that is actually a criticism

Me (Veronica) *(smiling knowingly)*: I'm not sure that would have deterred him. He seemed pretty determined to get attention.

David: You should have put him in his place the first time he spoke up. You let him go on for much too long.

DISCONNECTOR – **criticizing, judging, shaming, or blaming**, *specifically:*
  blame for not foreseeing and preventing problems

DISCONNECTOR – **lecturing or admonishing**, *specifically:*
  "you should have…"

What I'm feeling

What? David's blaming *me* for how that went? It's all *my* fault for not stopping an unstoppable know-it-all? And why is David looking to diagnose and criticize everything he thinks I did wrong? I feel like a bug under David's microscope. I thought I sat down for lunch with a supportive friend, but I'm feeling under attack! David seems to think he knows the right way to handle everything, and apparently that entitles him to teach and correct me as though I'm a schoolgirl.

I always want to see how I can improve, but I didn't invite David to diagnose my mistakes! If he'd been at all sympathetic and hadn't immediately hammered me with his great wisdom, starting with "Don't you see," and then telling me exactly what I "should have" done, I probably would have asked for his feedback and suggestions pretty soon. I do respect his opinions and experience, but I feel disrespected by his lecturing me like that and, sadly, I've lost some respect for him as a result. I hadn't seen this side of him before.

What I needed instead

Me (Veronica): Yeah, that guy was really annoying. He was already interrupting before I had even finished presenting the agenda.

David: I noticed. I was definitely wondering how you were feeling up there on stage.

CONNECTOR – **offering an expression of interest and caring understanding**, *specifically: showing interest in the other's experience*

Me (Veronica): I have to admit, I found him annoying. He seemed pretty determined to get attention. I'm thinking about how I might have gotten him to shut up sooner …

David: Mmm … It would be useful to have some tactics ready for handling such people, wouldn't it?

CONNECTOR – **showing warmth and generosity of spirit**, *specifically:*
> *meeting the other right where she is with attuned helpfulness and fostering her next step of learning*

Me (Veronica): It really would. Some people just go on and on, and it's hard to find any gap for replying. Hmm – looking back at it, if I were in that situation again, I would overcome my usual politeness and simply interrupt him and tell him we'll address any additional questions afterwards when I'm through with the presentation. What do you think? What would you do?

David: I might head him off at the pass by telling the audience at the start to please hold questions until the end.

Me (Veronica): Ah, of course. Good idea.

In the "what I needed instead" version of the conversation, I appreciated David accompanying me with interest as I followed my own process of thinking about how I would handle such a heckler in the future. When David shows respect for my ability to find solutions, then I'm happy to listen to *his* ideas because I retain my feeling of agency.

CONNECTOR – **supporting others' agency and autonomy in their lives**

Questions for discussion

1) Can you describe a situation in which you felt someone was diagnosing how you handled a particular situation, when you would have preferred to do your own processing? How did you feel in response?
2) What do you think leads someone to lecture and try to direct how another person deals with a difficult situation?
3) Do you sometimes feel as if you know better about what's going wrong in another person's life? How do you handle that feeling?
4) What ideas do you have for handling an unruly participant in a group you are leading?

Story 13: Jonathan

Background

Hi. I'm Jonathan. I commented the other day to my best friend Ben about our other friend Dennis.

What happened

Me (Jonathan): I'm pretty sure Dennis is going to fail the math test.

Ben: You're just saying that because you're jealous of him because his parents were nice and let him go on the exchange trip to Spain, and your parents didn't let you go.

DISCONNECTOR – ***telling rather than asking***, *specifically:*
> *explaining what the other's inner thoughts, feelings, and intentions are*

DISCONNECTOR – ***making assumptions that disconnect***, *specifically:*
> *believing "I know better than you what you're thinking"*

What I'm feeling

Annoyed! Yeah, *really* annoyed at Ben for thinking I'm that petty. He's my best friend and he doesn't know me any better than that? He seems to think he knows what's going on in my head better than I do, and that's super annoying, too. It's true that I'm still angry at my parents for not allowing me to go on the exchange. But it has nothing to do with what I said about Dennis and the math test. Why did Ben have to bring that up and use it to put me down like that?

What I needed instead

Me (Jonathan): I'm pretty sure Dennis is going to fail the math test.

Ben: What makes you say that? I mean, did he tell you that he didn't study or something?

Me (Jonathan): Yeah, he doesn't like our math teacher, and he said he's not even going to do the homework anymore.

Ben: You sound worried about him. What do you think, should one of us talk to him about it?

CONNECTOR – **active listening**, *accurately and empathically reflected*

CONNECTOR – **asking interestedly**, *specifically:*
inviting expression of thoughts and feelings

Questions for discussion

1) Can you describe a time when your listener jumped to an incorrect negative conclusion about you and your feelings? How did you feel?

2) Have you ever tried to correct your listener's incorrect interpretation of your motives? Describe that experience.

3) Are there times when you want to know how your listener is interpreting what you're saying? Describe such a circumstance.

4) Are you sometimes aware of yourself having an interpretation about what's going on inside another person? Under what conditions could it make sense to check with the other person about the accuracy of your interpretation?

Story 14: Chantal

Background

Dear readers,

You're most likely not just readers, but also shoppers. I'm Chantal, and I sit at the cash register in a chain discount store that does lively business all day. I work day shifts (from 10 a.m. to 6 p.m.), so the end of my work day is the beginning of the evening rush. What I'm trying to say is that I get tired and look forward to going home at exactly the hour when the lines get long and the customers become impatient.

The other day I had a surprising interaction, short but memorable. While I was waiting for a slow-moving woman to find her money in her purse, I was using every second to organize my receipts and coupons and wipe the workstation with spray cleaner, so I'd be ready to leave on time.

What happened

Customer *(with a smile)*: Wow, you have a lot to do!

*CONNECTOR – **acknowledging what you're noticing**, specifically:*
        simple acknowledgement of the other's human moment

What I'm feeling

She sees me as a person! All day long, the customers behave as though I'm an extension of the cash register: I say the amount, they hand me their card, I hand them the receipt, etc. But in this case, the customer saw me, first and foremost, as a human being trying to do a complicated job well. After my long day of slogging through impersonal coldness, that sudden little ray of personal warmth felt really good.

I mean, it was only a few seconds, but I had the impression that the customer was actually thinking about how it is to be in my position. I'm not sure why such a brief bit of thoughtful regard would give me such a lift, but it did.

I thought about it later and saw that the customer simply put into a few words her recognition of what she saw me doing. It was so simple, with no assumptions about how I might feel about my job or what kind of a mood I might be in. How could a few words from a stranger make me feel more seen than I've felt in quite a while?

Questions for discussion

1) Do you work or have you ever worked in a retail or service type of job in which you have frequent contact with the general public? If so, describe an interaction in which you felt particularly seen, heard, or appreciated by a customer.

2) If you've worked in such a job, describe an interaction with a customer in which you did not feel seen, heard, or appreciated.

3) When you've been in the customer role recently, have you had any contact with store personnel that had a noticeably humanizing or dehumanizing quality for that person? In hindsight, what do you wish you had said or not said?

4) Has living through a pandemic changed your perception of store personnel and the work they do? Have you communicated anything about that to them?

Story 15: George

Background

Hi, I'm George. Even though it's the middle of the semester, I'm new on campus because I just transferred from a different school. I fell in step with Elizabeth after class yesterday.

What happened

Me (George): Nice campus. Those flower baskets on all the lamp posts look so cool!

Elizabeth: What? I can't believe you just noticed those. How can you be so unobservant? They've been up for ages.

*DISCONNECTOR – **criticizing, judging, shaming, or blaming**, specifically:*
seizing opportunities to deliver shaming and establish one's superiority

What I'm feeling

I'm shocked speechless. Why did she turn my friendly comments into ammunition for machine-gunning me? Uh-oh, is this how people are in this school?

What I needed instead

Me (George): Nice campus. Those flower decorations on all the lamp posts look so cool!

Elizabeth: Yeah, they're really nice. I still enjoy them, even though they were put up last year.

Me (George): Oh! Well, I'm new here.

Elizabeth: In that case, welcome to our campus! And let me know if there's anything I can do to help you settle in.

*CONNECTOR – **showing warmth and generosity of spirit**, specifically:*
offering assistance with kindness

Questions for discussion

1) Can you describe a situation in which you were unexpectedly pounced upon with criticism or shaming?

2) How did you react outwardly? What were you feeling inside?

3) If someone you're with regards your viewpoint or assumptions as mistaken in some way, what do you feel is the best way for that person to say so?

4) What do you think and feel inside, and how do you respond, when you're with someone and you see a significant mistake in that person's views or assumptions?

Story 16: Jim

Background

Hi. I'm Jim. I've had a long career working in sales, and I'm good at what I do. I've been told I'm very persuasive. But of course, you win some and you lose some. It's part of the game, as I see it.

At the beginning of the year I got a new boss, Susan. She's only 32, so she certainly doesn't have as much real-world experience in sales as I do, but I was open. Fresh ideas are always welcome. What quickly jumped out at me, however, is how often she tells me what I "should" do or what I "should" have done with a given client. In these few months of working under Susan, I've become over-reactive to hearing the word "should" – allergic, you might say. It's gotten so bad that I snapped at my wife the other day when she lovingly said, "You should have told me you were tired. I would have been happy to drive." I apologized to her later for my sharp reaction. But with Susan there's no such easy cleanup after each incident.

What happened

Susan: So, Jim, how did it go this morning with the Jenson people? Are they going to sign the contract?

Me (Jim): I'm not convinced. It wasn't an outright no, but they're having doubts about working with a small firm like ours. They were pretty open about the fact that they're negotiating in parallel with a larger company.

Susan: And you let them go without a commitment? You should have prolonged the conversation with stories about the successes we've had with clients on an international scale! *That* definitely would have worked! That's what you should have done.

DISCONNECTOR – ***lecturing or admonishing***, *specifically:*
    blame for not preventing problems; implying incompetence

DISCONNECTOR – ***giving unsolicited advice or giving advice prematurely***, *specifically:*
    knowing better what would succeed

What I'm feeling

Unfairly judged! She wasn't even there, yet she assumes that her formulaic solutions would have made the sale. And I feel talked down to, as though I'm a rank beginner and she's the pro, when it's the other way around! She shouldn't be so quick to pass judgment on my performance. Sometimes things just don't go our way, and she shouldn't automatically turn that into blaming me for doing it wrong. A little trust in my experience and skill would be nice. It's not that I'm not open to her advice, but she shouldn't jump right to it before hearing why I handled it the way I did.

What I needed instead

Susan: So, Jim, how did it go this morning with the Jenson people? Are they going to sign the contract?

Me (Jim): I'm not convinced. It wasn't an outright no, but they have misgivings about working with a small firm like ours. They were pretty open about the fact that they're negotiating in parallel with a larger company.

Susan: I see. Sounds as though you were in a tight spot there. Do you think it might help increase their trust in us to tell them about our successes with large international clients?

*CONNECTOR – **asking rather than telling***

Me (Jim): Hard to predict, and they probably already noticed that in our brochure, but that's certainly worth trying. We left the door open, and I'll point that out when I check in with them next week.

Susan: Okay. If I can support you in any way, let me know.

*CONNECTOR – **showing warmth and generosity of spirit**, specifically:*
  offering assistance with kindness

Questions for discussion

1) Can you describe a situation in which someone told you what you "should" or "shouldn't" do, in effect implying that you lack competence or skill? How did you feel? How did you react?
2) Have you experienced a boss being supportive of you not only during your successes but also during your failures or problems?

3) Can you describe a situation in which you told someone what he or she "should" or "shouldn't" do? Had the other person specifically asked for your advice or guidance?

4) Have you experienced a time when you were tempted to tell another person what he or she "should" or "shouldn't" do, but you decided not to say it? What led you to make that decision?

Story 17: Ramona

Background

Hi, I'm Ramona. I'm feeling worn down and irritable because today so many things have gone wrong. And then, along with everything else, I had to wait in a ridiculously long line at the post office to mail a package.

What happened

The woman in front of me in line turned around and smiled and said, "Hi." I gave her a perfunctory smile. She then said, "We knew each other about ten years ago, from the karate school. Do you still go there?" I said, "No. I injured myself and don't do karate anymore." I didn't ask about her. I was in a bad mood.

She smiled understandingly and turned back around and faced the front of the line.

CONNECTOR – *acknowledging what you're noticing, specifically:*
respecting and cooperating with the other person's signals of unreceptivity

What I'm feeling

I'm grateful that she's leaving me in peace. Not that she was difficult in any way, but I just don't feel like making polite conversation today. I think that must have been plainly apparent to her. I mean, she must have noticed that my tone of voice, my words, and even my posture were all saying, "I don't have what it takes to be friendly right now." What I appreciate is that she noticed and respected that and didn't even seem to take it personally.

I have to admit, the kindness I saw in her brief smile surprised me. I guess what I expected to see in her face was a sort of dismissive or indignant look, as though her reaction would be, "Wow, that Ramona is an unfriendly bitch. And I was being so nice to her!" Makes me realize that in my life, receiving kind understanding when I'm upset isn't something that's happened much – or at all, maybe.

Questions for discussion

1) When you are having a particularly bad day, what do you most need from the people you come into contact with?
2) What do you think enabled the woman in front of Ramona to smile understandingly, rather than become unfriendly?

3) Can you describe a situation in which you could tell from someone's tone of voice and manner that the person wanted to be left alone? How did you feel about that preference?

4) Can you describe a situation in which you wanted to be left in peace, but someone else didn't get your message? How did you handle that?

Story 18: Manny

Background

I know I'm old and cranky. I can't help it – that's just how I am. I've had a rough life, abandoned as a kid, working low-wage jobs since I was 14 to try to make ends meet … For the last 12 years, at least I had my dog, Cowboy, for company. He was always at my side, always happy to see me, never got annoyed or insulted when I was in a bad mood. Cowboy died last week. Now I live alone, and nobody cares.

What happened

Neighbor: Hey, Manny, how's it going?

Me (Manny): Bad. Cowboy died.

Neighbor: Well, at least now you can move to a smaller place and don't need a yard anymore. You're always complaining about how much work the yard is.

DISCONNECTOR – **disregarding signals** *of distress*

DISCONNECTOR – **counteracting others' feelings, views, or actions**, *specifically: focusing on a positive "bright side" of the situation*

What I'm feeling

Not one damn ounce of sympathy! I should have known better than to even mention it. Damn, I let my guard down. I really should have known better, dammit! Yeah, he's my neighbor, but so what? He's *people*, and people are how they are. I tell him my only friend is gone, and all he can think about is that now I don't need my yard. Well, it's my own fault for trying for a few seconds of sympathy in this world.

What I needed instead

Neighbor: Hey, Manny, how's it going?

Me (Manny): Bad. Cowboy died.

Neighbor: Oh, I'm really sorry to hear that! He was your good buddy, I could see that.

CONNECTOR – *offering an expression of interest and caring understanding*

Me (Manny): Yeah, he sure was … Okay, see you around.

Questions for discussion

1) Have you experienced someone deflecting when you hinted about being deeply sad about something? If so, how did that feel to you, or how do you imagine that would feel to you?

2) Do you know any people who are possibly lonely much of the time, but you haven't considered that to date?

3) Can you describe someone you know who regularly complains about something? What do you think and feel when this happens, and how do you respond?

4) Do you ever complain about something? When you do, what response from your listener would really satisfy you? How might your expression of a particular dissatisfaction, hardship or distress be different from "complaining"?

Story 19: Courtney (part 1)

Background

Hi, everybody. My name is Courtney. I'm a full-time mom of three, and I'm married to a very difficult man who has some strong need to make everything my fault. I've tried to deal with this as best I can for years, largely for the kids' sake, but recently I've been noticing that it's even having a negative effect on the kids. The oldest one has started copying his father and making everything my fault. I'm seriously considering taking the kids and leaving – again, for their sake. But how can I take them away from their father? I'm full of inner turmoil!

I had a routine appointment with my physician a few weeks ago and asked for a referral for psychological counseling. She gave me the name and number of a local psychotherapist, so I made an appointment, which took place last week.

What happened

Me (Courtney): My husband is mean and negative toward me almost all the time! It wasn't always that way, but for the last two years he's made it clear that he has no love or respect for me. And I'm starting to see the same behavior in the kids. It's such an unhealthy environment for them that I feel I should protect them by separating, but maybe that could harm them in other ways. I don't know what to do, and I need help.

Psychotherapist: I'm willing to work with you, on one condition: You have to leave him first.

DISCONNECTOR – **undermining the other person's autonomy or agency**, *specifically: dictating what the other should do*

What I'm feeling

Whoa! Who do you think you are? How can you push me to do that without even knowing what's going on in my world? This has to be *my* decision, based on *my* knowledge and feelings about what's best for my children.

What I need from a professional counselor (or anyone, for that matter) is basic respect for my capabilities in dealing with my life situation. I need a counselor to help me get to my own clarity about the terrible tradeoffs I'm facing.

What I needed instead

Me (Courtney): My husband is mean and negative toward me almost all the time! It wasn't always that way, but for the last two years he's made it clear that he has no respect for me. And I'm starting to see the same behavior in the kids. It's such an unhealthy environment for them that I feel I should protect them by separating, but maybe that would harm them in other ways. I don't know what to do, and I need help.

Psychotherapist: Yes, that's often a very, very difficult decision for a loving parent to make. Of course, I can't make any decisions for you, but I can help you find your way in your decision-making process.

CONNECTOR – **active listening**, *reflected empathically, specifically:*
   acknowledging the difficulty of the dilemma

CONNECTOR – **supporting others' agency and autonomy in their lives**, *specifically:*
   acknowledgement of making one's own choices

Questions for discussion

1) Can you describe a potentially life-changing decision that you've made or are considering in the future? What is your experience with talking to others (friends, family, professionals …) about your decision-making process? Did you feel pushed into any particular choice by anyone?
2) Was it ever useful to you to hear about what others have experienced or what decision others would make in your situation?
3) What do you imagine or wish for when you read, "… I can help you find your way in your decision-making process"?
4) Have you ever tried to help another person with his or her decision-making process by telling that person what *you* would do? Did that seem to be helpful to the other person? If not, why do you think it wasn't?

Story 20: Courtney (part 2)

Background

Hi, readers, it's me again, Courtney. These recent weeks have felt like the longest weeks of my life. I finally made the painful decision to start separating from my abusive husband, but I haven't yet managed to move out with the kids. What a balancing act! There are very few people I can to talk to about it since it's essential for my husband to know nothing of my decision yet, but I'm too alone in my volatile and dangerous situation and have a burning need to feel seen and understood by someone.

Sitting at my desk at work, I must have had a troubled look on my face that a friendly coworker noticed, and he came over to me, and I took the spontaneous risk of confiding in him.

What happened

Coworker *(with just a touch of concern)*: Hey – how are you?

Me (Courtney): Oh, gosh – that's so kind of you. Actually, yeah, well, I decided yesterday that I have to leave my marriage. It was a really hard decision, and for now I have to keep it to myself.

Coworker: Wow, that's rough. I know you have kids. What a complicated situation for you. I hope you'll soon be able to tell some friends or family you trust.

CONNECTOR – *acknowledging what you're noticing*, *specifically:*
responding to indications of distress or need

CONNECTOR – *showing warmth and generosity of spirit*, *specifically:*
expressing empathic understanding with kindness

What I'm feeling

I'm sort of blown away by how much relief I feel from his simple words of understanding. I could have cried from the relief of feeling understood and suddenly so much less alone in my crisis, but I managed to hold back those tears. He really gets it! I'm so grateful, and that little conversation is helping to sustain me at this really vulnerable, pivotal moment in my life.

Questions for discussion

1) Can you describe a situation in which you were in some distress and received empathy for your feelings?

2) Can you describe an interaction in which you were able to understand another person deeply? How did you show your understanding to the other person? How do you think the other person felt?

3) Can you describe a situation in which another person did not empathize with your distress? Did that person instead offer advice or voice a positive outlook? How did you feel? What do you imagine got in the way of simply empathizing with you?

4) Can you recall a situation in which you were not able to empathize with another person's feelings? What was going on for you that got in the way of your being able to empathize?

Story 21: Bethany

Background

Hi, everybody! I'm Bethany. I'm 5 years old. My big sister is helping me write this story, because I only know how to write a few words so far.

The story is about a picture I drew in my room yesterday. I drew the same things I always draw: a brown tree and green grass and a yellow sun. This time I tried to draw a gray horse running through the grass, but I didn't think it really looked like a horse and I was getting mad about that.

Mommy came into my room to see what I was doing.

What happened

Mommy: What are you doing, Beth?

Me (Bethany): Drawing.

Mommy: Nice. Can I see your picture?

Me (Bethany): Okay … but I don't like it.

Mommy: But it's beautiful! You're a wonderful artist.

*DISCONNECTOR – **implying "you shouldn't feel how you feel,"** specifically:*
arguing against clearly expressed feelings

*DISCONNECTOR – **praising, presented as fact**, specifically:*
attempting to dispel a negative self-evaluation

What I'm feeling

Now I'm also mad at Mommy because she isn't listening to me about how unhappy I feel with my drawing. Now I'm *really* mad. When I'm unhappy about something, I need Mommy to understand what I'm unhappy about, but she doesn't. She tries to make me think everything is fine and there's no problem.

What I needed instead

Mommy: What are you doing, Beth?

Me (Bethany): Drawing.

Mommy: Nice. Can I see your picture?

Me (Bethany): Okay … but I don't like it.

Mommy: Hmm … Is there some part of the picture that you're not happy with?

*CONNECTOR – **asking rather than telling***

Me (Bethany): Yeah, the horse!

Mommy: Oh, the horse isn't how you wanted it to be.

*CONNECTOR – **active listening**, accurately reflected*

Questions for discussion

1) What do you imagine were the motivations of Mommy in praising Bethany and calling her "a wonderful artist"?
2) Did receiving or not receiving praise ever have a big effect on you?
3) Can you describe a situation in which you were dissatisfied with your own performance, and you expressed this to another person? How did the other person react? Was this helpful or unhelpful to you? In what ways?
4) Can you describe a situation in which another person expressed being dissatisfied with his or her own performance? How did you respond?

Story 22: Sem

Background

Hi, people. My name is Sem. My story is about my old clique of friends from when we were at university together, a decade ago. There are five of us, all guys. We were really close for the four years we spent there, and when we get together now it's like old times – funny and wild!

Given that four out of five are married, three of us have children, and we don't all live in the same city anymore, you can imagine that it's not easy to find a weekend that works for all five of us. But as the organizer of our yearly events, I'm persistent. We're very loyal to each other and look forward every year to our next get-together.

So you can imagine my surprise when I saw the email from Kai one week before our planned date, saying that he wasn't going to make it. His explanation was simply that he had scheduled something else on that weekend without realizing there was a conflict.

Well, I know Kai pretty well, and there isn't much that could come between him and the rest of us. I also know that he sometimes feels insecure about being the only member of the group without a partner. I decided to assume that his cancellation probably had something to do with a new relationship and that he'd tell us about it in due time. What else could be more important than reconnecting with us? So I wrote back "Good luck!" and smiled to myself.

What happened

The long-awaited weekend finally arrived. The four of us were sitting at our regular table at our favorite pub and enjoying a cold beer. I leaned forward conspiratorially and addressed the others.

Me (Sem): So … um … anybody know what's going on with Kai?

Yannick: Ha, I knew you'd be pissed at him!

ouch!

DISCONNECTOR – **telling rather than asking**, *specifically:*
explaining what the other's inner thoughts, feelings, and intentions are

Me (Sem): What are you talking about? I'm not pissed. I'm dying of suspense!

What I'm feeling

Yannick was so sure that he knew me so well that he could know in advance that I'd be pissed at Kai, but he was wrong. I guess it sort of hurts my feelings that Yannick sees me that way – a person who'd get angry at Kai for this. Wow, after all this time he *doesn't* know me so well. That's pretty disappointing. He was so into having me all figured out in his own mind that it never occurred to him to *ask* me how I felt about Kai.

What I needed instead

Me (Sem): So … um … anybody know what's going on with Kai?

Yannick: I could only guess. What do you think?

Me (Sem): I bet it's a woman. What else would be that important?

Yannick: Are you annoyed that he canceled on short notice?

CONNECTOR – ***asking interestedly***, *specifically:*
                     enquiring about the other's actual experience

Me (Sem): No, not at all. I'm kind of disappointed that he's not here with us, but I hope he's doing something very cool!

Questions for discussion

1) Have you ever experienced someone who was certain about what *you* were feeling, but who was totally wrong? How did or would that feel to you?
2) Have you ever experienced someone who was certain about what you were feeling, and who was *correct*? How did or would *that* feel to you?
3) Can you describe a situation in which you were sure you knew what another person was feeling, although the person had not communicated those feelings to you? Were you able to confirm your interpretation?
4) Can you describe a situation in which a person you know well behaved in an unexpected way? Were you able to form an explanatory interpretation? Did you ultimately gain any understanding about what actually happened?

Story 23: Carl

Background

Hello. My name is Carl. I retired recently from a management position at an international company. I always put my all into that job, even neglecting some of my family's needs along the way, although I didn't realize that at the time. You can't turn back the clock, but you can aim to do things differently in the future.

I had a mild heart attack during my last year on the job, so I'm paying more attention to my health these days. I'm still energetic enough to dive into big projects, and I've been looking forward to renovating an old house I bought a few years ago so that my daughter and her family can move in there.

I don't know what any of our lives will be like by the time you read this, but right now it's April 2020 and most of us are in the midst of the coronavirus crisis. It's terrible timing – not that there's such a thing as good timing for a pandemic. I have all these plans, but we're in lockdown now. I know it's necessary, but I'm so frustrated! I've waited all these years to retire and be able to choose how I spend my time, and now I can't move forward on my project. Due to my heart attack I'm considered a high-risk patient and I have to be especially careful not to come in contact with the virus. So I'm homebound and feeling time just slipping away from me, with no end in sight to this state of limbo.

An old colleague of mine, Sonja, was in my area recently and suggested getting together. We met for a walk in a nearby park, keeping six feet apart.

What happened

Me (Carl): Sonja, long time no see. How are you coping?

Sonja: What an interesting period we're in! Everything's unpredictable, people are unpredictable … I see the opportunity for big changes in the society. It's a real chance to bring more attention to climate change issues.

Me (Carl): Hmm, maybe. So you're feeling optimistic, in spite of all the craziness.

Sonja: Yeah, that's a good way to summarize it. And what about you?

Me (Carl): Well, to tell you the truth, I'm frustrated right now. I had things I wanted to accomplish this year, things that are important for my family, and now it looks as if everything will be on hold for who knows how long. I feel I'm losing a year of my life! And I'm powerless to change it.

Sonja: Well, you always did emphasize risk analysis and seeing what could go wrong, Carl. But you shouldn't see this so negatively! Why don't you just –

DISCONNECTOR – *saying "always" or "never"*

DISCONNECTOR – *implying "you shouldn't feel how you feel,"* *specifically:* *offering a positive view to dispel distress*

DISCONNECTOR – *disregarding the deeper message, especially if it involves distress or* *need*

Me (Carl): Please, Sonja, I don't want your optimism right now.

Sonja: I only wanted to suggest –

DISCONNECTOR – *implying "you shouldn't need what you need,"* *specifically:* *disregarding and violating the other's clear communication of a* *boundary*

DISCONNECTOR – *giving unsolicited advice or giving advice prematurely*

Me (Carl): I don't want advice and I don't want to talk about it anymore.

Sonja: But you could –

Me (Carl): Sonja, what part of "no, thank you" don't you understand?

What I'm feeling

I'm as fed up with Sonja as ever for her condescending attitude. She asked me how I'm doing with the crisis, and then disregarded and tried to correct what I'm experiencing. She made me wrong for feeling what I'm feeling! And she characterized me as "always" focused on what can go wrong, invalidating my judgment, as though the losses and hardships I'm facing aren't 100% real.

I didn't invite Sonja to critique my values or perceptions. Her own judgment is so heavy on optimism that for me, her opinions are pretty much useless to me.

I also didn't ask for her advice, and I had to block her three times before she got the message that I didn't want it.

What I needed instead

Me (Carl): Sonja, long time no see. How are you coping?

Sonja: What an interesting period we're in! Everything's unpredictable, people are unpredictable ... I see the opportunity for big changes in the society. It's a real chance to bring more attention to climate change issues.

Me (Carl): Hmm, maybe. So you're feeling optimistic, in spite of all the craziness.

Sonja: Yeah, that's a good way to summarize it. And what about you?

Me (Carl): Well, to tell you the truth, I'm frustrated right now. I had things I wanted to accomplish this year, things that are important for my family, and now it looks as if everything will be on hold for who knows how long. I feel I'm losing a year of my life! And powerless to change it.

Sonja: Sounds as though you're feeling blocked by forces you weren't expecting.

*CONNECTOR – **active listening**, accurately reflected*

Me (Carl): Exactly, totally blocked by big forces I wasn't expecting, forces I can't change or control.

Sonja: No wonder you're frustrated.

*CONNECTOR – **offering an expression of interest and caring understanding***

Questions for discussion

1) Can you describe a situation in which someone tried to convince you that you should feel differently from how you in fact felt? How did that feel? How did you react?
2) Have you ever had the experience of needing to interrupt another person's well-meant but not useful advice? How did you handle that?
3) Can you describe a situation in which you were tempted to tell another person not to be so negative about something?
4) Did you, in fact, speak your thoughts to the other person? What were your motivations to do so or not to do so?

Story 24: Nate

Background

Hi, people. My name is Nate, and I'm 42 years old. I grew up as the middle of three brothers, and I kind of got lost in the shuffle a lot of the time. My older brother was the achiever who brought home the honors, so he got a lot of attention, not leaving much room for me. My younger brother was the athlete of the family and outgrew me by the time he was 10.

He had a ravenous appetite and grabbed half the food on the table for himself as a matter of course. The message I grew up with was: There's not enough to go around, there's not enough for me, so I'd better hoard and protect what I can get. And there's certainly not enough attention available for me, so I'd better not have any expectations of getting any or I'll feel painfully disappointed and neglected.

In my adult years I've lived alone, surrounding myself with books and old LPs and technological gadgets that no one can take away from me, and I haven't dated much. I don't expect much interest from other people.

When I don't feel like heating up a meal, I step out to the pizzeria across the street. They know me there, since I've been going at least once a week for years.

Last Monday evening I was there at the pizzeria, and business was slow. Sandy, the waitress, sat down at my table, something she hadn't done before.

What happened

Sandy: Hey, it's nice that you came in on a slow night. Now I have someone to talk to. Mondays are usually so boring.

Me (Nate): Oh! Glad to be able to help.

Sandy: Yeah, I felt like talking to you some other times, but there was always too much going on.

CONNECTOR – ***showing warmth and generosity of spirit****, specifically:*
expressing the feeling of wanting connection

Me (Nate): Really?

Sandy *(smiling)*: Really!

Me (Nate): *(looking at Sandy, speechless)*

Sandy *(jumping up)*: The cook made too much tiramisu today. I'll go get you a nice, big portion. Be right back.

CONNECTOR – ***showing warmth and generosity of spirit,*** *specifically:*
thoughtful, nurturing actions

What I'm feeling

I'm really disoriented! I *know* that people don't pay attention to me, and here's Sandy not only paying attention to me but also admitting that she's been paying attention to me and interested in connecting with me for a while. And then her impulse to bring me tiramisu took me totally by surprise. I even caught myself half expecting her not to return from the kitchen. She's giving me not only attention, but also food?! In my experience, food isn't something that gets shared so easily. I'm suddenly full of stirred-up, unhappy childhood memories, and it's hard to sort out what's really going on.

Sandy's whole manner was so open and direct that the genuineness of her wanting to visit with me got across to me. I could see that she was actually happy to see me. To put it mildly, I'm not used to that! It seemed so simple for her to answer "Really!" as if she heard and understood my surprise.

Questions for discussion

1) Have you ever had an interaction in which you discovered that you mattered to the other person much more than seemed possible? How did you, or how might you, react to that?

2) Have you felt the kind of emotional confusion that Nate describes, in which a long-held assumption about the way the world works has met up with a contradictory experience?

3) What do you imagine made it possible for Sandy to be so plainly open with Nate about wanting his company?

4) Why do you think it's hard for most people most of the time to express affinity openly the way Sandy did?

Story 25: Simeon

Background

Hi, people. My name is Simeon. I'm 16 years old. I live with my parents and my younger sister. I consider myself to be an environmental activist. I do volunteer work after school and on weekends for a group that organizes live demonstrations and online petitions and that lobbies the government to help keep our country green and livable.

My Dad was a political activist against racism when he was young, but he had some bad experiences, including getting seriously injured at the hands of the police when a demonstration went out of control. He's on a different path now. He writes posts in forums, but he doesn't go out in crowds anymore. I can understand his feelings, but what's true for him isn't necessarily true for me. I don't feel a need to avoid those physical dangers.

A few days ago I was telling Dad about our highly secret plans for a demonstration to block the construction site of a waste processing plant in an environmentally delicate area that won't survive additional air and water pollution. It's a hot topic among the locals. We're planning to chain ourselves to nearby structures and to each other. It can get pretty intense when we chain ourselves to things and the police come with their metal-cutting shears. I was enthusiastically describing our plan …

What happened

Dad *(interrupting me)*: Sim, Sim — it's hard for me to listen to this right now. I know you're excited about this action, and I remember what it felt like to do these things at your age. But I'm your father and I'm thinking of your safety above and beyond every other consideration. I'm sorry, but I really can't listen to all the details you want to tell me. It makes me too nervous. I'm not going to try to stop you from doing it — I know better than that. And I trust you to be alert and use good judgment at all times. But I can take in only so much of this at a time! I hope you can understand that.

CONNECTOR – *using I-messages*

CONNECTOR – *using transparency in communication*

CONNECTOR – *offering an expression of interest and caring understanding*, specifically: *showing concern*

What I'm feeling

Well, on the one hand I'm kind of disappointed and frustrated that he's cutting off discussion. My Dad is my biggest role model and I want to share everything with him. On the other hand, I can really feel the caring and worry behind his words. I respect him for giving me so much freedom, and I respect him for explaining his own need so honestly, in a way that doesn't make me feel as if I'm doing anything wrong.

Questions for discussion

1) Imagine being in the father's position. Would you be able to listen calmly to Simeon's plans for the demonstration, given your past traumatic experience of being attacked and seriously injured in exactly that kind of situation? How do you imagine you would respond to Simeon?

2) Simeon's father ended the conversation sooner than Simeon would have wanted. What do you think enabled Simeon to accept the discussion being cut off in this way without feeling opposed or criticized?

3) Can you describe a situation, if you have one in your memory, in which someone you loved willingly put him- or herself in harm's way? How did you feel about that? What did you communicate to that person? Did you express your own feelings?

4) Have you ever knowingly put yourself in a risky situation? If so, was there someone whose objection was hard for you to take in? What might have better enabled you to understand that person's concerns?

Story 26: Destiny

Background

Hi,

My name is Destiny. I'm 11, and I'm in sixth grade. I've been noticing recently how much easier it is to talk to Mom than to Dad about some things. Here's an example from yesterday. It was the last day of school before the holidays, and we got our report cards and went home much earlier than usual. When I arrived, Dad was home already, but Mom wasn't yet.

What happened

Dad: Hi, honey. Was it a good day at school today?

Me (Destiny): Yup.

Dad: You must be happy that the semester's over!

Me (Destiny): Sure.

Dad: Oh, did you get your report card?

Me (Destiny): Yup.

Dad: Happy with your grades?

Me (Destiny): Yeah … I guess …

Dad: That's my girl.

ouch!

DISCONNECTOR – **asking leading questions**, *specifically:*
requiring only positive feelings and attitudes

DISCONNECTOR – **asking closed (yes or no) questions**

What I'm feeling

His questions let me know that he wants to hear only happy good news, nothing about anything negative. When he asks, "Was it a good day at school today?", I sense his need to hear that it was a good day. Or when he asks, "Happy with your grades?",

I hear the word "happy" and feel as if I have to be happy for him. I mean, I know he really, really loves me, but I can tell he doesn't want to know what I'm really feeling or what really happened in my life that day. I give him the answers he wants, but all I can manage is one- or two-word replies with half-dead energy because actually it's kind of depressing. I guess I wish he'd notice that and ask me about what's really going on with me, but he almost never does. He's happy with my phony positive answers and goes on his merry way.

What I needed instead

Here's what happened later in the evening when Mom came home. It felt good to be able to share more of my experiences and let off some steam.

Mom: Hi, Des – how was school today?

CONNECTOR – **asking interestedly**, *specifically:*
    enquiring about the other's actual experience

Me (Destiny): It was good, especially because it was a short day. We got our report cards and had only three periods. That's always fun. So I went to Jane's for lunch before I came home.

Mom: Oh, right, today was report card day. How did it go?

CONNECTOR – **asking open questions**

Me (Destiny): Pretty good. The only thing that surprised me was that I got a C in art! How do you get a C in art? Who is *she* to tell me that my artwork isn't good enough? I was annoyed for a while, but then Jane and I played games after lunch and I forgot about the stupid art teacher.

Questions for discussion

1) Is there a relationship in which you tend to answer in short or one-word answers? What do you observe about the communication pattern with that person? How do you usually feel in that relationship?
2) Think of a relationship in which you tend to answer with more extensive or deeper information. What about the communication in that relationship enables you to share more of yourself? How do you feel overall in that relationship?

3) What do you think might be the reasons for Destiny's father angling for positivity? Do you know someone who does that? How does that person continue the conversation when your response isn't positive as expected?

4) How do you imagine that Destiny's mother's life experiences differed from those of her father, such that her mother asks open-ended questions that invite Destiny to express the full truth of her experiences? How might Destiny be feeling in life if her mother had the same style as her father?

Story 27: Matt

Background

Dear reader,

I don't know whether you're used to hearing from a kid, but I really need someone to take me seriously, so thanks for listening. My name is Matt, and I'm 10 years old.

My parents and I were in the car on our way back from spending a weekend with our relatives. It's about a three-hour drive, and we headed out earlier than usual on Sunday because I had soccer practice that afternoon.

What happened

Me (Matt): I'm hungry.

Mom: We just had brunch!

ouch!

DISCONNECTOR – *implying "you shouldn't feel how you feel"*

Me (Matt): But I'm hungry anyway.

Mom: Hmm, we don't have anything in the car, and if we stop anywhere, you'll be late for soccer.

Dad: Stop complaining. Just try to sleep until we get there.

ouch!

DISCONNECTOR – *disregarding signals of distress or need*

DISCONNECTOR – *implying "you shouldn't need what you need,"* specifically:
  defining distress due to an unmet need as weakness and poor character

What I'm feeling

First of all, I'm still feeling hungry, no matter what they say. And the fact that we just had brunch doesn't change that. Isn't that obvious? And yet my mother doesn't want to believe me that I'm already hungry. That feels really bad.

Second of all, I feel so insulted by Dad! His way of ignoring that I'm hungry is to call it "complaining," as if it's fine to ignore somebody who has a complaint. And he also *ordered* me to "stop complaining," as if I'm some sort of robot with an on-and-off switch.

What I needed instead

Me (Matt): I'm hungry.

Mom: Uh-oh, I didn't plan for that right after brunch! Wow, what an appetite my growing boy has! Hmm, we don't have anything in the car, and if we stop anywhere, you'll be late for soccer. I'm so sorry, honey, but you might have to tolerate feeling hungry for a while. It might not last the whole ride.

*CONNECTOR – **offering an expression of interest and caring understanding**, specifically: showing empathy*

Dad: I know how awful that feels. When I was little, I had a trick for dealing with that. You wanna hear it?

*CONNECTOR – **active listening**, empathically reflected*

*CONNECTOR – **asking rather than telling**, specifically: asking whether advice is welcome*

Me (Matt): Sure.

Dad: On long car rides, I tried to sleep as much as I could, so I wouldn't even notice the time going by. How about trying that?

Questions for discussion

1) Do you remember how it felt to be a kid on a long car ride? How did your family handle challenges like this one?
2) If you were one of the parents, how would you respond in this situation?
3) What might the mother have been feeling when she learned her son was hungry and she hadn't brought any food?
4) Do you think there are times when parents are justified in giving orders? If so, can you give examples?

Story 28: Ina

Background

Hi! I'm Ina, a full-time mother of two wonderful daughters. The older one, who's 11, dances ballet pretty well for her age. I try to encourage her to go to class regularly but without putting too much pressure on her.

We recently attended a recital of prize winners from a local dance competition. The performers were 16- to 18-year-olds, some of them quite impressive, in fact I'd say they already have a level of virtuosity. Afterwards we happened to encounter one of my daughter's ballet school friends and her mother, Angie.

What happened

Me (Ina): What a lot of talent we have in our town!

Angie: Yeah, they're amazing, these young people. They've probably been dancing since before they could talk.

Me (Ina): In five years that'll be our kids up there on the stage.

Angie: Our kids? I don't think so. They'll never be that good.

DISCONNECTOR – ***counteracting others' feelings, views, or actions***, *specifically: implying you shouldn't have those hopes and aspirations*

DISCONNECTOR – ***making assumptions that disconnect***, *specifically: believing "I know better than you about your child's capabilities and potential."*

What I'm feeling

How dare you make a negative prediction about my child?!?! You can talk negatively about your own child as much as you want (which I think is also terrible), but don't presume to know anything about my daughter's potential! Keep your pessimistic opinions about my child to yourself!

What I needed instead

Me (Ina): What a lot of talent we have in our town!

Angie: Yeah, they're amazing, these young people. They've probably been dancing since before they could talk.

Me (Ina): In five years that'll be our kids up there on the stage.

Angie: Is that a goal your daughter has?

*CONNECTOR – **asking interestedly***

Me (Ina): Hmm. Interesting question. After seeing this performance tonight, I think I'll feel her out about that.

Angie: Yeah, my daughter's been having some doubts about how much talent she has for ballet – just between you and me. She's actually thinking of quitting ballet and starting baseball.

*CONNECTOR – **speaking for oneself only**, specifically:*
   confiding about a delicate area of vulnerability

Questions for discussion

1) What do you think might have motivated Angie to say, "Our kids? I don't think so. They'll never be that good"?
2) If you were Ina, how would *you* react to that remark from Angie?
3) What do you think might have motivated Ina to say with apparent certainty, "In five years that'll be our kids up there on the stage"?
4) When you hear people speak with certainty about their future glories, how do you feel and respond?

Story 29: Nancy

Background

Hello, dear reader,

I'm Nancy. I'm remembering a conversation from many decades ago that significantly affected my future and my fate. It was a short conversation, but I've never forgotten it.

It was 1986, I was 28 years old, and I was at the movies with my boyfriend, Terry. Everyone said we were good together, and we'd cautiously started having talks about maybe becoming engaged.

We were leaving the movie theater after having seen *Hannah and Her Sisters*, a Woody Allen comedy-drama about a woman and her two sisters and their partners. As usual with Woody Allen movies, we laughed a lot, but it was also laced with some deep emotions, and as we were walking away from the theater, I was awash with thoughts of my recently deceased mother and her relationships with her two younger sisters.

What happened

Me (Nancy): There were some scenes in there that made me think so much of my mother. I really miss her, and I'm feeling so sad right now.

Terry: Have you stopped to think about the fact that you can choose to move past that? It's up to you, you know.

DISCONNECTOR – *implying "you shouldn't feel how you feel,"* *specifically: invalidating an ongoing grief process*

DISCONNECTOR – *giving unsolicited advice or giving advice prematurely*

DISCONNECTOR – *asking leading questions, specifically: a pseudo-question that means, "You should see this the same way I do."*

What I'm feeling

Hey, these feelings of missing and sadness are my love for my mother, and you're making me wrong for feeling them?! And I was feeling close to you until ten seconds ago, but not anymore! Now I'm feeling a really big gulf between us, and it's very upsetting. In fact, what you just did is so upsetting that you've succeeded in yanking me out of my feelings for my mom – and into doubts about us. Do you think I'd want to spend my life with someone who tells me what I should and shouldn't be feeling in my heart? Oh my God, I can't believe this crisis just came out of nowhere!

Terry, apparently *you* need to quickly "move past" distressing feelings or things that upset you. I hope your approach works brilliantly for you, but you make a big mistake in assuming it will work for me. Did I ask for your advice about how to deal with my feelings? No, I didn't. Yet you presume to foist it on me. Yikes, actually I'm lucky this showed up *before* we went ahead and got engaged.

It also bothers me that you made your condescending advice sound like a question, but it was one of those pseudo-questions people use to make their own point – and your point came across very clearly. When I have strong emotions, I have to find my own path, my own solutions, and my own timing. I'm sure you had good intentions and meant to be helpful according to your own perspective about feelings, but even so, this is a major difference between us and a major problem in our relationship.

What I needed instead

Me (Nancy): There were some scenes in there that made me think so much of my mother. I really miss her, and I'm feeling so sad right now.

Terry: I can see how that movie would bring up all those feelings about your mom.

*CONNECTOR – **active listening**, empathically reflected*

Follow-up to what happened

I did not marry Terry. I can't say that that conversation was *the* reason, but it began a reconsideration that helped me see a number of factors that finally caused me to end our relationship.

Questions for discussion

1) Can you describe a situation in which receiving unsolicited advice was exactly the wrong thing for you?
2) Can you describe a situation in which you definitely wanted another person's advice? Did you explicitly ask for it?

3) How could Nancy have expressed the distancing effect of Terry's reply in a way that he might have understood?

4) Imagine yourself in Terry's position. Do you think he was fully aware of what gave rise to his response? Can you think of both altruistic and non-altruistic intentions?

Story 30: Freddy

Background

Hi, guys, I'm Freddy, 23 years old. I just finished college and started my first job. It's great to have my own income, and I found a decent one-room apartment for a reasonable price near work. What a breath of fresh air after the years I lived with my parents during college!

I'm going all-in with creating a new life for myself. I joined a fitness club and got myself a dog for company. She's a mutt, but quite a beauty nonetheless, so I named her Bella. What she has in looks, however, she makes up for with stubbornness. I'm trying really hard to train her, using dog treats and affection for conditioning, but she insists on barking at all the wrong times, which is not making me very popular with my new neighbors. I'm feeling extremely frustrated!

I stopped by my parents' place for dinner last Sunday.

What happened

Mom *(passing a helping of home-made lasagna to me)*: And how's it going with Bella?

Me (Freddy): Oh, man. She's unbelievably strong-willed and stubborn. Or else I'm doing something wrong. It feels like a battle, and she's winning!

Mom: Are you being completely consistent in when you reward her?

Me (Freddy): I think so. And I don't want to have to use punishment. But when she wakes me up by barking in the middle of the night, I get so furious at her that I want to throw her against the wall to make her stop!

Mom *(looking aghast)*: How can you even say such a thing? Where did *that* mean streak come from? The poor dog!

ouch!

*DISCONNECTOR – **implying "you shouldn't feel how you feel,"** specifically: condemnation of dark thoughts that arise under extreme stress*

*DISCONNECTOR – **moralizing***

What I'm feeling

Betrayed. I felt really vulnerable in showing my mother my true level of frustration and anger about the dog. I love Bella and feel committed to her, long-term, but at that moment I was admitting that I'm really struggling with this. That's not the moment to criticize me or take the dog's side.

The look on Mom's face was as if she thought I were a murderer or something. I realize I may have shocked her, but doesn't she know me well enough to know I was just letting off steam and would never harm a dog? Why did she need to judge me so negatively? That certainly shut me up and made me regret that I had confided in her.

Follow-up after about ten minutes

Me (Freddy): You know, Mom, now that I've calmed down somewhat, I can understand why you were upset by what I said about the dog. I know it alarmed you, but I needed some sympathy, and instead got condemnation.

Mom: Sorry, I really didn't mean to mouth off at you. And I do get how frustrated and desperate you feel with Bella in the middle of the night.

CONNECTOR – *repairing rifts, specifically:*
apologizing and expressing empathic understanding of the other's experience

Me (Freddy): Yeah, it's okay. I was just letting off steam.

What I needed instead

Mom *(passing a **helping of home-made lasagna** to me)*: And how's it going with Bella?

Me (Freddy): Oh, man. She's unbelievably strong-willed and stubborn. Or else I'm doing something wrong. It feels like a battle, and she's winning!

Mom: That sounds challenging. Hmm … I'm wondering … Are you being completely consistent in when you reward her?

Me (Freddy): I think so. And I don't want to have to use punishment. But when she wakes me up by barking in the middle of the night, I get so furious at her that I want to throw her against the wall to make her stop!

Mom: That's true desperation! First you're jolted awake by the barking, then you can't get her to stop! And you have to get up early for work the next day.

CONNECTOR – **active listening**, *accurately and empathically reflected*

Me (Freddy): That's it, exactly. On the weekends I don't care so much. I can sleep late, but during the week it's seeming impossible.

Questions for discussion

1) Have you ever admitted to "socially unacceptable" feelings and thereby made yourself vulnerable, as Freddy did? How did the other person handle it?
2) Can you describe a situation in which you held back from revealing feelings that in some way seemed unacceptable to share, because you did not want to make yourself vulnerable?
3) Can you think of a time when you felt judgmental or appalled by something someone said, although you basically liked and respected the person? How did you react?
4) What was that person's response? What do you think he or she was feeling?

Story 31: Linda

Background

Hi, friends. I'm Linda, 63 years old, and a happy mother and grandmother. I have certain memories, both good and bad, of moments in my own childhood that are still crystal clear, as if they had happened yesterday. My parents were loving, good people. However, as soon as any of us kids expressed any strong, negative emotion, our parents became agitated and would do whatever was necessary to change the topic or the focus. I think now that they simply felt helpless and didn't know what to do with their own discomfort. It never occurred to them to just give us some understanding of what was distressing us or what our need was.

Here's an example from when I was 4. I was furious with my father because he wouldn't let me kiss our pet bunny rabbits. He was afraid they might scratch me in the face, but I wanted to cuddle them. Since I had already learned that openly expressing my anger in words was taboo, I expressed it in the only slightly less direct way of becoming a furious, charging bull, using my pointer fingers as horns, and I raced at him in all my rage, stamping, making aggressive, snorting sounds and glaring at the floor.

What happened

Daddy: Ha ha, you're a really cute little bull. Look at me, smile at me. May I pet you? I've never petted a bull before.

*DISCONNECTOR – **implying "you shouldn't feel how you feel"***

*DISCONNECTOR – **disregarding signals** of distress or need*

*DISCONNECTOR – **deflecting, distracting, or evading**, specifically:*
        failing to engage with bad moods or painful emotions

What I'm feeling

Now I feel even *more* angry at Daddy, because I really want him to feel my angry protest at him for not letting me kiss the bunnies, but he's completely ignoring how upset I'm feeling. So now I'm also feeling helpless because I can't get Daddy to care about how unhappy I feel, and that makes me also feel desperate and scared. I'm just swimming in so many really awful feelings, and Daddy is smiling and amused with me. In these moments I'm learning to expect to be disregarded whenever I need to express distress to others, a pattern that has stuck with me all my life, even today.

What I needed instead

Daddy: Oh, this raging bull is very angry at me, because I'm not letting her kiss those bunnies! Well, I *didn't know* that a big bull would really *really* want to kiss bunnies! Yes, they are snuggly, cuddly little things, aren't they? How 'bout we take a look at one of them together and figure out what parts are cuddly and what parts are sharp and scratchy? We'll figure out how to kiss them without your face being scratched and hurt, okay?

CONNECTOR – acknowledging what you're noticing

Questions for discussion

1) Can you describe an experience in which you were angry about something and your anger was not taken seriously?
2) Can you think of a situation in which your listener seemed uncomfortable with the emotions you were expressing and deflected the conversation to another topic or focus?
3) What do you imagine Daddy might have been feeling when little Linda charged at him?
4) Can you describe a situation in which someone expressed anger at you? What feelings came up for you? How did you respond?

Story 32: James

Background

Greetings to all, far and wide. My name is James, and I'm what many would call a globetrotter: born in Ghana, undergrad in the U.S., grad school in China, and now I live with my young family in Japan.

You can imagine that in some ways I've gotten used to being the outsider, the foreigner. Sure. I'm the one who chose to live in new places where I've had to learn new languages and customs. And I've always made an effort to learn the local language and adapt to the customs and unwritten rules of whatever society I'm currently living in. My U.S.A.-born wife and I usually speak English to each other at home.

I can accept the inevitable curiosity and even a certain level of ignorance (I use that word without value judgment) on the part of people who, for example, have never before met a Black African.

What's hard for me to understand or accept, however, is people being so stuck in their preconceptions or biases that they cannot hear or see the truth of what they're experiencing with their own five senses. What I'm about to share with you happens to me on a daily (!) basis here.

What happened

We were in the food court of a shopping mall on the outskirts of a large city. My wife and I went to a counter to order our food. I ordered in fluent Japanese, and the woman understood me and typed the order into her terminal, and then she turned to her coworker and said in Japanese:

Worker: Oh, they're just foreigners.

Then she turned back to me and told me the price in broken English.

DISCONNECTOR – not registering or responding to what was just said

DISCONNECTOR – believing and asserting stereotypes

The worker completely disregarded my speaking Japanese to her, even though she had understood me. Her mental stereotype of foreigners was so strong that it literally deafened her to what her own ears had just heard. Based solely on my appearance, I couldn't possibly be speaking her language.

What I'm feeling

I'm feeling as though I'm interacting with someone who is sleepwalking, or thoroughly brainwashed, or in the kind of profound spell you read about in Grimm's fairy tales. I'm feeling completely invisible behind her projection of her cultural or racial stereotype onto me. And it feels a bit eerie – even though, as I mentioned, I encounter the same thing frequently. It would feel demeaning if I were to take it personally, but it's so clear to me that this isn't something to take personally at all. It's sad and troubling to come face-to-face with this extreme degree of other-izing that humans indulge in all over the world.

I wanted to respond by saying something neutral very slowly and extra-clearly in Japanese, to make her wake up and hear that it's Japanese I'm speaking and realize her error, but I stopped myself from doing that because I thought that might plunge her into shame, and I didn't want to risk that or do that to her.

What I needed instead

I needed simply to be heard for what I was plainly communicating, irrespective of my appearance: I have learned your language and I am using your language for ordering this food. Period.

Worker *(to me in Japanese)*: Thank you for your order. That will be 3,250 yen.

CONNECTOR – **having assumptions that connect**, *specifically:*
    perceiving others as unique individuals and learning who they are from their actual behavior

Questions for discussion

1) Is there a particular aspect of your own person (accent, size, age, skin color, disability, gender, etc.) that people sometimes react to when it's not relevant from your point of view? How do you wish they would instead handle their noticing of that aspect of you?

2) Have you ever had the experience of not being heard because the listener became preoccupied with something about your appearance? What for you would be the optimal way of responding to that?

3) Are there times when you are distracted by some external characteristic of another person and have difficulty staying focused on what the person is saying? Describe such a situation and why that external characteristic is such a strong distraction for you.

4) Can you remember an experience of meeting someone from a particular unfamiliar culture for the first time, and you were unsure whether the person spoke your language? How did you handle the communication?

Story 33: Magda

Background

Hi to all you readers!

My name is Magda. I'm 29 years old. I just got back from a bicycling vacation through France with my new boyfriend, Fernando. Sounds romantic, right? It was, for the most part. But I guess there will always be some confusing or upsetting situations when you're just getting to know someone, and being together day and night for two weeks was new and very intense. So there are some things I'm still puzzling over and trying to understand exactly what went wrong, and how I really feel about them.

I'm not as physically fit as Fernando, so we were riding at a moderate speed when a bunch of serious male cyclists passed us, and two of them commented audibly to each other in French how large my derrière looked from behind. Charming, don't you think? I was mortified that Fernando might have heard them, so I was really relieved when I realized that he hadn't understood what they said.

What happened

Fernando: What were they laughing about? Did you understand what they said?

Me (Magda): Yes. It wasn't funny.

Fernando: What did they say?

Me (Magda): They were making fun of me.

Fernando: But what exactly did they say?

Me (Magda): Something embarrassing. I don't feel like repeating it.

Fernando: Tell me!

ouch!

DISCONNECTOR – **disregarding signals** *of distress or need, specifically: pushing past an emotional boundary*

DISCONNECTOR – **demanding or ordering**

Me (Magda): It's very awkward …

Fernando: Oh, come on! Don't you trust me? How bad can it be that you can't tell me?

ouch!

DISCONNECTOR – **shifting the focus onto oneself**, *specifically:*
> *eclipsing the other's need with one's own*

DISCONNECTOR – **counteracting others' feelings, views, or actions**, *specifically:*
> *pressuring by an accusation of mistrustful attitude*

DISCONNECTOR – **undermining the other person's autonomy or agency**, *specifically:*
> *disallowing freedom of choice;*
> *demanding that something private be revealed*

DISCONNECTOR – **minimizing or trivializing** *strongly expressed feelings*

Me (Magda) *(silent, trying to figure out what to say and do)*

Fernando: This is ridiculous! Some strangers say something that I simply didn't catch, and you won't tell me what it is.

Me (Magda) *(explosively)*: They were making fun of my anatomy, okay?

Fernando: That's all? And you made such a big deal over it, as if you didn't even trust me. What exactly did they say?

ouch!

DISCONNECTOR – **implying "you shouldn't feel how you feel,"** *specifically:*
> *dismissing and invalidating vulnerable feelings*

DISCONNECTOR – **interrogating**

Me (Magda): That I have a big rear. You satisfied now?

Fernando: Yeah … but it's not really *so* big.

Me (Magda): *(Long silence.)*

What I'm feeling

I'm mortified and I'm really angry over being pressured to submit and allow my emotional boundary to be violated. He pushed and pushed, ignoring the vulnerability and embarrassment that I clearly expressed, until I did what he wanted.

He didn't acknowledge my signals of vulnerability and embarrassment at all, and instead focused totally on his own issue of not feeling trusted by me.

In hindsight (no pun intended!), I can't believe he actually ordered me to tell him what they said. I'm shocked, really, to discover that he assumes he gets to order me to meet a need he's suddenly feeling.

He also seems to assume that he gets to define for me what's important and what isn't. Well, it's my body and my feelings, and if something *is* "a big deal" to me, he should respect that, not invalidate it!

What I needed instead

Fernando: What were they laughing about? Did you understand what they said?

Me (Magda): Yes. It wasn't funny.

Fernando: What did they say?

Me (Magda): They were making fun of me.

Fernando: Oh, how rude!

Me (Magda): Very.

Fernando: Do you feel like telling me what they said?

*CONNECTOR – **opening the door to supportive conversation***

Me (Magda): Not right now. Maybe later, okay?

Fernando: Okay.

*CONNECTOR – **supporting others' agency and autonomy in their lives**, specifically: respecting boundaries and feelings*

Questions for discussion

1) Can you think of a sensitive topic in your life (as body size was for Magda) that you might not be ready to discuss openly with a new friend or acquaintance?

2) Can you describe a situation in which you gave in to someone else's pushing, although giving in violated a boundary and you later regretted it? In hindsight, can you see why you didn't remain firm for yourself?

3) Have you ever felt annoyed or left out because someone wouldn't share private information with you? What do you think their reasons were? How did you handle it?

4) What do you surmise was Fernando's strong need to pressure Magda to tell him what she heard?

Story 34: Ginny

Background

Dear reader,

Hi. I'm Ginny. When I was a kid, a long time ago, I passionately loved roller skating. For many years, I went to an indoor skating rink several times a week right after getting home from school, sometimes staying until dinner time. Skating felt like flying and dancing all at once to fun music, and the kids there were unbelievably cool.

When I was 12 years old (but looked 15), a 21-year-old guy took an interest in me and asked in a suggestive tone whether I could meet him "out in back" when I was done skating. As young and inexperienced as I was, I did know that the cool older kids went out in back to make out and do stuff where the adults wouldn't see them.

I felt scared, confused, and embarrassed, without understanding why I had those feelings. My father was outside waiting for me in our car at the appointed time, so when I was done skating, I jumped gratefully into the car. I was unusually quiet on the way home.

The next day after school, my dad asked me whether I'd be going skating.

What happened

Me (Ginny) *(flatly)*: I don't feel like going. I don't want to skate anymore.

Father: That's a shame. But you need the exercise. I guess you could go to gymnastics instead, like your sister.

DISCONNECTOR – **disregarding signals** *of distress or need*

What I'm feeling

Doesn't he want to know *why* I'm stopping? Isn't it obvious that something bad must have happened? Wow, he's not really thinking about how I am or what's happening with me.

What I needed instead

Me (Ginny) *(flatly)*: I don't feel like going. I don't want to skate anymore.

Father: You're not enjoying it anymore?

Me (Ginny): No.

Father: I sure had the impression that you always had a lot of fun at the rink. Did something happen to make it stop being fun?

*CONNECTOR – **acknowledging what you're noticing**, specifically:*
    inquiring about distress signals

Me (Ginny): Yes.

Father: If you'd like to tell me about it, I'm here to listen.

*CONNECTOR – **opening the door to supportive conversation***

*CONNECTOR – **showing warmth and generosity of spirit**, specifically:*
    inviting open communication about what's distressing instead of leaving the
    person alone in it

Me (Ginny): Maybe I'll tell Mommy.

Father: Hmm. Okay. Sounds important, so can I count on it that you'll tell Mommy?

*CONNECTOR – **offering an expression of interest and caring understanding**, specifi-*
    cally: showing concern; arranging for communication to end isolation

Me (Ginny): Okay, I will.

Questions for discussion

1)   Can you describe a situation in which you felt that someone understood your literal words, but not the deeper emotional message you needed the person to hear?

2)   Have you ever given someone a superficial reason for your decision, when in fact your reasons went much deeper? Describe your feelings and motivations for making that choice.

3)   Are there times when you as a listener stay on a superficial level in a conversation, although you sense that the other person has more complex material that could be shared? Describe your feelings and motivations for making that choice.

4)   Can you give an example of a personal topic you might have had difficulty talking about as a child, but which you can now talk about easily? What has changed that enables you to do that?

Story 35: Mitchell

Background

Hi, everybody, this is Mitchell writing to you.

I have a story I'd like to share with you about how someone listened to me in a curious and understanding way, and how that really helped me to understand and accept *myself* better.

I had been critical of myself my entire adult life for the kind of performance pressure I put myself under at work. I come from a perfectionist kind of family. Both of my parents had jobs involving a lot of responsibility, and I learned that it's not acceptable to give less than 100%.

So what career did I choose? Air traffic controller! Maybe I was trying to outperform my high-performance parents. In any event, I expect absolute perfection from myself at work.

At some point it occurred to me that there might be something wrong with me for putting myself under all this performance pressure, especially since over the years I've gotten criticism from friends who called me "workaholic" and "type A personality." One girlfriend complained all the time about my needing at least an hour to unwind after work and not paying attention to her immediately.

I wondered whether my attitudes were a result of the heavy conditioning I had gotten from my parents and whether I was even free to decide on my own how I wanted to perform at work. In my mind I started seeing myself as abnormal, maybe even compulsive.

An old school friend, Louis, a very laid-back kind of guy, wanted to meet up for a beer, and my concern over my work style came up in the conversation, since it was on my mind.

What happened

Louis: So how's the job?

Me (Mitchell): I don't know. I mean, it's great, in a way … It's what I always dreamed of doing. I guess I'm lucky in that way.

Louis: You don't sound completely convinced.

CONNECTOR – *acknowledging what you're noticing*, *specifically:*
observing doubtfulness

Me (Mitchell): Ha. Is it that obvious? You're right, I'm not completely convinced.

(Then I was lost in thought for a minute or so, and, amazingly, Louis just waited without saying anything. That in itself was an unusual experience for me.)

CONNECTOR – *allowing time and space for one's individual process to unfold*

Me (Mitchell): Sometimes I think there might be something wrong with me. When I'm at work I don't think about *anything* else. I'm so totally focused that it's as if the rest of the world doesn't even exist. And I have this ridiculous expectation of myself that every bit of my work has to be absolutely perfect, so I'm always under that pressure.

Louis: Yeah, sounds intense, and also really tense.

CONNECTOR – *active listening*, *empathically reflected*

CONNECTOR – *maintaining focus on the speaker*

Me (Mitchell): It is. It really is.

Louis: You called it a "ridiculous expectation." *(silence for another minute …)*

CONNECTOR – *acknowledging what you're noticing*, *specifically:*
perceiving self-invalidation

Me (Mitchell): Well, people outside the job have said that.

Louis: Right, people who don't do that kind of work.

Me (Mitchell): That's true.

Louis: And on the inside, among your coworkers?

CONNECTOR – *asking interestedly*

Me (Mitchell): Actually, I get a lot of positive feedback for my commitment and focus.

Louis: Hmm, that sounds rewarding. How do you feel about the work itself?

Me (Mitchell): Oh, I'm totally in a state of flow. You know, suddenly it reminds me of how it felt during a game when I was on the varsity basketball team in college: intense pressure but all flow. I love being on duty. I feel effective and I'm doing something important.

Louis: Wow, that doesn't sound bad at all. I'm curious whether there are also any downsides about the job.

Me (Mitchell): Maybe only that I get tired from the concentration, so I need a certain amount of time to regenerate when I get home after a shift. But I guess that's pretty normal when you give your all. I *have* to give it my all. It's an all-or-nothing type of work. There are people's *lives* depending on me, so *of course* I have to pay attention totally and be at the top of my game!

Louis: So it feels as if the performance pressure is somehow appropriate to the situation?

CONNECTOR – **active listening**, *accurately and empathically reflected*

Me (Mitchell): Now that you put it that way … yes, *completely* appropriate, in fact.

Louis *(with a twinkle)*: Well then, I'm relieved that I'm not spending the evening with a neurotic, workaholic guy who can't get a grip on himself at work.

Me (Mitchell): You know, I've been telling myself for years that there's something wrong with me for pushing myself so hard on the job. Suddenly I can see that it's fine, in fact it's totally *appropriate* to be a perfectionist in a high-stakes situation. And as long as I enjoy it, and as long as I unwind and enjoy other aspects of my life, there's not really anything wrong with me. Ha! That's honestly a whole new way for me to look at it.

Louis: Yeah, it's funny – we're both sitting here getting to know you better.

Me (Mitchell): Ha! Yeah, you know, Louis, I think you're the first person who hasn't offered advice or criticism about me and my job. Thanks, man.

What I'm feeling

I feel deeply relieved! It's the first time in my adult life that I've felt that maybe there's basically nothing wrong with me. In fact, maybe I'm really fortunate to be doing work that I love, even though it's necessarily a high-pressure experience. I feel lighter and more at ease in my own skin.

And I'm really appreciating Louis. Our conversation was so helpful, and yet I have the impression that he didn't do anything other than simply want to understand my experience. At least, that's how his questions felt to me – just his curiosity to understand more about whatever he heard me say about my experience. And I did feel understood by him, really deeply – wow, maybe more than by anybody, ever. That felt great in itself. I didn't thank him for that part, but I will when we get together again.

Questions for discussion

1) What do you think enabled Louis to be capable of tracking Mitchell so well and keeping himself and his own opinions out of it?

2) Can you describe a situation in which you stayed fully focused on someone else's personal sharing and kept yourself and your opinions out of it? What in that situation enabled you to do that?

3) Can you describe a situation in which you replied to the other person's personal sharing by making comments about yourself or your opinions? What led you to respond that way in that situation?

4) Do you notice any general patterns across situations where you do or don't stay fully focused on the other person's personal sharing?

Story 36: Eric

Background

Hello, folks. I'm Eric, I'm 41, and I live with my wife and kids in Virginia. I've kept in touch over the years with my old college housemate, Drake, who lives in Oregon. I have to admit I've sensed a diverging of our views with regard to political topics in the last few years, so I was wary about venturing into the vaccination debate with him. But Drake surprised me in a good way. We sure don't see eye-to-eye about it, but we were able to have a constructive conversation. What struck me was all the things he *didn't* do that I've unfortunately gotten used to recently: He didn't call me names or use disparaging labels; he didn't interrupt me or yell over me; he didn't tell me I'm wrong. Astounding! So it *is* possible to have differing opinions and still stay friends? If we can do it, why can't other people manage it?

What happened

Me (Eric): Well, I probably should congratulate you on your promotion, but hey – does it really make sense to be happy for somebody who's setting up deck chairs on the *Titanic*?

Drake: What do you mean?

Me (Eric): Soon there won't be anything left of our individual rights! Civilization as we know it is going down the tubes. Can you believe the government is trying to force us to get those f★★★ing vaccinations?

Drake: Um … yeah … Sounds as if you don't think it's a good idea.

Me (Eric): A good idea? For chemicals that have hardly been tested to be shot into my body? And my kids' bodies? It's the only body each of us has, and it's my right and my duty to protect them. I'm watching out for the well-being of my family!

Drake: Ah, so you don't trust that the vaccinations have been sufficiently tested.

*CONNECTOR – **active listening**, accurately reflected*

Me (Eric): Absolutely not. It all happened so fast, and the pharma industry is making so much money off this. And you know how strong their lobby is and how much money they contribute to politicians. Sorry, old pal, but that's not a set-up I can trust. Especially when I'm also being forced into it.

Drake: So the element of being forced into it by law is a big factor in your feelings, too, sounds like.

*CONNECTOR – **active listening**, accurately reflected*

*CONNECTOR – **maintaining focus on the speaker***

Me (Eric): You got that right! Total non-starter.

Drake: And how does your wife see it? After all, you guys are making decisions on behalf of your kids.

*CONNECTOR – **asking interestedly***

Me (Eric): Basically she agrees with me, though she does worry that one of us could get badly sick. But you can get badly sick from lots of different things. You can get hit by a car tomorrow. You can't plan for all eventualities.

Drake: That *does* have a certain kind of logic to it, I suppose. I'm trying to take this all in …

*CONNECTOR – **having assumptions that connect**, specifically:*
the other's responses and behaviors have an underlying coherence

Me (Eric): Well, that's just how it is for us, and nobody's going to change my mind, so don't even try.

Drake: Hmm, so you're probably already thinking that I see this differently. Well, I'm not out to change how you think … but I'm wondering if you're interested in knowing my thoughts anyhow.

*CONNECTOR – **asking rather than telling***

Me (Eric): Sure, why not …?

Drake: Okay, here goes. First of all, sure, big pharma is profit-driven and pours money into corrupt politicians, and yes, they're capable of really bad stuff, so I factor that in, but I also follow what the actual lab researchers are saying. I've personally known a lot of science researchers in my life, and all the ones I've known are sincere and honest about doing science to find what's true. That's what attracted them to science research in the first place. Sure, there are some bad apples, there always are in any field, but when lab researchers from all around the world are reporting pretty much the same results, which is that the Covid vaccines are as safe as – or safer than

– a lot of other drugs that have been well tested, I feel I can trust that information. Just saying my point of view, not trying to convince you.

Me (Eric): Good. You aren't.

Drake: Didn't expect to. Thanks for listening anyway. And I agree with you that it doesn't make sense to worry about or plan for all of the many different dangers in the world. But when there are easy precautions to take for a clear and present danger, it makes sense to me to do that. I feel more danger from the Covid virus than from the Covid vaccine, so I get the vaccine. And hey, I don't mind the government telling me I can't drive faster than the speed limit, which exists for everyone's safety, and so does the vaccine requirement. Okay, now I'm done.

Me (Eric): That was quite a speech! Ha ha. I bet it's not the first time you've explained all that to someone. Sounds as if you've put a lot of thought into it.

Drake: Yeah, I have. Thanks for being willing to listen, even though it's not at all how you think about it.

Me (Eric): Well, you have to do what feels right to you. And I'll do what feels right to me.

Drake: Yep, I guess we have to agree to disagree on this topic. I wouldn't want it to come between us.

CONNECTOR – **supporting others' agency and autonomy in their lives**, *specifically: expressing recognition of the other's position*

Me (Eric): Yeah, same here. You know, we don't talk so often, but when we do, it always reminds me why we got along so well back then. Take good care, my friend, and give my best to your family.

Drake: Same! Be well. And stay healthy, please.

What I'm feeling

I'm surprised, because I was expecting Drake to argue with me and disapprove and try to convince me to change my views. This vaccination debate has lost me some friends in the last couple of years, and it's a new experience for me that someone with a totally different opinion on this hot topic is still capable of listening respectfully and not making me into a villain. Wow. I really underestimated Drake. Remarkable, really.

Questions for discussion

1) What have you glimpsed or surmised about the personal issues or inner factors that result in people adopting highly polarized, black-and-white views?

2) What connectors and disconnectors do you yourself tend to use during discussions of extremely hot issues? Can you describe a particular incident?

3) What feelings come up for you when listening to someone's views on a hot issue, when your views are diametrically opposed? How do you manage or cope with those feelings?

4) Whichever side you're on regarding the various hot, highly polarized issues of the day, can you imagine that the other side's views and positions have a coherent inner basis that could come into expression in response to good listening?

Story 37: Jennifer

Background

Hi. I hope somebody reads this. My name is Jennifer, I'm 13, and I need to get out of this house, but I don't know how to make that happen.

My stepfather has been touching me in creepy ways since I was 10, but Mom is so crazy about him that she doesn't believe me. Or maybe she sort of does believe me, but she's worried that if she makes waves, he'll leave her. Which would be the best possible thing in the world. Maybe *she's* afraid of him, too. I honestly don't know what Mom thinks or believes. It doesn't make any sense to me. I used to think she loved me. Now I'm not so sure. I've almost given up trying to get her attention, but I decided to try one more time before taking the step of talking to our school guidance counselor.

What happened

Me (Jennifer): Mom, *please* don't go out to your yoga class this evening. I've told you a million times, I don't want to be alone with *him*.

Mom: You don't like him just because he makes you do your homework and doesn't accept your excuses!

*DISCONNECTOR – **disregarding signals** of distress or need*

*DISCONNECTOR – **interpreting** feelings and motives*

Me (Jennifer): That's not true! He won't leave me alone when you're not here. I hate when he touches me! Just yesterday he tried to –

Mom: What kind of a tramp have I raised as a daughter who has to accuse her own stepfather of dirty things! You ought to be ashamed of yourself!

*DISCONNECTOR – **interrupting** mid-sentence*

*DISCONNECTOR – **criticizing, judging, shaming, or blaming**, specifically:*
name-calling and shaming the victim as a smokescreen to keep attention away from the real offender

Me (Jennifer): So now you're making it into *my* fault? I don't understand why you don't put your foot down and tell him to leave me in peace! Maybe if –

Mom: Look, he promised me that he would always treat you with respect. And I believe him. So ... topic closed.

*DISCONNECTOR – **interrupting** mid-sentence*

*DISCONNECTOR – **disregarding signals** of distress*

*DISCONNECTOR – **cutting off communication***

What I'm feeling

Unprotected. Abandoned. In danger. Unloved. It's my mother's job to take care of me and protect me, but she leaves me alone with this monster that she married even though I've told her that he touches me. If she loves me, she should care that I'm suffering and want to protect me from harm, right?

But instead she invents the idea that it's really about my not wanting to do my homework. And can you believe she called me a tramp? As if *I'm* making him come on to me! How does she even come up with such things?

And she kept interrupting me. She really doesn't want to hear what I'm trying to tell her.

What I needed instead

Me (Jennifer): Mom, *please* don't go out to your yoga class this evening. I've told you a million times, I don't want to be alone with *him*.

Mom: Tell me ... what's going on?

*CONNECTOR – **opening the door to supportive conversation**, specifically:*
offering understanding and accompaniment in honest communication

Me (Jennifer): It's hard to talk about … He keeps finding excuses to put his hands on me and it's really creepy! So you have to stay here!

Mom: Well, we have a real problem, then. I see that. Of course I'll stay home with you! Come, let's go into your room and shut the door so we can figure this out.

Questions for discussion

1) Can you describe a situation in which you, as a youth, felt vulnerable or unsafe around an adult? Did you talk to anyone about it at the time?

2) How do you – or would you – handle unwanted or inappropriate sexual advances?

3) Why do you imagine that Mom was unable or unwilling to hear and recognize what Jennifer was suffering?

4) Have you ever felt caught in the conflicting needs operating in two or more relationships? What do you see as the best way out of such a difficult bind?

Story 38: Henry

Background

To all of you readers: This might seem obvious, but I need to say it anyhow. Sometimes people go through a crisis, and then they really, really need to be listened to and actually *heard*. And not pushed to do things the way other people want them to, even if the other people think they're helping.

I am currently in a significant life crisis. My name is Henry, and I'm 38. I've been in a relationship with Sandra for ten years, and it was obvious to us and everyone else that we were planning to get married and start a family soon. We'd talked about it for a long time now, and we both wanted that. So we started planning.

Six weeks ago, a friend hinted to me that Sandra was sleeping with my best friend! At first I was 100% sure that couldn't be true. But, you know, once you have a suspicion, you start seeing a lot of little things through a new lens, little things that would otherwise never have attracted your attention.

I started noticing how when we were out with the gang, the two of them tended to be away from the group – just "happening" to go to the bathroom at the same time. Also, sometimes she ended a phone call abruptly when I walked into the room.

Last week I confronted her, and she admitted the affair. What makes it even worse (as if it could get any worse!) is that this has been going on for a year-and-a-half, while we were making engagement and marriage plans. I spent the last week trying to give her, and myself, a chance to calm down and look for a solution. But it's not working. I asked her to move out yesterday, which she did. Ten years of my life – down the tubes! Partner gone. Best friend gone. How could I have been so blind? Needless to say, I'm devastated.

Friends and family are rallying around me, trying to console me, which I appreciate, although I can feel that getting over this, if at all possible, will take a long time. Sometimes I want company, and sometimes I just want to be alone. There are people who can listen and accept that. But my father … He's never been good at letting me be in charge of my own life. He always has his own ideas, whether it's what college I should go to or how to mend heartbreak.

What happened

Dad: I knew I should have come over sooner! You're letting things go to wrack and ruin! The yard is a disaster, but don't worry, I'll take care of it.

DISCONNECTOR – **criticizing, judging, shaming, or blaming**, *specifically:*
scolding, berating

DISCONNECTOR – **undermining the other person's autonomy or agency**, *specifically:*
presuming to take control of the other's home situation

Me (Henry): No! Do not do anything! The yard is the last thing I care about right now.

Dad: I said I'll take care of it. You don't have to do anything.

Me (Henry): Leave my yard alone! It's my yard!

Dad *(to Mom, while getting into the car)*: Come, dear. The gardening supply store is still open; we'll just make it before they close. *(To me)*: See you in about an hour.

DISCONNECTOR – **disregarding signals** *of distress, specifically:*
ignoring objections

What I'm feeling

The fury I'm feeling at my father is so familiar! Yet once again he's assuming he knows what's right for me, taking control of my situation and taking away *my* control of my own life! That was bad enough before, but right now it's far worse. I can't control how Sandra behaves, I can't control what my best friend does, I can't control my feelings of loss, betrayal, rage, sadness … and now I can't even control my own yard!

I feel completely disempowered by my father scolding me about the yard, adding *that* to the towering pile of evidence that I can't manage my own life. Thanks, Dad!

What I needed instead

Dad: We got here as soon as we could. How're you doing?

Me (Henry): Terrible. I still can't believe it.

Dad: Yeah … I can only begin to imagine … Anything I can do to help you? Should I do some yard work for you, so you don't have to worry about that?

Me (Henry): No! Do not do anything! The yard is the last thing I care about right now.

Dad: Ah, okay. Just let me know what you need …

CONNECTOR – *supporting others' agency and autonomy in their lives*

Me (Henry): Thanks, Dad. Everything's so crazy right now, I have no idea what I need. Maybe I need help making sense of how this train wreck happened.

Dad: Well, that's what we're here for.

Questions for discussion

1) Can you describe an experience of feeling that someone was inappropriately trying to take control of some aspect of your life and defining that as helping you? How did that feel to you? What did you do?
2) Have you had the experience of fervently and clearly expressing objections and the other person ignoring your protestations? Did you start to wonder whether you were the one being unreasonable?
3) What do you imagine was the underlying emotional need that was motivating Henry's father to override Henry and take control of Henry's yard?
4) Can you describe a situation in which a friend or family member was in crisis and you wanted very much to be of help? Did the person express his or her needs clearly? What role did you play or try to play in that crisis?

Story 39: Jeffrey

Background

To all of you sensitive souls out there who've ever been bullied, I'm one of you. I feel your pain, because it's my pain too. My name is Jeffrey, and I'm grown up now, so I can talk about it more easily than I could back then.

As a kid, I was small for my age, and I was shy. Great combination for the jungle that is grade school, wouldn't you say? I especially remember a kid named Barry. He was a big bruiser, not too bright, but full of self-righteousness, and he was always hungry. On this particular day, he had just stolen and eaten my lunch for about the tenth time.

I was crying as I told my father about it when he picked me up after school.

What happened

Me (Jeffrey): Daddy, I'm never going back to school! That big idiot Barry stole my lunch again today. I hate him!

Daddy: First of all, stop crying!

*DISCONNECTOR – **demanding or ordering***

*DISCONNECTOR – **implying "you shouldn't feel how you feel"***

*DISCONNECTOR – **disregarding signals** of distress or need, specifically:*
        total lack of empathy

Daddy: If you cry over these things, of course the other kids won't respect you. Jeffrey, you've got to toughen up and be a man. That bully won't leave you alone until you show him you're just as tough as he is.

*DISCONNECTOR – **giving unsolicited advice or giving advice prematurely***

What I'm feeling

I can't tell whether Daddy is blaming me or trying to help me. I'm confused. I didn't cry in school, only with Daddy. I can never be as tough as Barry is – he's so big and mean, and I'm small. Maybe it means I have to pretend not to be scared about being bullied.

Daddy told me to stop crying as if it's something I can just turn on and off. But it isn't! Now I'm worried that Daddy won't love me as much if I can't get control over my crying.

What I needed instead

Me (Jeffrey): Daddy, I'm never going back there! That idiot Barry stole my lunch again today. I hate him!

Daddy: Oh, boy, that was a nasty thing for him to do! I can understand that you're upset.

*CONNECTOR – **offering an expression of interest and caring understanding***

Me (Jeffrey): I sure am! I never want to see him again.

Daddy: Yeah!

Me (Jeffrey): And I'm never again gonna show him what I have for lunch. He's like the Cookie Monster, except he's an Everything Monster. He eats everything. No wonder he's so big and fat!

Daddy: Does he take other people's lunches also?

*CONNECTOR – **asking interestedly***

Me (Jeffrey): Yeah. Yesterday he took Kevin's, Jacky's, and mine. What a pig!

Daddy: And how do Kevin and Jacky feel about that?

Me (Jeffrey): They hate it, too. Today they waited until Barry was looking at them and then they spit on their own lunch so he wouldn't want to take it. It was so funny! I'm gonna do that tomorrow.

Daddy: Good plan!

Questions for discussion

1) In the "What I needed instead" section above, what did Daddy do differently that led to Jeffrey finding his own solution for how to stop Barry from stealing his lunch?
2) Can you describe a situation in which you felt that your listener was imposing an interpretation or advice for your situation, but was an outsider to that situation? How did you feel about that?

3) Have you ever arrived at important new clarity regarding a dilemma as a result of your listener empathetically understanding and asking about your situation?

4) Have you ever felt uncomfortable or disapproving toward someone's tears or strong emotions? How did you handle that?

Story 40: Jamal

Background

Hi, I'm Jamal. I'm 17, and I live at home with my parents and two little sisters. My father is a computer engineer, and he thinks that logic can solve any problem in life. The story I'm about to tell you was not the first time that his logic wasn't helpful.

My girlfriend split up with me just a few days ago, which was very painful for me. My father noticed that I was down, and he asked me about it.

What happened

Me (Jamal): Yeah, Pops, I'm depressed. Katherine and I split up.

Pops: Oh, I'm sorry to hear that. She's a nice girl. What happened?

Me (Jamal): What happened is that she ended it. She left me. And I wasn't expecting it.

Pops: Well, don't despair. Think of it this way: You once told me she was a one-in-a-million. That means that in this city there are two others who are a good match to you, since there are three million people. And a total of 16 good matches in this state. And … just imagine if you learn a foreign language! You'd be expanding the pool of candidates by many millions! And you're intelligent and good-looking, which helps your odds significantly.

DISCONNECTOR – *making assumptions that disconnect*, specifically:
    "I have to give him a solution that would help end his unhappiness."

DISCONNECTOR – *implying "you shouldn't feel how you feel"*

DISCONNECTOR – *using logic to dispel feelings*, specifically:
    trying to allay despair

DISCONNECTOR – *reassuring inappropriately*, specifically:
    trying to help relieve distress by offering positive thinking

What I'm feeling

I'm feeling that Pops and I live on different planets. He's in his own tidy world of logic, and I'm in the messy world of people and feelings. I don't want a solution (especially *his* solution) right now. I just want someone to understand what I'm experiencing while I'm going through these intense feelings. So, basically, right now I feel really alone in all this pain.

I know Pops was trying to be helpful by using his logic to reassure me that my future is bright. But I was really hurting over losing Katherine and didn't want a new girlfriend, so his logically positive outlook had no meaning for me, except to imply that I shouldn't feel as bad as I was feeling.

And how logical is it for Pops to reassure me about my intellect and looks? Obviously those things weren't enough for Katherine!

What I needed instead

Me (Jamal): Yeah, Pops, I'm depressed. Katherine and I split up.

Pops: Oh, I'm sorry to hear that. She's a nice girl. What happened?

Me (Jamal): What happened is that she ended it. She left me. And I wasn't expecting it.

Pops: I see … You didn't see it coming. I can imagine what a shock that was.

*CONNECTOR – **active listening**, empathically reflected*

Me (Jamal): Yeah, a shock. That's a good word for it. I think I need a few days just to get used to the idea that we're not together anymore. It's hard to believe. And it hurts. Maybe I'll go out to the gym now. That might help take my mind off her for a couple of hours.

Just those few words of understanding from Pops would have helped me. At least I wouldn't have felt so alone in my state of shock and pain. It's so much worse when you're feeling all alone in it!

Questions for discussion

1) Can you describe a situation in which you were communicating on an emotional level about a problem, and the other person responded with logical arguments? How did you feel? Were you able to find a common level for viable further communication?
2) Have you experienced feeling quite down and your conversation partner tried to reassure you? In what ways was this helpful or unhelpful (or both) to you?

3) What do you imagine Pops' motivations were in reassuring Jamal about his future prospects?

4) Can you describe a time when you used a logical argument to try to talk someone into or out of feeling a certain way? How did the person respond?

Story 41: Philip

Background

Dear reader,

My name is Philip, and I'm 43 years old. I left home at 16, and then kept my parents at arm's length ever since. I couldn't really tell you why if you'd asked me before recently. I also never thought about how that was for my parents. I just always knew that I was more comfortable living in a different city and seeing them only occasionally.

For Christmas two years ago, my wife and kids and I spent two days at my parents' house, and it just sort of happened that my mother and I were the last ones still up at night after everyone else had gone to sleep, and somehow we slipped into an honest kind of conversation, the kind that happens more easily when you're tired and your defenses are down. It was just a couple of minutes that went like this:

What happened

Mom: I can't tell you how wonderful it is to have you all here. I've been looking forward to this for months!

Me (Philip): Yeah, it's nice. Once or twice a year.

Mom: Aha ... not too often ...

*CONNECTOR – **active listening**, accurately reflected*

Me (Philip): Right.

Mom: I have to admit, I've wondered about that over the years.

*CONNECTOR – **using transparency in communication***

*CONNECTOR – **asking interestedly**, specifically:*
        inquiring further with interest and curiosity

Me (Philip): About what?

Mom: About not too often. And about you living so far away.

Me (Philip): Hmm. Like ... you wonder if there's a reason?

Mom: I'm sure you have your reasons. I guess people always have their reasons.

CONNECTOR – *having assumptions that connect, specifically:*
assuming there are important reasons for a person's choices

CONNECTOR – *supporting others' agency and autonomy in their lives, specifically:*
expressing respect for personal choices

Me (Philip): What if I give a reason that's upsetting for you?

Mom: Well … I'm your mother. I want to understand you and know what's going on in your life. Whatever you want to tell me, I'm here to listen. And I'm no stranger to hearing things in our family that are upsetting, okay?

CONNECTOR – *showing warmth and generosity of spirit, specifically:*
offering listening and caring understanding

CONNECTOR – *attending to the other's pressing needs first*

Me (Philip): It's strange – if it were only you, I'd probably come to visit more often. I think it's Dad I'm allergic to in large dosages. Huh. I didn't realize that until now.

Mom: Mmm. That's an important realization.

Me (Philip): Yeah. Somehow I always have the feeling he's judging me, and there's no way I can ever live up to his expectations.

Mom: I can certainly see how you might want to avoid large doses of that.

CONNECTOR – *active listening, empathically reflected*

CONNECTOR – *maintaining focus on the speaker*

Me (Philip): For sure. But it wasn't even clear to me until just now when I said it to you.

What I'm feeling

I've been feeling some relief from having this new understanding about why I keep my distance from my parents. I think somewhere deep down I've regretted not bringing my kids and my parents together more often. In fact I'm realizing I've felt a little judgmental toward myself about that, so it's a relief to know that I've had a good reason all along. That doesn't solve the problem, of course, but at least now I know what the problem really is, and it gives me a new way to think about it.

It surprised me when my mother said, "I have to admit, I've wondered about that over the years." In our family, no one ever talked openly like that about how we're really feeling or what's really going on. So that was a new move by Mom, and I really appreciate it. It let me realize something important, and it brought us closer together than we've been in a long, long time.

When I thought about that conversation the next day, I realized that Mom must have had her own needs and feelings about family visits. I'm sure she wants to see her grandchildren more often. Yet she put her own feelings aside in order to give me a chance to come out with something I've been keeping buried inside for a long time.

Questions for discussion

1) What family dynamics might have been preventing discussion of Philip living far away for all those years? What connectors made it possible for Philip and his mother to finally address this delicate area?

2) Can you think of a topic in your own family that remains unspoken and undiscussed? Can you imagine how discussion might be approached?

3) Philip says that the main problem hasn't been solved. If you were in Philip's position, what next steps might you take based on seeing that it went well with Mom?

4) Can you describe a situation in which you put your own needs and feelings aside in order to give your full attention to listening to what another person needed to communicate about the same matter? How did you feel about that interaction afterwards?

Story 42: Grace

Background

Dear reader,

Hi and thanks for listening to me. My name is Grace, and I'm 18. I just graduated from high school, and I'm having major conflicts with my parents about my future. Basically it boils down to whether I take a year off to travel and work before going to college (my idea) or I start college immediately after the summer vacation (my parents' idea).

What happened

Me (Grace): I've been in school since I was 5! A change of pace would be great.

Mom: College would be a change of pace. A whole new place with new people.

ouch!

*DISCONNECTOR – **disregarding signals** of distress or need*

Me (Grace): Can't you understand? College is still school, still studying, still writing papers with deadlines, still taking tests … It's more of the same thing, always doing what other people tell me to do. I need a break from all that!

Dad: A college education is the most useful thing you can do for your future. Neither your mother nor I had that opportunity at your age, but *you* have it, and you ought to take advantage of having it.

ouch!

*DISCONNECTOR – **disregarding signals** of distress or need*

*DISCONNECTOR – **giving unsolicited advice or giving advice prematurely***

*DISCONNECTOR – **moralizing**, specifically:*
> *"You don't recognize or appreciate the opportunity we've provided you with."*

*DISCONNECTOR – **undermining the other person's autonomy or agency**, specifically:*
"You should have the same priorities and reasoning as we do."

Me (Grace): Well, I'm not you! And you're talking as though I'll never go to college if I put it off for a year. I know it's important for my life, and I'm going to do it, but you're trying to *make* me do it on *your schedule*. What part of "I need a break" is too hard for you guys to understand?

What I'm feeling

This is so frustrating! They didn't even acknowledge what I was clearly telling them I need, a break from school. How can they be so locked onto *their* need for me to jump right into college that they totally ignore what I'm telling them *I* need? Do they really think they can logically *convince* me to not need the break that I desperately need? I wish I had parents who want to understand what I'm feeling!

What I needed instead

Me (Grace): I've been in school since I was 5! A change of pace would be great.

Mom: Wow, that's 12 years! And you've been a good student!

*CONNECTOR – **active listening**, empathically reflected*

Me (Grace): Exactly! I really need a break from constantly studying and writing papers and taking tests and doing what teachers tell me I have to do. I need a year of doing what *I* want to be doing – maybe some traveling and seeing whales and visiting my cousins in Denmark and reading whatever *I* want to be reading.

Dad: I can see how appealing all of that feels to you at this point. At the same time, there are other considerations that I'm thinking about. Can I share my thoughts with you?

*CONNECTOR – **active listening**, empathically reflected*

*CONNECTOR – **supporting others' agency and autonomy in their lives**, specifically:*
asking whether input is welcome

Me (Grace): Sure.

Dad: Mom and I know how hard the job market can be for people without a college degree, and we think it's important for you to stay on track for that.

Me (Grace): Well, I'm definitely planning to go to college, and if I start fresh after a one-year break and actually *want* to begin college, I'll do better, and I don't think any career opportunities will go down the drain in that amount of time.

Questions for discussion

1) How have you felt and responded when someone was lecturing you about the "right" way to handle or think about something?

2) Have you ever tried hard to convince and pressure someone to do what you "knew" was best for him or her? From the way things then turned out, what have you learned from that whole process?

3) Can you think of a time when your own concerns and notions regarding another person's well-being made it difficult for you to hear and acknowledge that person's feelings, desires, or sense of what was right for him or her?

4) Conflicts between parents and children over the children's future are quite common. Describe such a conflict that you have experienced, either with your own parents or, if you have children, with your own children. What do you see now, in hindsight, that would have brought about more effective communication?

Story 43: Francine

Background

Hi, everybody. My name is Francine, and I'm 55 years old. I was a stay-at-home mom, and now my kids are all out of the house and I'm enjoying my freedom. I decided last year that I'd have even more freedom if I learned to drive a car, which is not so easy after a life as a non-driver.

I've been practicing for eight months, with help from both a driving teacher and my son when he has time. I refuse to practice with my husband because he loses his patience easily and yells at me.

I took my driving test two weeks ago, and ... I failed it. I don't know how that happened! I know everything and I can do everything, but I got nervous and forgot to use the blinker before changing lanes, something I would normally never forget! I'm so upset with myself, and I keep thinking about what went wrong inside my head that caused me to be distracted and make that dumb mistake. I'm thinking that there's no sense making an appointment to retry the test before I've figured out how to avoid the same thing happening again.

Then I made another foolish mistake: talking to my husband about it over dinner.

What happened

Me (Francine): I'm still trying to understand why I'd get nervous enough to make that silly mistake during my driving test. It's strange. In school I never got nervous about taking tests. I wonder why this was so different ...

Husband: It was two weeks ago. Get over it!

DISCONNECTOR – **disregarding signals** *of distress or need*

DISCONNECTOR – **implying "you shouldn't need what you need"**

DISCONNECTOR – **giving unsolicited advice or giving advice prematurely**

DISCONNECTOR – **demanding or ordering**

What I'm feeling

For a minute or two I'm totally confused and almost dazed by his sudden, disdainful scolding of me for trying to figure out what happened. He's so certain, so he must be right. And he's *ordering* me to stop thinking about it, so my continued thinking about it must be *seriously* wrong to do and he'll lose all respect for me if I ever mention it again. He already seems disgusted with me over this.

I'm feeling fear over being so unacceptable to my husband, but then somehow, some other part of me inside manages to think, "Wait a minute, I'm not a bad little girl, I'm a grown woman trying to learn from a mistake I made. Two weeks doesn't seem like a long time to be figuring out something really important that took me by surprise and went unexpectedly wrong. I *need* to figure it out!"

Then I look over at my husband, seeing that *he* is the one making a big mistake by being so judgmental and harsh, and my fear is gone, replaced by a deep sadness that I'm so alone and unsupported in my marriage.

What I needed instead

Me (Francine): I'm still trying to understand why I'd get nervous enough to make that silly mistake during my driving test. It's strange. In school I never got nervous about taking tests. I wonder why this was so different …

Husband: It's still on your mind?

Me (Francine): Yes, because if I don't see why it happened, it could happen again, even though I've practiced so much.

Husband: Well, that makes sense. Any insights yet?

CONNECTOR —*active listening* with *reflected understanding*

CONNECTOR – *asking interestedly*, *specifically:*
        inquiring further in caring accompaniment

Me (Francine): Mmm, maybe. I think the tester guy made me nervous. There was something about him … Maybe he reminds me of someone. I'm not sure. I'll have to think about that. Yeah, in fact, now that I think about it, I had a bad feeling as soon as I saw him, and it went downhill from there. Okay, seeing that feels helpful. That isn't likely to happen again. Thanks. I got further from describing it to you than from my inner ruminating.

*CONNECTOR – **allowing time and space for one's individual process to unfold***

Husband: Good.

Questions for discussion

1) Has anyone ever told you to "get over it" (or some similar message)? How did you interpret that message? What effects did that have on you?

2) Have you ever felt that another person was taking too much time to process an upsetting experience? In what ways did you feel uncomfortable about what you were witnessing?

3) Can you describe a situation in which you needed days, weeks, or even months of processing before you could let go of a painful experience, or before it lost most of its intensity? What changed that enabled you to move on?

4) Do you have a painful experience in your past that has such a deep meaning for you that you continue to think about it now, many years after the actual occurrence? What would you need in order to be more finished with that experience?

Story 44: Clint

Background

Hi, readers. My name is Clint. I just turned 40, and I can feel myself slipping into a depression again. I've been in therapy for years, and the depression comes and goes. My mother suffered from depression her whole life, so is mine genetic or the result of growing up in my mom's dark cloud? I'll probably never know. If you look at it objectively, I have a good life. I'm in a long-term relationship with my partner of many years, Kenny. I have a good, stable job, and otherwise I'm healthy.

If it gets really bad, I'll go back onto a regimen of antidepressants, but due to the unpleasant side effects I tend to put that off as long as possible. This phase of feeling the depression coming on but not yet being willing to start the meds is a scary time.

What happened

Kenny: Aren't you getting up? You'll be late for work.

Me (Clint): I'm going to call in sick.

Kenny: Are you sick?

Me (Clint): I guess that's a matter of opinion. I can't go to the office today. I can't face anyone.

Kenny: Oh, no, are you getting depressed again?

Me (Clint): Either that, or someone put a huge gray blanket over the world.

Kenny: I don't understand you. What do you have to be depressed about? We have each other, we have our work, we have our friends, we have enough money …

ouch!

DISCONNECTOR – *implying "you shouldn't feel how you feel"*

DISCONNECTOR – *counteracting others' feelings, views, or actions*, *specifically:*
  citing positive facts to dispel depression

DISCONNECTOR – *making assumptions that disconnect*, *specifically:*
  "If I can't make sense of you, that means you aren't rational."

What I'm feeling

As Kenny said, he doesn't understand me, and that's exactly what I'm now feeling – in addition to being depressed. Kenny just doesn't get that my depression has nothing to do with those good things. And if I knew how to avoid it, I certainly would! I'm not depressed because things aren't good enough for me! When Kenny lists all the reasons why I should feel happy, I wonder if he thinks I'm being a spoiled brat or a stupid idiot.

What I needed instead

Kenny: Aren't you getting up? You'll be late for work.

Me (Clint): I'm going to call in sick.

Kenny: Are you sick?

Me (Clint): I guess that's a matter of opinion. I can't go to the office today. I can't face anyone.

Kenny: Oh man, are you feeling a depression coming on?

Me (Clint): Either that, or someone put a huge gray blanket over the world.

Kenny: I'm so sorry about that. Yeah, stay home, keep things simple. Would you like me to bring you a cup of coffee?

Me (Clint): Yeah, thanks.

Kenny: Okay, coming right up. You must be wondering about starting meds again. If talking that over would help, we could do that this evening when I'm home from work.

CONNECTOR – **opening the door to supportive conversation**, *specifically:*
expressing empathy and willingness to help

CONNECTOR – **showing warmth and generosity of spirit**, *specifically:*
inviting open communication about what's distressing instead of leaving the person alone in it

Questions for discussion

1) Have you ever been seriously incapacitated or ill? What were the most helpful or supportive reactions from other people? What reactions were least helpful or supportive?

2) Can you describe a situation in which you were helpful or supportive to another person who was incapacitated or very ill? What type of feedback did you receive from the other person about your efforts?

3) Have you had the experience of feeling impatient or ungenerous with another person's depression or disability? Were some needs of yours in conflict with the other person's condition or needs?

4) From your point of view, would it be better or worse for Kenny if he were to find that the cause of his depression was entirely psychological, not genetic? Why would this matter?

Story 45: Suyin

Background

Hello, dear readers, I'm Suyin, mother of a 7-year-old son. I lost my husband — and my son lost his father — two years ago unexpectedly in a car accident. We still miss him terribly.

I *am* making some progress in navigating life as a single parent. A cousin of mine was fortunately in a position to hire me part-time at her store, so my son and I have enough money to keep a roof over our heads, and I can still get home in time to be there for him after school. It's hectic, and it's a challenge for me to make ends meet, but we're managing.

I hadn't heard from my old friend Nora in a long time, so I was glad when she suggested getting together for a cup of coffee. I arranged a play date for my son so I'd have a Saturday afternoon free to see Nora. She looked radiant, and told me in glowing terms about her new partner. I was happy for her, although I also felt some wistfulness remembering better times in my own life. Then I told her about the process I'm still in the midst of, adapting to life as a single parent.

What happened

Me (Suyin): Well, I don't cry every day anymore. That's progress, actually. It turned out that there was a lot more to the grieving process than I ever imagined. A *lot* more. At this point, though, the main challenge of being a single mother is financial. Now it's totally on me to keep us afloat.

Nora: Oh, I wish from the bottom of my heart that you'll find a new partner soon!

DISCONNECTOR – **disregarding signals** of distress or need

DISCONNECTOR – **making assumptions that disconnect**, specifically:
     presuming to know what the other person needs

What I'm feeling

What? Did you even hear what I said? I was talking about my grief feelings and the burden of making money, and you respond about a new partner? It feels like being in two different films that were spliced together arbitrarily. Well, old friend, you couldn't have made it clearer that you don't want to hear about my struggles. I was needing and expecting you to give me some understanding for what I'm going through, so I'm really disappointed in you.

Apart from her dodging my need to share about my struggles, I'm sure Nora had the best of intentions in wishing that I'll have a new partner soon, but she was making a very big and very incorrect assumption that she knew what I need or want. She said it in a big-hearted way, but she was in her own world and wasn't tuning in to me at all. In fact, I felt invisible.

What I needed instead

Me (Suyin): Well, I don't cry every day anymore. That's progress, actually. It turned out that there was a lot more to the grieving process than I ever imagined. A *lot* more. At this point, though, the main challenge of being a single mother is financial. Now it's totally on me to keep us afloat.

Nora: So you've been moving through a difficult emotional process reasonably well, but now it's the material managing of life that you're up against.

CONNECTOR – **active listening**, *accurately and empathically reflected, specifically: maintaining focus on what the speaker has expressed*

Me (Suyin): Exactly. The emotional process keeps unfolding and still needs some time. And patience with myself. But yes, the financial constraints are what I have to deal with now. I'm looking into the possibility of training as a real estate broker. It's pretty expensive, so things could temporarily be even harder before they get easier, but once I have my license, I'll be able to earn far better.

Questions for discussion

1) Have you experienced someone wishing something for you that was not in alignment with your own needs or wishes? How did you respond?
2) Can you bring to mind a situation in which you caught a friend up on some big changes in your life? Did you feel satisfied with your friend's listening and understanding? Why or why not?

3) What would you guess may have led Nora to respond with, "I wish for you from the bottom of my heart that you find a new partner"?

4) Can you describe a situation in which you felt you knew just what would help dispel or solve a friend's dilemma? Did you express this to the friend? If yes, how did you express it? And how was it received?

Story 46: Sage

Background

Hello, readers! I'd like to tell you about an interaction with a dear friend who simply listens to what I share and accepts me as I am.

My name is Sage. I suspect I'm not the only person who feels ashamed of having a messy apartment, but my feeling of shame might be more intense than most people's. I had a lot of pressure from my mother when I was growing up about how a "proper" young lady conducts and presents herself. Having a disorderly household was a huge no-no.

Every so often I do a major cleanup, and then I feel good about it for a short while. But then I get busy with life and work and friends, and my place goes back to wrack and ruin, and stays that way most of the time.

For that reason, I like to meet friends at a nearby coffee shop, especially if it's a spontaneous get-together. No muss, no fuss, as they say. My sister is the only person I don't feel embarrassed in front of when the apartment is a mess, so she's allowed to drop by unannounced, but nobody else, please!

My friend Miriam lives nearby and likes to ring my doorbell on her way back from doing errands.

What happened

Me (Sage): Hello?

Miriam: Hey, it's me. Wanna hang out? You have time now?

Me (Sage): The place is a mess, as usual. I'll come down. Be there in three minutes.

Miriam: Okay, I'll be at the coffee shop at our usual table.
    (a few minutes later …)

Me (Sage): Nice to see you! Sorry I didn't invite you in.

Miriam: That's okay. I know you don't like me showing up when you're not expecting me.

CONNECTOR – ***showing warmth and generosity of spirit,*** *specifically:*
        expressing caring thoughtfulness of needs previously communicated

Me (Sage) *(responding in kind to Miriam's relaxed openness)*: Yeah, thanks, but it's not just you. In fact, it's not about you at all!

Miriam: No? Good! I've been wondering ... so I'm glad to hear that.

CONNECTOR – **showing warmth and generosity of spirit,** *specifically:*
expressing feelings of wanting connection and togetherness

Me (Sage): Yeah. It's my embarrassment with *anyone* seeing my messy place. I always had such heavy pressure from my mother. She still expects me to keep my apartment neat, the same way she always made me clean up my room at home.

Miriam: Ah, so your mother has a kind of primal authority on what a household should look like.

CONNECTOR – **active listening,** *accurately reflected*

Me (Sage): She sure does! I wish I could shake it off. I'm the most loyal customer at this coffee shop thanks to my mother. She's the reason I meet people here instead of at home.

Miriam: That's interesting.

Me (Sage): It is, actually, now that I think about it. Every time I come here, it's because I'm deferring to my mother's standards on housekeeping. I'm going to remember that from now on, every time I walk through the door of this café.

Miriam: You mean, remember that you're doing it *her* way and not *your* way?

CONNECTOR – **active listening,** *accurately reflected*

Me (Sage): Yeah, that I'm always making the decision in this automatic way, based on what's not acceptable to *her*, and that I'm not even asking myself what's okay with *me*.

Questions for discussion

1) Have you ever experienced new insights about yourself by having a listener who simply kept "getting" what you were saying and letting you know what he or she was understanding from you?

2) None of Miriam's responses to Sage in this dialogue consisted of giving advice or reassurance. What might that indicate about Miriam's basic view of people and personal relationships?

3) Sage has an automatic behavior (not letting people see her messy home) that is driven by the feelings of shame and incompetence induced by her mother. Do you know someone who exhibits similar behavior? Is there something you might adopt from Miriam's style of listening that might be helpful for that person in some way?

4) When a friend or family member is mentioning to you something about a difficulty, which type of response do you tend to make – giving advice, giving reassurances, or giving understanding of what you're hearing about the difficulty?

Story 47: Nicola

Background

Hi, people. My name is Nicola, and I'm 13 years old. My new hobby is playing chess, and everybody says I'm pretty good at it, considering I started only last year. I'm in the chess club at school and I play on the junior team, and I'm going to be in my first tournament in two weeks – so exciting!

And then this happened: One of the older kids on the senior chess team was in a skiing accident over the weekend. He's in the hospital with a couple of broken bones, and the coach asked me if I would substitute for him on the senior team. Me! On the senior team! It's a big honor, but I'm really nervous. I still feel like a baby at chess. I know the standard moves, but there are lots of strategies that I haven't learned yet, and I know I can't possibly learn all of them in two weeks. Getting good at chess takes years of experience.

What happened

Me (Nicola): I'm going to my room, Dad, 'cause I have to practice for the chess tournament. I can't imagine how I can possibly be ready in two weeks.

Dad: You're really very good at chess, you know.

Me (Nicola): Well, for my age maybe. But not in comparison to the kids on the senior team.

Dad: That's what you think, but I don't really think you have anything to worry about. You're pretty close to them in skill.

*DISCONNECTOR – **reassuring inappropriately***

Me (Nicola): Not really, Dad. I need a couple of years of playing regularly before I'll have their level of skill. I'll be playing against kids who've been playing for years. I can't catch up in two weeks! Agghh!

Dad: Don't make yourself crazy over it. The coach believes in you, so that should be enough to give you confidence, don't you think?

DISCONNECTOR – *implying "you shouldn't feel how you feel"*

DISCONNECTOR – *counteracting others' feelings, views, or actions*, *specifically:*
citing positive facts to invalidate realistic concerns and sensible anxiety

Me (Nicola): No! You don't understand. I don't feel ready, and two weeks is a really short time! I want to do this, but it stresses me out.

Dad: I don't think you're being realistic about this.

DISCONNECTOR – *disregarding signals of distress or need, specifically:*
total lack of empathy

DISCONNECTOR – *counteracting others' feelings, views, or actions*, *specifically:*
how you view and feel about this are wrong, and I know what's realistic and right

Me (Nicola): Why don't you ever listen to me?!

What I'm feeling

I was already pretty stressed, and now I'm *really* stressed by Dad telling me over and over that I'm wrong and stupid to feel stressed about playing against the experienced seniors! He wouldn't listen to anything I explained! He just wouldn't see the problem I'm facing. But I see it! Him telling me I shouldn't be worried doesn't make the problem or my worry go away. I can't switch off my worry just because Dad wants me to! His reassurances were so lame! He really doesn't get it! I know he's trying to be helpful in his own way, but that doesn't count for much because he makes me feel so much worse!

I won't talk to Dad about feeling stressed or worried about anything anymore. He makes it much worse. I think I'll just lock myself in my room now and just practice chess as much as I can.

What I needed instead

Me (Nicola): I'm going to my room, Dad, 'cause I have to practice for the chess tournament. I can't imagine how I can possibly be ready in two weeks.

Dad: Feeling the time pressure, huh?

*CONNECTOR – **active listening**, accurately reflected*

Me (Nicola): You can say that again! I need a couple of years of playing regularly before I'll have their level of skill. I'll be playing against kids who've been playing for years. I can't catch up in two weeks! Agghh!

Dad: Yeah, you need two years, but you have two weeks! I get what you're saying. What ideas do you have about how to get as ready as you can in the available time?

*CONNECTOR – **active listening**, accurately reflected*

*CONNECTOR – **asking interestedly**, specifically:*
inviting further problem-solving with caring accompaniment

Me (Nicola): Coach gave me some sample games to work through. He said he thinks I'm going to surprise myself. I have to admit that helps.

Dad: I bet it does! Well, I'll leave you to your practice. If you need anything, just give a shout.

Questions for discussion

1) Have you ever experienced the same kind of futility that Nicola described, in which you tried unsuccessfully multiple times to get someone to understand your dilemma or distress, and the other person just kept trying to show you how wrong you were to feel negatively? How did you, or might you, handle that conversation?

2) Have you expressed insecurity or worry to someone and been met with positive reassurances? How did that feel to you, and then how did you respond to that reassurance?

3) What do you imagine might have been motivating Dad to be so unaccepting of Nicola's anxiety and so determined to reassure her out of her anxiety?

4) Can you describe a time when you felt it was necessary, or kind, or helpful, to reassure someone who was feeling worried or insecure? What effect did your efforts have? Under what circumstances might reassurance be useful to another person, and when is it not helpful?

Story 48: Yolanda

Background

Dear readers,

I'm Yolanda, a 60-something Manhattanite with the good fortune of having a close circle of friends. We've known each other forever and a day, it seems. Some of us have partners, some don't, some are childless, some have kids who've moved far away, so it's us "oldies" relying on each other to be there when someone needs help and to celebrate birthdays and major holidays together.

We know a lot about each other, but we don't know everything, of course. Most of us came from somewhere else and moved to New York as adults, gradually building shared experiences. Building a clique as an adult offered me a chance to try some things in a new way and find fresh priorities in my relationships. I dropped some old expectations and kind of reinvented myself. I have the impression that that's true for some of my friends, too.

A couple of weeks ago I got a call from Stacy, a childhood friend from up in New England. We hadn't seen each other in several years, and she was planning to be in Manhattan on business for two weeks and wanted to get together. Since she'd be here over a weekend, I invited her to come along to the birthday dinner for Angeline, one of the women in my clique. I'll admit that I had some misgivings about how it would go, but I knew Stacy to be empathetic and people-oriented, so on our way to the dinner I just mentioned with a smile, "Don't give away any of my deep, dark secrets, okay?" and pushed any doubts aside.

My city friends enjoyed Stacy, who entertained them with stories of silly things the two of us had done in grade school.

What happened

Angeline: Sounds as if you two led adventurous lives. Whoever said that growing up in farm country was boring?!

Stacy: Yeah, it was never boring with Yolanda around. We went through a lot together: We were partying when we should have been studying, and we'd get lost in the woods on what was supposed to be a short hike. But to me the craziest adventure of all was her marriage and divorce.

Angeline: What? Yolanda? Your divorce was here in New York. What's Stacy talking about?

DISCONNECTOR – **disregarding signals** *of distress or need, specifically:*
violating an expressed need for not revealing personal information

Me (Yolanda): Um, yeah, I was married before. Not something I particularly enjoy talking about.

What I'm feeling

How could Stacy betray me like that? I *told* her not to mention dark things from our past! I'm really shocked at how careless she was with my privacy! And I'm embarrassed in front of my friends because now they think I'm hiding something terrible or shameful in my past. I also feel worried that my friends are upset with me for keeping secrets from them, although I had my reasons. They're *my* reasons. It's *my* life. I'm allowed to decide how much personal information I share with whom.

What I needed instead

Angeline: Sounds as if you two led adventurous lives. Whoever said that growing up in farm country was boring?!

Stacy: Yeah, it was never boring with Yolanda around. We went through a lot together. Yolanda, what stories have you told your friends about our colorful past?

CONNECTOR – **showing warmth and generosity of spirit**, *specifically:*
expressing caring thoughtfulness of needs previously communicated

Questions for discussion

1) Have you had an experience in which someone who knew you well shared something personal about you when you felt it was inappropriate, carelessly violating your privacy? How did or would that feel to you? If that were to happen in the future, how would you want to respond?

2) Do you have a story about meeting a friend's friends or family and cautiously wondering what personal information might not be okay to share? What questions did you ask yourself?

3) Have you ever revealed something personal about a friend or relative and then regretted having done so? What was, or would be, your motivation to reveal such information? What questions could you ask yourself before sharing information about another person?

4) Have you ever tried to clear up any such missteps with someone? If so, how did that go? If not, why not?

Story 49: Judith

Background

Dear readers,

My name is Judith, 65 years old. I recently retired from my job as a school secretary for 24 years, and I live alone. I realized just recently that I miss having people around me all the time, as I did at school, so I've been keeping my eye out for a part-time job somewhere in the neighborhood.

I was in the local copy shop last week at a time when it was quite full. I was copying a card I designed that I'm thinking of sending out for Christmas this year. Anyway, while I was paying, I spontaneously mentioned to the young guy at the cash register that I'm available to work a few hours a week in case they need anyone. I left my phone number with him, and he promised to pass it along to the owner.

The owner, Henry, did contact me, but it went in a truly bizarre direction. I've copied below the exact wording of the text messages, as well as the timing of them – on a Sunday, when the shop was closed.

What happened

1:25 a.m.

Hello, good morning Judith,

Thank you for offering to work for us and leaving your card with my employee. How can we make this happen? Please call me as soon as possible. My cell phone: (123) 456-7890.

Henry

(I saw this message at 9:00 a.m. while drinking my coffee. I went out jogging and thought about how I wanted to respond. When I got back, another message from Henry was waiting for me.)

9:30 a.m.

You'll have to find a job somewhere else! I can see that you already read my message, but you couldn't be bothered to answer. No answer means no job!

(I then responded:)

10:00 a.m.

Dear Henry,

I was planning to answer you. Why quickly jump to such extreme interpretations? It does seem that we don't really overlap in our sense of timing. What a shame!

Regards,

Judith

(Then came this shocking response:)
2:50 p.m.

> You could have simply written "I'll get back to you later," but you didn't. Or you could have written "I'm not interested," but you didn't. Instead, you read my message and chose not to answer! Given such behavior, I can't imagine us working together. A woman in her 60s should be mature enough to handle a simple text message about a part-time job, don't you think? Sorry, it's a no-go.

DISCONNECTOR – **implying "you shouldn't need what you need,"** *specifically: disallowing and invalidating the other's need for time and space to arrive at a reply*

DISCONNECTOR – **criticizing, judging, shaming, or blaming,** *specifically: scolding, berating; expressing negative judgments of the other's character; demeaning, denigrating*

What I'm feeling

I feel attacked, harshly judged, berated, demeaned, and rejected by Henry for not meeting his strict, extreme rules and standards of behavior, which he seems to assume are obvious, universal truths. What a tyrant! Whew, I'm really lucky I *didn't* reply right away! If I had, his ugly tyranny might not have emerged until after I was working for him! And it's also a good thing I have those 24 years of knowing that I'm a responsible, conscientious worker who gets along well with many different people! *I'm* immune to Henry's demonizing, fortunately, but someone with shaky self-esteem could be seriously damaged by him! I'd bet that has actually happened more than once. Oh gee, I hope he doesn't have any children! The thought makes me shiver. Needless to say, I have no further desire to have anything to do with Henry or his shop, and I'll be looking for another copy shop in the future when I want to copy anything!

What I needed instead

Just look at how many times he wrote *you, you, you*! What I needed was for Henry to talk in *I-messages*, which I learned to do long ago, rather than in you-messages, like this:
1:25 a.m.

> Hello, good morning Judith,

Thank you for offering to work for us and leaving your card with my employee. How can we make this happen as quickly as possible? I actually need someone to start tomorrow, Monday. Could that work for you? Please call me as soon as possible. My cell phone: (123) 456-7890. –Henry

9:30 a.m.

I might have to try to find someone else if I don't hear from you in the next hour or so, since I'm under time pressure, but I'd be happy if this could work out.

CONNECTOR – **using I-messages** *to express needs*

10:00 a.m.

Dear Henry,

I was planning to answer you shortly. I can stop in tomorrow and give it a try. What time should I show up? Thanks for giving me an opportunity.

Regards,

Judith

Questions for discussion

1) What do you think may have been going on emotionally or psychologically for Henry that led him to form such an extreme interpretation of Judith and express himself using accusatory you-messages?

2) Have you been on the receiving end of blameful, judgmental you-messages? How did you or would you feel, and respond, as the recipient of that?

3) Can you remember a situation in which you expressed your own upset feelings using you-messages toward another person? How did the other person react? Can you think of a way to express yourself in that situation using I-messages?

4) Have you witnessed a conflict situation in which someone used I-messages? Can you sense the different trajectories created by I-messages versus you-messages?

Story 50: Amber

Background

Dear readers,

Hi, my name is Amber, and I'm 31 years old. I got married several months ago, and I was thrilled that I got pregnant soon after the wedding! My husband and I are from the U.S.A. but we're living in South America right now, and I try to keep up with my relatives in the U.S.A. by talking to them online every few weeks.

I'm quite close with my Aunt Jody, who's only eight years older than I am. She feels more like a sister than an aunt. Funnily enough, Jody also got married last year. Her new husband, Zane, pops into view onscreen briefly every time I'm online with Jody. It's okay that he does that, since he's well-meaning. He probably thinks I'll be offended if he doesn't say hi (although that's not really the case).

The thing is, I find myself feeling slightly annoyed at him every single time we interact, and I'm trying to figure out why, since he's clearly making an effort and he wants me to like him.

What happened

Me (Amber): Hey, Zane, how ya doing?

Zane: Good. And you? I see you're doing great! I'm sure you're super excited about everything!

ouch!

DISCONNECTOR – **making assumptions that disconnect,** *specifically:*
presuming to know what the other is experiencing

Me (Amber): Well, yeah, I guess so, but right now I'm just feeling so heavy and awkward, and I'm having trouble sleeping at night.

Zane: Hey, that'll be the least of your problems once the baby comes. Your whole life is going to change. You'll never have a minute to yourself, so enjoy it now!

ouch!

DISCONNECTOR – **disregarding signals** *of distress or need*

*DISCONNECTOR – **making assumptions that disconnect**, specifically:*
presuming to know what the other will experience

*DISCONNECTOR – **giving unsolicited advice or giving advice prematurely***

Me (Amber): Well, see … I was just saying how *hard* it is to enjoy it now!

Zane: Okay, always good to see you. I'll just sign off for now.

ouch!

*DISCONNECTOR – **disregarding signals** of distress or need*

*DISCONNECTOR – **not listening, literally***

What I'm feeling

Bored, watching Zane onscreen blowing hot air. It's similar to how it feels when you're watching a stand-up comedian who isn't funny at all. I'm also annoyed, as I mentioned, because Zane just keeps delivering his one-liner notions of me, except it has nothing to do with me at all. Never once has he *asked* me about me. Maybe he's nervous with me and very different with Aunt Jody. I sure hope so.

What I needed instead

Me (Amber): Hey, Zane, how ya doing?

Zane: Good. And you? How're things coming along?

*CONNECTOR – **asking rather than telling***

*CONNECTOR – **asking interestedly**, specifically:*
expressing interest in the other's actual experience

Me (Amber): Oh, man … Right now I'm just feeling so heavy and awkward, and I'm having trouble sleeping at night.

Zane: Agghh! Being sleep-deprived is no joke. May this difficult phase end immediately! Good to see you again!

*CONNECTOR – **active listening**, empathically reflected*

Questions for discussion

1) In your opinion, in reply to Zane saying, "I see you're doing great! I'm sure you're super excited about everything!" would it have been okay if Amber had said to Zane gently, "Well, I'm sorry to disappoint you, but actually …"? Why, or why not?

2) How would you have responded in Amber's position when Zane said, "Your whole life is going to change. You'll never have a minute to yourself, so enjoy it now!"

3) How have you dealt with the problem of being forced to interact with someone you don't enjoy?

4) It probably would help Amber connect with Zane if she knew what Aunt Jody enjoys, appreciates, and values him for. Can you think of how Amber could elicit some of that information from Aunt Jody without criticizing Zane?

Story 51: Liam

Background

Hi, people,

My name is Liam, and I'm 32 years old.

My girlfriend Willow is incredibly knowledgeable about European history. Some people say she's actually obsessed with it, but since I'm drawn to certain historical times too, I can understand her passion.

She tries to share her fascination and her knowledge with me, which I appreciate, at least in principle, or at least when I think about it rationally, but I somehow usually end up feeling stupid and ignorant. I don't really think that's her intention, since I know she loves me. But how she tells me things often doesn't go well for me, and I wind up looking at her in stony silence and don't want to listen to her anymore.

What happened

Willow *(excitedly showing me an online article)*: You won't believe it, but F. A. Lindemann actually recognized the dangerous developments in Germany in the early 1930s!

Me (Liam): Um … Who's F. A. Lindemann?

Willow *(in a tone of annoyed disbelief)*: Don't you recognize *that name*?

DISCONNECTOR – **criticizing, judging, shaming, or blaming**, *specifically:*
regarding not knowing something as a shocking, shameful failing

Me (Liam): Doesn't sound familiar.

Willow: You mean you've never heard of him?

Me (Liam): If I had, I'd tell you.

Willow: Gosh! He was *only* Churchill's top scientific advisor during the war and had a major influence on British policy!

*DISCONNECTOR – **lecturing or admonishing**, specifically:*
using sarcasm to shame the other for not knowing something

*DISCONNECTOR – **disparaging** the other person for being ignorant of a fact*

What I'm feeling

It's a cringing feeling of embarrassment for being ignorant of things Willow assumed I knew. It's as if she's discovering I'm not her equal, right before my eyes. She's really surprised at what I don't know, and not only surprised, but also sort of disappointed and critical, like when she said, "Don't you recognize that name?" That doesn't feel like a real question. In my mind, I hear it end with, "… you idiot!" And then she rubs it in, with "he's *only*" or "it's *only*" sarcasm. To tell the truth, on some days this puts me into feeling inadequate and sheepish to such a degree that my libido is nowhere to be found, if you know what I mean.

What I needed instead

Willow *(excitedly showing me an article on her laptop)*: You won't believe it, but F. A. Lindemann actually recognized the dangerous developments in Germany in the early 1930s!

Me (Liam): Um … Who's F. A. Lindemann?

Willow: Lindemann was Churchill's top scientific advisor during the war, and he had a major influence on British policy.

*CONNECTOR – **showing warmth and generosity of spirit**, specifically:*
sharing knowledge with kind helpfulness

Me (Liam): Oh, interesting. Wow, imagine what their conversations must have been!

Willow: Yes! And I find it fascinating to discover that he was recognizing trouble in Germany already in the early 1930s!

Questions for discussion

1) Can you recall an interaction with someone in which you felt embarrassed or troubled about not knowing something? Can you define what would lead you to feel that way?

2) Do you know someone who frequently calls attention to her or his superior knowledge, sometimes in contrast to someone else's lesser knowledge? How do you feel about that person in such situations?

3) Have you ever been surprised by another person not knowing something (a fact, a famous person, etc.) that you assumed *everyone* knew? Did you express your surprise to the other person? Did you feel a negative judgment toward him or her?

4) Are there any particular areas of knowledge that you consider to be a *must,* in the sense that you *would* feel judgmental toward someone who lacks that knowledge? If so, what are those areas?

Story 52: Lisa

Background

Hello, dear readers:

My name is Lisa. I'm 57 years old, and I've been on the lookout for a new partner for a couple of years. I'd like to tell you about a recent short relationship I had, how it fell apart, and how I ended up stronger and more peaceful by really listening honestly to myself.

What happened

I met Victor online on a dating portal, and it was exciting right from the beginning. We had so much in common, and every communication between us, whether online or in person, felt deep and meaningful to me, just as I had been longing for.

It built and built over the first four weeks, and then, inexplicably from my point of view, he started pulling away, just at the point where I had allowed myself to feel fairly trusting and confident in exploring the possibility of a future together. I couldn't get an explanation out of him that made sense to me.

I couldn't help but continue writing Victor emails expressing my feelings, my love, my commitment, all to no avail. At first he was patient and kind in his responses. And then came the email that changed everything. He said that he had never really believed in our potential together, it had been just a short adventure anyway, he was convinced that my feelings for him were nothing more than a "projection" of my own desires onto him, and that I completely failed to see the reality of the situation. That really hurt.

What I'm feeling

Here's my best effort to reproduce the evolving conversation I had with myself over the next few days after reading that email from him:

- Oh my God, how stupid of me! How blind I've been! He's right, of course. I must be so desperate that I see only what I want to see, and I'm incapable of seeing reality. I feel so exposed and shamed. So undeserving of respect in how I handled this.
- Wait. I'm starting to feel pissed off. What am I angry about?
- What makes me think I have to accept his view of what happened? Why does *he* get to write the history and presume to know what was going on inside *me*?

- Memories of a previous intense relationship are coming up. After that breakup, my ex went around telling lies about what had happened. He gaslighted me and everybody we knew, and they all believed him. My believing Victor's version feels similar, and it makes me furious! I think some of my current fury is coming from anger I never expressed back then. I accepted it then because I didn't trust or listen to myself.
- What if I'm right about what happened with Victor? What if I have the right to listen to *my* version and write my own history? Let me explore this …
- My feelings were certainly real. The depth of my commitment was real. My whole experience felt real. Just because he experienced something different doesn't make my experience less real or valid.
- So there's not just one reality that Victor saw clearly and I failed to see. I'm starting to think that there's *his* true experience and there's *my* true experience. I guess I can give him that … that his experience and decisions were as real and right for him as mine were for me.
- I see that Victor's true experience and my true experience don't overlap very much. It's painful to admit that, since I fervently wanted a different outcome, but I'm starting to think I can live with how this went, as long as I really listen to my true experience and trust it. I might have to mourn this loss for a while, but I'll be okay.

In the past I've always pressured myself to get over sad or painful things quickly because I felt as if my intense feelings were a burden to my friends. It's a new experience to give myself all the room I need to keep listening to myself and acknowledge my feelings. That has really helped me make sense out of what had happened and be able to move through my grieving process and move on.

CONNECTOR – **active listening**, *empathically reflected, specifically:*
listening to and trusting one's own experience

CONNECTOR – **allowing time and space for one's individual process to unfold**

Questions for discussion

1) Can you recall a time when you allowed yourself to receive the full focus of your own listening skills, and you took the time and space to find your deeper truths? Would you benefit from doing that in some particular area now?

2) What do you think about the differing concepts of, on the one hand, there being a single reality with right and wrong interpretations, and, on the other hand, each person having a unique, subjectively true experience that can be that person's firm ground only by listening to it and trusting it?

3) Have you been in a relationship that ended in such a way that you could describe it today as two different experiences of the relationship that didn't overlap enough?

4) Are there other people in your life – your parents, or siblings, or your own children, for example – whose inner worlds of meaning and resulting feelings and behaviors have become understandable to you only after the passage of time? What enabled that to become possible?

Part 2

It's all about connection

DOI: 10.4324/9781003288589-2

Part 2 provides further insights into the connectors and disconnectors that make all the difference in how our interactions leave us feeling, as shown by people's stories in Part 1.

The importance of using good listening skills, including the use of connectors and the avoidance of disconnectors, of course depends on the nature of the conversation. When the content is deeply personal, heavy, or important to the relationship, then our skill as listeners has a great effect and is especially important. When it's more of a lightweight banter, the conversation can usually flow along well without our being particularly careful about our listening quality. And yet, such low-key, more superficial conversations provide a great opportunity for practicing listening and communication skills with minimal risk.

Right alongside our skillful responses as listeners, our *intent* and good will are noticed, felt, and valued, in and of themselves, by a person wanting to be heard and understood. A simple statement such as, "I'm hearing you, and I'm starting to get what you mean," lets the person know you're doing your best. However, sometimes a listener doesn't yet "get" what the other person means. It's valid, then, to say simply, "I don't yet understand what you mean." That shows interest in achieving understanding.

Connectors illuminated

As we've seen throughout the stories in Part 1, most of us want and need to be seen, heard, listened to, and understood in order to feel the satisfaction, comfort, support, and security of *connection*. And listening well to *oneself* creates inner connection, reducing or even resolving areas of internal conflict that are inherent in being human.

Whenever we're listening, the more we assume that people's thoughts, emotions, and actions make some sort of sense to *them* (even if they perhaps don't yet make sense to *us*), the easier it is to connect with others. You might be surprised at how the doors of mutual understanding fly open as a result of holding that assumption of inner *coherence*, which is simply the understanding that how each of us thinks, feels, and acts fully makes sense based on what we have learned about the world from our lifetime of experiences. When we cannot *see* any sense in someone's thoughts, feelings, or actions, it's common to jump to the conclusion that the person is being "irrational," but if we are assuming coherence, we know that we simply aren't privy to how it all does make sense within that person's own inner world of meaning. There's more about coherence below in discussing the connector "having assumptions that connect" on page 148, and also in Part 3.

146

These connectors are more fully considered on the following pages:

Having assumptions that connect

We wouldn't be able to navigate life without making a great many assumptions! Each of us has learned through our life experiences a huge amount about how the world works and how people are – and no two of us have learned all the same things. As we move through life, we are guided by our learned expectations, based on those life experiences, of how the world around us will most likely be, and how the people around us will most likely behave. We are almost continually predicting, but without awareness of doing so, and making choices accordingly. Paleolithic humans made predictive assumptions based on experience, for example, about the danger of certain animals or of sudden changes in weather. Their assumptions were necessary for adapting and surviving in a complex, changing world.

Today, we humans share many predictive assumptions that are based on our life experiences, such as taking for granted that automobile drivers will stay on the proper side of the road. Other assumptions are unique to the individual, such as knowing how to endear ourselves to others – which for one person might be through a sense of humor and for another person might be through flouting the law. Our assumptions today also arise out of needing to adapt and survive in a complex world.

There are assumptions we can make about people that function as *connectors*, because they lead us to respond in ways that strengthen and deepen relationships. For example:

- We can assume that a person's thoughts, feelings, and behaviors are coherent, because they make sense to that person (whether or not we know or understand the other's framework of sense-making). When we approach people and relationships with this assumption, it is much more likely that we can have satisfying, interesting, respectful interactions and connect at a meaningful level.
- We can assume that each of us is the "single source of knowledge" about our life learnings, our frameworks of meaning, and our emotional truths – in short, our inner coherence. When we make this assumption, we are able to support others in finding solutions and adaptations in life that are well tailored and optimized for *their* own lives, rather than assuming we know better according to what would be best in *our* own life.
- We can assume that every person is complex and unique and, therefore, differs from ourselves in ways that might be understood through good listening.

Alongside those connection-building assumptions, we may concurrently have other assumptions, largely unquestioned and outside of our awareness, that could cause disconnections. We are usually unaware of *having* most of our guiding assumptions in the first place, so we are unaware of how they control and limit us. Our assumptions seem to be simply the immutable truth of *how the world is* or *how it is necessary to be* in the world as it is. And some of our own potent assumptions are likely to be contrary to the above assumptions that connect. Consider, for example, the unquestioned assumption, "When you tell me about your needs, it means you're telling me I'm an inadequate partner." What a powerful effect that one assumption has within a couple's relationship! Imagine the surprise felt by that assumption's owner after it comes into awareness and is expressed, and the partner then explains, "That isn't what it means to *me* at all when I tell you about an unmet need of mine. It means I'm making a request *so that we can be closer and happier together*, because that's what I want for us." One of the most fruitful effects of good listening skills is the revealing of limiting, implicit assumptions that *dis*connect, allowing them to be revealed as untrue.

How, then, can we develop and strengthen the assumptions that generate responses that best connect us to others? The most connecting thing we can do is to try to see inside that person's subjective world view, the way an anthropologist enters into the world of meaning of an unfamiliar culture. This can be an expansive, new adventure of discovery and connection. In that process, of course, one inevitably realizes that one is already making assumptions that aren't true about the other person's world. Discovering how our assumptions are off track is an awareness-expanding moment! For example, when a friend tells me a story and I say, "Wow, that sounds scary," and she answers, "No, it was actually an educational experience," then I can take note of this "course correction" and recognize that I *assumed* my friend would react a certain way – and yet she didn't. That's a normal part of endeavoring to understand other people.

The connector **having assumptions that connect** is illustrated in the following stories:

Story 32: James
Story 36: Eric
Story 41: Philip

Attending to the other's pressing needs first

Whenever two or more interacting people are having problems at the same time, with each one needing the other(s) to listen, a constructive outcome may be possible only by allowing someone to be given adequate listening first.

The biggest challenge occurs when people are simultaneously deeply involved in their own uncomfortable experiences and don't readily find the capacity to sense what the other is experiencing, so it doesn't even occur to them to ask themselves whose need to receive listening is more urgent at that moment. An extreme form of this occurs when a parent is so chronically troubled that the normal, everyday needs of a child cannot be perceived and met.

In some situations it's clear to us immediately that either the other person's need is more urgent than our own or the other person acutely needs listening and understanding before being capable of listening to our issue. Imagine, for example, calling a friend to vent your frustration about something relatively minor, only to find out that the friend's father had just suffered a heart attack. Then we're usually willing and able to contain and hold our own pressing issue for the time it takes to be a supportive listener to the other party. This valuable skill of putting our own issue on hold for a time may be motivated by caring or generosity, by the pragmatic aim of calming and deescalating the situation, or by recognizing that *we* will get to be heard only after giving listening to the other person (or even not at all).

In other cases, however, it's not immediately clear to us on an emotional level how to proceed with the conversation. We may feel torn between listening and talking, without seeing any way to discern whose need seems most urgent or any reason to give priority to the other's need to be heard first.

It's often useful to recognize that a truly *important* matter does not necessarily have *urgency*, in the sense that immediate action is not necessary to avoid dire consequences. Our own need or issues may be genuinely important, yet we may recognize that the other person's need has an urgency that ours does not.

And yet many situations remain unclear. How can we find our way in the midst of such situations? A constructive, depolarized interaction can emerge through the use of *transparency*. We simply comment on the dilemma just as it is, including our own lack of seeing a resolution yet. Imagine saying, for example, "Hang on a second. We're both having pretty strong reactions right now, aren't we, and neither one of us is feeling heard by the other." A next step could be, "Maybe just one of us at a time could talk and be listened to. How does that seem?" A further step might be, "I think I can put my 'stuff' on hold for a while and concentrate on really listening to you first." If that doesn't feel doable, we can say, "I'm so riled up right now, I need you to listen to me first before I'll be able to do the same for you. Could that work?"

Using transparency in such ways requires the ability and willingness to step outside of the immediate happenings, mentally, in order to look at the situation from an observer's perspective to some degree. We discuss this skill further for the connectors "using transparency in communication" and "using meta-level communication" on pages 164 and 165.

The connector **attending to the other's pressing needs first** is illustrated in the following story:

Story 41: Philip

Maintaining focus on the speaker

When a person communicating with us has expressed some degree of need or distress – not even necessarily anything intense or dramatic – that person's human need to be acknowledged, listened to, and understood should have priority in the conversation, as a rule, until it's clear that the need is satisfied. The focus, then, should remain on that person, to whatever extent possible. If the listener instead switches to talking about him- or herself, that is likely to come across as a hurtful lack of caring, which of course is a potent disconnector.

Listening in a conscious way with focus on the speaker means putting any unrelated thoughts and personal concerns on the back burner, knowing we can deal with them at a later time. Minimizing distractions, making eye contact, and using other appropriate facial expressions (if physically or virtually together) are additional ways we can let the speaker know he or she has our attention.

Ways of maintaining focus on the speaker include:

• inviting the expression of thoughts and feelings
• expressing interest and caring toward the other's experience
• inquiring further with interest and curiosity

A good question to ask ourselves as listeners is: "Am I making this be about myself?" It's often tempting to do that, especially if we've had our own experience with the area the other person is addressing. We can easily plunge into "Oh, yeah! The same thing happened to me when …," and before we know it, we've made it be about ourselves for too long and the other person feels left by the wayside.

If we notice that we've strayed from keeping our focus on the speaker, we can usually repair things easily by transparently directing attention back to the speaker by saying, for example, "You were describing xyz just before. Please tell me more about that …," or even more explicitly, "Sorry, didn't mean to interrupt. I'm interested in hearing what happened next …."

The connector **maintaining focus on the speaker** is illustrated in the following stories:

Story 35: Mitchell
Story 36: Eric
Story 41: Philip

Acknowledging what you're noticing

The idea of acknowledging what you're noticing couldn't be much simpler at first glance. And yet it's a crucially important capability that threads its way throughout the entire set of listening skills supporting interpersonal connection.

You might express what you're noticing as "I see you're troubled" or "We're having a difference of opinion" or "You seem fulfilled by your work" or "I'm enjoying how well we're understanding each other about this." Each of those four examples consists simply of an explicit, transparent, honest naming of what *kind* of personal experience is happening, whether for the other person, or for oneself, or in the interaction, without getting into the particular contents of the experience. We can develop the habit of momentarily taking a bird's-eye view and asking ourselves, "What's happening here in the room right now?"

Some people find it easier to comment on what's happening in the room when it's something positive or uncontroversial. However, when we've noticed the other person give some indication of distress or a troubling situation, perhaps indirectly, it's then particularly important to acknowledge the difficulty of the dilemma – rather than going along with disregarding it – even if doing so might feel somewhat awkward. A broadly useful response is along these lines: "You mentioned that you're dealing with xyz. I imagine that could be challenging." That clearly acknowledges the distress signal with a tactful touch of sympathy, and respectfully leaves it to the other person to decide whether or not to say more about it. If the other person is clearly expressing distress and we're not sure how to approach that but want to respond with acknowledgement, we might say, "Oh, I see, that's quite a troubling situation. I wonder if it's preoccupying you …?"

The connector **acknowledging what you're noticing** is illustrated in the following stories:

Asking interestedly

As a listener, one doesn't always immediately experience the speaker's comments as being interesting and worthy of further time and attention. However, there is a fairly easy way out of that initial dilemma: asking a pertinent question that could elicit material that *would* be interesting to you, and asking that question interestedly. Here are two examples:

Speaker: My sister and her family visited us over the long weekend. We all went for a walk in the hills, played board games, and watched movies online.
Listener: How was it? Family visits can be full of complexities, can't they …

Speaker: Hey, I lucked out: During the week, the Mets had night games I could watch, and then all weekend they had a series of games in Chicago!
Listener: Wow! So that gets me wondering: What is it about them that's most interesting to you? Is it their overall identity as a team? Or maybe the personal stories and qualities of individual players?

By asking such questions about the speaker's topic with interest and curiosity, you rescue yourself from helpless boredom, but there's more going on than meets the eye. You're also communicating implicitly a respectful regard of the speaker as a full person who has inner substance that's worthy of enquiring about and understanding. So, as simple as this type of response seems, it is a valuable gift, and it contributes to well-being, whether or not the speaker consciously recognizes or appreciates that gift.

The essence of this way of interacting is simply to follow your own interest and ask a question that really would make the conversation interesting and meaningful to *you*, while remaining fully focused on the speaker's experience and concerns.

For further guidance on asking questions, see "asking open questions" on page 161.

The connector **asking interestedly** is illustrated in the following stories:

Story 8: Tiffany
Story 13: Jonathan
Story 22: Sem
Story 26: Destiny
Story 28: Ina
Story 35: Mitchell
Story 36: Eric
Story 39: Jeffrey
Story 41: Philip
Story 43: Francine
Story 47: Nicola
Story 50: Amber

Active listening

This refers to the practice of reflecting back to the speaker, accurately and empathically, what you have understood about his or her experience. You stay as close as you can to the speaker's own phrases and meanings, not taking liberties of interpretation or elaboration, though never seeming merely to parrot back what's just been said. Rather, you speak with some degree of sensitive understanding of the other's subjective experience. Active, empathic listening is a skill that's fundamental in creating meaningful connection to another person.

Listening in this way is comprised of a large array of capabilities, many of which we have expanded on in this book, including:

- recognizing the speaker's need for being listened to and letting the interchange be about that person
- showing interest and warmly accepting the other person's state of mind
- giving responses, both verbal and nonverbal, that express the intention of understanding
- leaving responsibility and agency to the "owner" of the problem to find solutions
- expressing empathy for the message and the underlying feelings, but not overdoing it
- remaining nonjudgmental
- meeting the other person right where he or she is and acknowledging that person's human moment

- putting aside any emotional agenda of one's own, at least for the duration of the listening portion of the conversation
- reflecting back and simply saying what we're noticing, going to the meta level and being transparent as needed
- initiating the repair of any disconnects that develop interpersonally

There are numerous examples of active empathic listening throughout this book.

If we find ourselves unable or unwilling to listen and reflect in this manner, we can embark on our own inner discovery process by experimenting with these sorts of open-ended questions:

- If I imagine listening to this person right now and maintaining an anthropologist's stance of "not knowing" what's going on in the other person, what do I notice happening in myself?
- If I imagine freeing myself as much as possible from unquestioned assumptions about right and wrong when listening to that person, what comes up for me?
- If I imagine being intentional about offering understanding and empathy, what do I feel?

If we're nonjudgmental about our own reactions and allow any lurking discomfort to bubble up into conscious awareness, that will lead to understanding ourselves better.

The connector **active listening** is illustrated in the following stories:

Story 2: Manuela
Story 3: Glenn
Story 10: Christopher
Story 13: Jonathan
Story 19: Courtney (part 1)
Story 21: Bethany
Story 23: Carl
Story 27: Matt
Story 29: Nancy
Story 30: Freddy
Story 35: Mitchell
Story 36: Eric
Story 40: Jamal
Story 41: Philip

Offering an expression of interest and caring understanding

Empathizing is one of the greatest connectors on earth! It's an absolutely essential component of understanding anyone at a deeply meaningful level. Empathizing means that as the listener, we're aiming to experience a vicarious sampling of the other person's subjective experience. How does it feel to be that person in that situation? We can't really know, of course, but we can try for a degree of such intersubjective understanding through a combination of close listening and our emotional openness to feeling the other's experience.

Empathizing leads us to respond with a comment such as, "So, you're feeling very worried about her, aren't you …?" Receiving such empathy is an experience of "feeling felt" (a beautifully apt phrase coined by psychiatrist Daniel Siegel). The person feels caringly accepted, rather than criticized or pathologized, for how he or she is, and might then move on toward further self-understanding or problem-solving, to whatever extent is fitting. Compare that response to, "You worry too much about things." Empathizing is completely devoid of criticizing or pathologizing, as well as advice-giving or any attempt to fix or change anything. Empathizing is such a precious gift because it enables other people to feel not only seen and understood in what they are experiencing, but also to some degree tenderly *accompanied*, which reduces aloneness. The accompaniment itself is deeply valuable because it tells people that they are not all alone with whatever is being experienced and felt.

Concern about reinforcing negative feelings or beliefs stops some people from expressing empathy, but that is a mistaken view. Nor does expressing empathy mean that the person empathizing shares or is agreeing with the other's views or feelings. It means only that the empathizing person is able, to some extent, to have a subjective sense of what the other is experiencing, and to let the other know that. Often there comes a clear response from the other person indicating that he or she feels intimately understood.

A surprising discovery that many people make when practicing empathetic listening is the large overlap among us, at the deepest level, of our basic human needs. We all thrive when receiving thoughtful, nurturing connection.

The connector **offering an expression of interest and caring understanding** is illustrated in the following stories:

Story 1: Olivia
Story 11: Deborah
Story 12: Veronica
Story 18: Manny
Story 23: Carl
Story 25: Simeon
Story 27: Matt
Story 34: Ginny
Story 39: Jeffrey

Showing warmth and generosity of spirit

Who comes to mind when you read the phrase "warmth and generosity of spirit"? Something in us instinctively admires and values people who radiate those qualities. Being on the receiving end of such kindness is a true blessing.

As listeners, we have the opportunity, every day, over and over, to emit some warmth and generosity of spirit. Whenever it's apparent that someone is in need or distress to any degree, that's a very real opportunity to be kind and generous in response, without expecting anything concrete in return.

Of course, it's a choice that has to be made in the moment. Sometimes one's own situation or state of mind really requires letting that opportunity pass. In that case, it's still always possible to disengage with a touch of kind regard rather than cold disregard – for example, by saying sincerely, "Sorry, I'm really on overload right now. I wish you all the best, though!" It can be interesting to examine which needs of one's own are standing in the way, which also opens up the opportunity to explain some of that transparently to the other person, if appropriate.

If, however, that choice is yes, then we can offer listening, caring, and understanding to the person in need, and possibly even some practical, helpful action. This surely is one of the greatest gifts we humans can give each other.

The connector **showing warmth and generosity of spirit** is illustrated in the following stories:

Story 1: Olivia
Story 4: Annie
Story 6: Emma
Story 11: Deborah
Story 12: Veronica
Story 15: George
Story 16: Jim
Story 20: Courtney (part 2)
Story 24: Nate
Story 34: Ginny
Story 41: Philip
Story 44: Clint
Story 46: Sage
Story 48: Yolanda
Story 51: Liam

Allowing time and space for one's individual process to unfold

People's inner processes move at their own speed. For quality listening, sometimes slower is faster: The listener patiently allows the time needed for the speaker's communication process to unfold. It also requires that the listener have sufficient inner space, or capacity, and openness to receive, hold, and understand the other person's communication.

Each of us is truly unique and complex, particularly in our feelings. Finding our way forward in life, especially when feelings are involved, is a personal process that doesn't necessarily or inherently conform to any externally visible rules or timeline. A given step or process of change may be more complex for one person than for another, so sorting things out may need more or less time, accordingly. We're giving something precious to people when we let them know – both explicitly and non-verbally – that we as listeners are aiming for a sensitive understanding of their inner process, unhurriedly, without constraints or pushback, and with sufficient "space."

Often there's a significant difference between a listener's sense of timing and the pace of the speaker's process of articulating what is inside needing to be communicated somehow. Listeners tend to move through the process more quickly than would be optimal for a person whose own process is emerging and unfolding while speaking. In order to be sure of offering sufficient listening time, we suggest trying out one or more of these responses to communicate interested expectancy of the speaker's next words:

- Hmm … (then pause and notice whether the speaker appears to need more time, and likewise for the next two phrases)
- I see …
- Tell me more, if you'd like …

The speaker or even the listener may be in need of more time or space (or something else) before being ready to continue the conversation. Awareness of such needs and the ability to express them openly and transparently are sometimes the critical factors that allow communication and connection to develop satisfyingly.

If we as listeners are under time pressure or feeling impatient with the other person's pace or process for any reason, we can consider postponing the conversation to another time when we have the desire and capacity to listen and support. Often it's best to be transparent and say that this isn't a good moment for being a good listener (and possibly what the reason is, if the reason isn't hurtful), and then offer a different time to follow up.

The connector **allowing time and space for one's individual process to unfold** is illustrated in the following stories:

Story 2: Manuela
Story 5: Emily
Story 35: Mitchell
Story 43: Francine
Story 52: Lisa

Opening the door to supportive conversation

Sometimes we pick up on signals from others that there's something they want or need to share, or they seem uncertain and are looking for a safe place to figure something out. That's an opportunity to consider opening the door – figuratively speaking – and inviting a person into supportive conversation.

In order to open the door to someone, we ourselves need to feel receptive to at least the other's first indications of what he or she wants to express. We can keep the door open to the extent we're able to remain attentive and nonjudgmental about what emerges. A listener in that stance is a safe space for the speaker. If at some point that stance no longer feels workable to maintain, that can be expressed with gentle transparency, for example: "I can see that there's more you'd share about this, and I wish I had enough capacity to keep listening, but I'm sorry; I don't. Maybe we could come back to this area some other time."

This book is very much about opening the door of connection to people who are important to us. Door-opening signals can be verbal and nonverbal, including facial expressions of warmth and interest, body language that's open and relaxed, and a tone of voice that conveys the messages, "I'm interested and curious," "I'm here for you, in case there's something you'd like to share," "Let me know if you need me," "I'm ready to focus on you and your topics," and "I want to understand your inner world, to whatever extent you want to share it with me."

We can also open the door to people we simply happen to cross paths with, as in this example: You're standing in line at a local food store and notice that the cashier is stressed and being curt with customers ahead of you in line. When it's your turn to pay, you make eye contact warmly and say, "Gee, it's tough right now with so many customers, isn't it … and they're all in a rush …." The cashier will probably say something in response, such as "Yeah, it's been like this for hours!" in appreciation of feeling understood and receiving that empathy.

There may be times when you feel you *should* open the door and listen, while at the same time a voice inside says that it's not the right thing to do right now. The option of honoring that inner sense is important to allow and consider. We have no absolute obligation to open the door to everyone at every moment just because the other person has the need for a listener. We offer the highest-quality listening and caring when we willingly choose to give this gift, knowing that the act of connecting can do oneself as much good as it does the other person.

The connector **opening the door to supportive conversation** is illustrated in the following stories:

Story 11: Deborah
Story 33: Magda
Story 34: Ginny
Story 37: Jennifer
Story 44: Clint

Asking open questions

Asking "open" questions is one way of opening the door to someone and inviting substantive personal communication. Open questions invite more than a yes-or-no answer. Rather, they encourage exploration and introspection.

Examples of open questions are "How do you feel about ...?" "How did it go at ... today?" "How was it for you to get ... yesterday?" "What do you think about that ...?" "Where do you suppose that's heading?" "How are you faring with this?"

You can also ask such questions in a way that more personally expresses your interest, such as "I'm curious how you feel about ...," "I'm wondering how it went at ... today," and "I'd be interested in hearing how it was for you to get ... yesterday, if you want to tell me about that." As you see, those are actually statements (I-messages, in fact) rather than questions, though the questions are clearly implied.

An open question invites the other person to choose *what* to say and *how much* to say in reply. Ask open questions when you have the interest, time, and attention available to listen to the responses.

The connector **asking open questions** is illustrated in the following story:

Story 26: Destiny

Asking rather than telling

Examples of asking or inviting, rather than telling, are questions such as "Shall I share my thoughts with you?" or "How was it for you to win a prize in that competition?" or "I wonder how you felt when you found out your ex-wife remarried?" Telling, on the other hand, includes statements such as "Here's what I think you should do," "You must be thrilled to have won a prize in that competition!" and "Hearing that your ex has remarried is a real punch in the gut; I know."

Asking other people about themselves and their inner lives – their thoughts and feelings – functions nicely as a connector in several ways. It sends the message, "I feel interested in you and want to know more about you," while also respectfully acknowledging, "You know best about what's true for you" as well as "It's for you to decide what you want to share with me about yourself."

In contrast, *telling* others about themselves sends implicit messages that function as disconnectors: "Your views and feelings are going to be the standard, predictable ones, so I don't need to learn from you about you" and "I've got you fully figured out."

It's quite straightforward to recognize which you're doing – asking or telling – once you remember to stop and notice your own communication. Then it becomes clear whether you're letting others know that you're open and ready to learn about them, or wanting them to see how much you believe you already know about them.

We live in a world that rewards us when we know things and shames us when we don't, both in school and in the working world. Acknowledging that we don't know what's going on inside another person can make us feel vulnerable. It may take some time, practice, and introspection to start becoming comfortable with not knowing, which enables us to ask rather than tell.

The connector **asking rather than telling** is illustrated in the following stories:

Story 16: Jim
Story 21: Bethany
Story 27: Matt
Story 36: Eric
Story 50: Amber

Using I-messages

"I'm now feeling hurt and disappointed after learning that yet another clear agreement between us was forgotten." An I-message is a transparent revealing of one's own views and/or feelings in response to the other person, with a phrasing that avoids blaming, accusing, or vilifying the other person. In that sense, it is assertive but clean, so it is minimally provocative, escalatory, or open to challenge. The intent is to avoid making the other person feel attacked or defensive, while explicitly naming the issues at hand and the interpersonal process in play. Together with active empathic listening, I-messages constitute the fundamental basis of interpersonal communication that builds connection between people.

What do I-messages have to do with listening? They are entirely based on listening to oneself. Only by noticing and honoring what's going on inside ourselves can we possibly communicate our views, feelings, and needs clearly to others in I-statements.

An I-message is not just any statement that begins with "I." "I feel that you're an inconsiderate person" isn't an I-message (it's a blame-laden "you-message"), whereas "I need more consideration than that when plans we've made are being changed" is a pure I-message. Most I-messages begin "I feel/I want/I need/I think ...."

Making I-statements involves capabilities and intentions described elsewhere in this book, such as:

- communicating transparently about your own inner experience
- speaking for yourself only, without assuming that the other person is – or ought to be – having the same experience
- expressing your feeling of wanting connection and being together
- expressing your desire to offer ongoing contact and accompaniment through a period of distress
- assessing whether the other person is in a position to listen
- proactively repairing interpersonal rifts

Even with the necessary awareness of one's inner feelings and needs, the choice whether to make an I-statement in a particular situation has to be carefully considered. There is no guarantee of a harmonious, constructive process ensuing. The choice should take account of the gravity of the issue and whether you know the other person to be non-defensive and respectful of others' needs and feelings. If the matter involves a delicate area of vulnerability, how much risk for you is there? For instance, during a meeting with one's supervisor at work, it would generally be a low-risk I-message to say, "I usually feel most motivation for a project when I have some degree of creative freedom in it, and I'm hoping for that soon."

The connector **using I-messages** is illustrated in the following stories:

Story 5: Emily
Story 25: Simeon
Story 49: Judith

Speaking for oneself only

When we presume to express another person's truths or what we believe should be his or her truths, we can find ourselves on quite shaky ground. We can't possibly know for sure what another person understands, experiences, or feels in a particular situation.

The principle of speaking only for oneself is closely related to making as few assumptions as possible about the inner lives and workings of other people. Although we do need to make certain assumptions about others in order to function in this world, it's a balancing act, because people and their subjective experiences are unique.

One assumption that's usually safe to make is that we understand less about the other person than we think we do!

Instead of making a blanket statement about something, as if it were true for everyone, we do better by making a statement that represents only our own experience. Rather than saying, "The best thing to do about that breakup is to find the silver lining," say something like, "I know how I've dealt with breakups, but my way isn't necessarily your way," and perhaps continue with, "Let me know if you'd like to hear about what helped me."

We can practice starting any potentially helpful sharing with "I'm not sure about you, so I'll speak just for myself about this" or "I can't speak for you, of course, but for me, though, this feels ...."

The connector **speaking for oneself only** is illustrated in the following story:

Story 28: Ina

Using transparency in communication

Transparency in interpersonal communication is one of those skills that are simple in concept, yet not always so easy to put into practice. Any extended conversation generally is accompanied by private inner experiences on multiple levels at once, as a rule, including not only the topic at hand, but also how each person feels about the topic, the other person, the relationship, and how the conversation itself has been going. Transparency consists of choosing to express openly one of those normally private areas of experiencing while it's happening, in real time.

For example, two friends have been having lunch together for about half an hour and one of them suddenly says, "Well, we've been talking for a while now and I need to tell you that all along I've been looking for signals as to whether you still have any lingering feelings from our misunderstanding last month – but I *can't tell*, so now I'm coming right out and asking you: Is there anything that we need to address or clear up?" That example illustrates one of the most common uses of transparency: Revealing to someone the existence of a problem involving that person, which one has been trying and failing to solve alone, privately. A very nice result in such cases tends to be an enrichment of connection, authenticity, and openness in the relationship.

Communicating transparently requires paying attention inwardly and outwardly at the same time, and then stating clearly what we're noticing, either within ourselves or in the room, so to speak. An example of the former is: "I'm at a loss to find words of comfort." An example of the latter is: "I'm not sure why no one has commented on my very visible injury, so I just want to say that for me it's okay to talk about."

Of course, some things are best kept private. Terrible troubles and hurts are sometimes caused by the too-simplistic belief held by some people that "honesty" requires revealing *everything*. Transparency is a thoughtful, selective revealing based on awareness of having the option to express something you were holding privately.

The connector **using transparency in communication** is illustrated in the following stories:

Story 25: Simeon
Story 41: Philip

Using meta-level communication

In the context of interpersonal communication, connection, and relationships, we use the term "meta level" to refer to addressing the broader, previously unstated conditions within which the current communications are occurring. It means addressing the larger picture that is influencing or even shaping the current communications. It has a large overlap with the connector "using transparency in communication" on page 164.

As with transparency, this is a skill that is conceptually simple and yet not always easy to remember to implement in real time, at the moment when it would be most effective. Often we're so involved in the topics under discussion at the moment that we can't easily step outside of that focus and look at the bigger picture.

Statements at the meta level are typically reflections about the state of the communication or the situation at large, as in "We're accumulating quite a number of topics that we don't yet agree about" or "I think it would be good if we paused right here to decide together which of these many tasks have the highest priority" or "None of us is saying anything about the atmosphere of conflict that's surrounding us right now." Meta-comments expand the scope of what's being considered in order to include strongly relevant, larger-scale aspects that were going unaddressed.

The connector **using meta-level communication** is illustrated in the following story:

Story 5: Emily

Noticing incongruence among words, emotions, and behaviors

Our communication to other people comes across as most believable and authentic, and therefore serves as a connector, when all aspects of our behavior are consistent or *congruent* with each other. That means that our verbal communication matches our facial expression, our body posture, and our actions. When there are discrepancies, the non-verbal messages speak louder than words.

Imagine saying to someone, "I'm *so* glad you got that promotion!" in a nearly monotone voice as you look across the room at what others are doing. That person will notice and feel that your message of gladness isn't genuine. Imagine your partner saying, "I'm listening to everything you're telling me," but at the same time being visibly absorbed in some other activity. You won't be convinced that you have your partner's full attention at all.

Imagine asking a friend how things are, and that person replies "Everything's fine" while his or her face and gestures suggest worry and tension. That's your cue to consider checking more closely. "Glad everything's fine," you might say, "but is there something at the moment?" Lightly inquiring into the other's hint of distress is an important connector that signals, "You matter, and I care how you are." This opens the door for others to share more, if they choose to do so, without pressuring them to reveal anything they prefer to keep private. See the related connector "opening the door to supportive conversation" on page 159.

The connector **noticing incongruence among words, emotions, and behaviors** is illustrated in the following story:

Story 1: Olivia

Supporting others' agency and autonomy in their lives

How we listen and respond to others is shaped very strongly by our core attitudes toward people. An attitude that serves as a potent connector is recognition of the *agency* of each person in his or her own life. That means deeply respecting people's own capacity and entitlement to choose how to respond to the challenges and opportunities in their unique situations. With that attitude of respecting agency, one doesn't think, "I know what he should do" or "I know how she should feel about this." There is no attempt to impose any agenda of one's own, but rather a wish to support the other person in finding his or her own best way. Any response given from that perspective is likely to be a connector.

Specific forms of this connector include:

- respecting signals of unreceptivity
- acknowledgement of making one's own choices
- respecting boundaries and feelings
- expressing respect for autonomy and personal choices
- listening to and trusting one's own experience

When we've been listening closely and want very much to be helpful for the other's problem, it can take a lot of self-awareness to refrain from trying to take control of a matter that belongs to another person. There are so many ways we can cross that line, often without awareness of doing so. An inner look at *why* this desire comes up – and what happens if we don't act on it in a given situation – can be an interesting and valuable exercise in understanding oneself better. See also the connector "speaking for oneself only" on page 163.

The connector **supporting others' agency and autonomy in their lives** is illustrated in the following stories:

Story 12: Veronica
Story 19: Courtney (part 1)
Story 33: Magda
Story 36: Eric
Story 38: Henry
Story 41: Philip
Story 42: Grace

Repairing rifts

We refer to the presence of a strain, distance, or breach in a relationship as a rift – whether it existed only momentarily or has persisted over a longer period of time. It's a lapse or deterioration of connection within the relationship.

Rifts are created in myriad ways. A rift can result merely from one person misinterpreting another's benign words or actions. Within the large universe of rifts, what's relevant here is the sizable category of avoidable rifts that are created by communicating with disconnectors, illustrated in Part 1 of this book – as in statements such as, "You always become defensive when we disagree about something" or "Don't be so negative; just look at it this way …" or "You should definitely take that job" or "You're just saying that because you're jealous of him" or "I can't believe you just noticed that. How can you be so unobservant?"

A disconnector causes an "ouch" experience which, if not repaired, is likely to create some degree of rift. Rifts that are left unrepaired tend to persist, cooling the warmth of the connection, and sometimes can fester and intensify, with the potential for ruining a relationship. Repairing rifts is, of course, an important (re-) connector.

Choosing whether to attempt repair can be a difficult decision, depending on how important the person is to you, your sense of his or her capacity for non-defensively examining what happened, and whether the vulnerability entailed in revealing your "ouch" is an acceptable risk for you if the other person proves *not* to have the understanding and non-defensiveness required for successful repair.

Once you have decided that the relationship is valuable enough to risk the vulnerability and effort of repair work, repairing a rift involves:

- finding a time and place in which the other person will most likely have available attention and be open and receptive
- speaking transparently but tactfully – using I-messages – about what has gone wrong from your perspective, using connectors and avoiding disconnectors, and aiming not to *convince* the other person, but only to *explain* what you experienced (aided by your transparency and meta-comments about exactly that)
- listening to the other's view of what happened with the same respectful, empathic attitude that you need in *that person's* listening to *you*
- looking for common ground, a shared understanding of what happened that makes a repetition far less likely and dissolves the "ouch"

In order to be proactive in repairing a rift, one needs the willingness to move toward and into – not away from – what's really happening in the relationship. It's natural to be concerned that in trying for repair, some new misstep could make the rift even larger. If, due to that concern, you back away, remaining out of communication, that in turn *does* make the rift bigger, because now even more distance and disconnection have developed. In such situations, transparency can be very useful. We can say, for example, "Hey, you know, I've been feeling a little bit out of sync with you, and hoping to get back in sync by talking with you about it, and also hoping that my communication skills are good enough to make it simple and easy. I'd really hate to make anything more complicated than it really is. So, first let me ask: Is this a workable time for you for that kind of a talk? If not, we could do it some other time." Notice the very considerate meta-level question at the end of that (see page 165).

As we attempt a repair, it becomes apparent whether or not something also went wrong for the other person. If it did, we may discover that repairing the rift necessitates our offering both understanding and apology for our role in co-creating the rift, a role we may not have recognized previously. Our role may have been something we said or did that was unwittingly hurtful or offensive, or something we *didn't* say or do that the other needed from us. Repair can be helped along nicely by an apology wrapped in transparency, such as, "I see how my lack of awareness of that caused a bad experience for you, and I apologize for that. It's very helpful for me that you've pointed this out for me to see." Such an apology is not an admission of being a bad person. Rather, it is a powerful connector that shows caring, respect, self-responsibility, and the humility of acknowledging that each of us continues to learn from experience.

The connector **repairing rifts** is illustrated in the following stories:

Story 7: Paul
Story 8: Megan
Story 30: Freddy

Disconnectors laid bare

In reading the stories in Part 1, you've probably become aware of how frequently disconnectors are used in everyday conversation. The stories also show their wide range of impact. Some disconnectors have a relatively subtle effect, not causing significant harm but letting the opportunity for satisfying connection slip by and leaving one wondering why an unpleasant aftertaste remains. At the other end of the spectrum are disconnectors that hurt deeply and can cause lasting distress as well as lasting damage to the relationship.

Any degree of increased awareness of our use of disconnectors and *any* shift toward doing so less often begins a greater use of connectors, rewarded by the enhanced well-being that connectors produce for those we're in contact with as well as for ourselves as listeners. Being told, "Ah, this conversation has been *so good!*" gives you the small joy of knowing you've succeeded in giving the gift of listening.

On the following pages, the disconnectors are grouped according to similar functions in our communication (as well as listed separately in alphabetical order to make them easier to find). For instance, there is a group describing "disconnection due to trying to fix the other person's problem."

These disconnectors are more fully considered on the following pages:

Disconnectors in alphabetical order

Disconnection due to not taking in what the other person is communicating

Not listening, literally

Someone is trying to communicate, but the other person pays no attention. The (non-)listener might be inwardly preoccupied or outwardly occupied with something else entirely, or may only be waiting for the other to finish in order to resume being the speaker.

Attentive, quality listening isn't something that most people can do as part of multitasking, and if the listener isn't devoting adequate attention, that will rapidly become apparent to a speaker who really *wants* good listening and real two-way communication.

What constitutes "not listening" varies, depending on the situation. If, for example, we're on a train ride, sitting next to a friend who's telling lightweight family stories, it's probably fine to be watching the scenery at the same time as we're listening. That same behavior, however, could easily constitute "not listening" if our companion is relating a heart-wrenching experience and what's needed is our undivided attention.

Of course, there *are* people who talk on and on and are seemingly oblivious to their listener's quality of listening. They seem to want only to be heard talking and aren't in need of a true listener. If we sense clearly that our active, close listening isn't what's wanted, then it's only natural to feel like doing something else at the same time!

What if you find yourself unable or unwilling to listen to someone? In such cases it's helpful to reflect on whether the blockage is specific to that particular speaker (for example, "I find her attitude about this topic really annoying") or whether it arises from a more general issue in one's own life (for instance, "Nobody has ever listened to *me*, so why should I listen to anyone else?") or is due to an urgent, current need of your own (as in "I just got home from a tiring trip and want nothing more than a warm bath!"). Recognizing the true nature of the blockage will be helpful in deciding how to deal with it.

The disconnector **not listening, literally** is illustrated in the following story:

Story 50: Amber

Cutting off communication

Cutting off communication with another person is, by definition, disconnecting from that person. To cut off communication is to no longer be available for listening. At times this can be an intentional and carefully considered step chosen because of a felt need to create or maintain emotional distance from a person. With awareness of such needs and feelings, we can evaluate whether to communicate an explanation of the reasons for cutting off communication. The cut-off may be temporary, as in the case of not having the capacity to listen on a particular occasion, or it may be permanent, as in the case of realizing that the ongoing experience of a particular relationship doesn't feel suitable.

Communication can also be cut off unintentionally by a listener who is not aware of having underlying needs, feelings, or motivations that are leading to that response. In these cases, the person on the receiving end of the cut-off very likely has an "ouch" experience of some kind, such as feeling disregarded, or insulted, or hurt, or not seen, or unworthy, or any number of emotionally distressing meanings.

We cut people off when we interrupt them to put the focus on our own point or topic. We cut them off when we unilaterally say "End of discussion!" without finding out whether the other person is also ready to end it. We cut off communication when we walk out of the room while the other person is still speaking. These actions may at times feel necessary and appropriate, and as usual, there is no universal right-or-wrong rule about this. It's important, however, to look inside and recognize what's going on that is making it feel necessary to resort to harsh disconnection. Asking oneself these questions can be useful:

- Will I feel okay with myself later about cutting off the communication in this way now?
- What's making it feel necessary to do this right now?
- What am I needing to protect myself from?
- Is this relationship or this person deserving of an explanation from me in the form of a clean I-message?

The disconnector **cutting off communication** is illustrated in the following story:

Story 37: Jennifer

Disregarding signals

Usually there is much more to notice about what others are communicating than is obvious at first glance. It's not only the spoken words that express what people are experiencing, but also their tone of voice, their posture, their tempo, their eye contact or lack thereof, and much more. Skilled listeners notice all of these signals, guiding them to respond in sensitively attuned ways that can connect deeply.

We humans, though, are so often focused – first and foremost – on our own experiences, expectations, and needs, and we perceive other people and their communications through our own, very personal filters. These filters can lead us at times to miss or disregard the signals that others are sending.

Often the most difficult signals to receive and recognize from others are signals of distress and unmet needs. Such signals may feel burdensome, or we may feel too unskilled and unequipped to address such areas, or a current difficulty with our own circumstances or state of mind could make it unworkable to focus on the other person's emotional dilemma.

For tips on responding to people in ways that acknowledge their signals, see the connector "acknowledging what you're noticing" on page 152.

The disconnector **disregarding signals** is illustrated in the following stories:

Story 1: Olivia
Story 8: Megan
Story 11: Deborah
Story 18: Manny
Story 27: Matt
Story 31: Linda
Story 33: Magda
Story 34: Ginny
Story 37: Jennifer
Story 38: Henry
Story 39: Jeffrey
Story 42: Grace
Story 43: Francine
Story 45: Suyin
Story 47: Nicola
Story 48: Yolanda
Story 50: Amber

Disregarding the deeper message, especially if it involves distress or need

As mentioned in the descriptions of "noticing incongruence among words, emotions, and behaviors" and "disregarding signals," there is often considerably more happening emotionally for a person than what has been communicated verbally. An extreme example is the classic depiction of a couple where one partner asks, "What's wrong, dear?" and the other glares, arms folded defiantly, and says, "Absolutely nothing!" But it's the much milder version of that scene that is more to the point here, where one partner's mood is only slightly yet noticeably reserved and distant and, when asked if anything is wrong, says "I'm fine."

If a person seems to be sending mixed or understated messages and we, as listener, interpret the speaker's words entirely at face value, we may be bypassing crucial, deeper messages. Listeners may do that (whether knowingly or not) because they don't want to engage with those hinted-at, problematic levels of what the speaker is experiencing, and it's easier, quicker, or more comfortable to go along with the superficial content. However, that disregard of the distress signal has a high price, because it has the effect of being a disconnector.

People usually *want* to feel heard and understood on a more substantive, personally meaningful level, no matter what they say, and when that kind of listening isn't forthcoming, disconnection is perpetuated. What may have been the speaker's disconnection from his or her own feelings is now compounded by a disconnection between speaker and listener.

Working creatively with this dynamic requires becoming aware of one's own tendency to disregard others' hints of distress. With that awareness, it becomes possible to inquire about whether the speaker *wants* us to pick up on the fact that a message is coming across to us as mixed. One possibility is to use transparency and observe out loud, for instance, "You're *saying* that the situation is fine, and yet I get the sense from you that maybe there's also another side to it." Children in particular usually don't have the vocabulary to verbalize their inner experience readily, so it's especially important to invite expression of the deeper message when they show any unexplained signs of disturbance or distress.

If we find that we're reluctant to make such an inquiry, then it might be interesting to do some of our own digging and find out what's underneath that reluctance.

The disconnector **disregarding the deeper message, especially if it involves distress or need**, is illustrated in the following stories:

Story 7: Paul
Story 23: Carl

Deflecting, distracting, or evading

When a person is talking about a personally important topic, anything a listener does to move away from – rather than toward – that topic is an unwelcome, unhelpful response and a disconnector, as a rule.

Deflecting means changing the course of the conversation by changing the topic, either by doing so oneself or by getting the speaker to shift topics. Example: A woman says to her partner, "I feel really hurt by your tone of voice," and the partner replies, "Oh, you're just overly sensitive when you have your period." Deflecting an incoming message about oneself is like holding up a shield in order to prevent the message from reaching us and to send it off in a new direction. This change of direction may deflect attention from the listener back to the speaker when the listener feels uncomfortable in some way.

Distracting is used by listeners for similar reasons and causes a shift in the focus of the conversation. Example: A teenager, just back from an exchange program in Paris, tells her mother, "I feel so nostalgic when I hear the song 'Sous le ciel de Paris.' I could just start crying." Her mother, feeling uncomfortable with her daughter's emotions, answers, "It's so cute how you pronounce French words."

Evasion consists of pretending not to know or not to be sure of something. It's similar to deflecting and distracting, in that the listener is moving away from, instead of toward, what a speaker is communicating. The listener, for his or her own coherent reasons, is avoiding connecting with the speaker and the speaker's topic. Example: In a group discussion, a man intentionally ignores an individual asking a question that feels uncomfortable to him, evading that topic by turning to a different member of the group and talking about something else.

Deflecting, distracting, and evading are disconnectors that can have many possible effects on the speaker, depending on what meanings he or she makes of the listener's behavior. The speaker may feel personally diminished and unimportant to the listener altogether, or may feel that the listener regards the particular topic as unimportant. Feelings of confusion, shame, or regret, for example, or of being "too much" in some way, may result. People often have a sense of being left alone with their problem when a listener directs attention away from the topic they've addressed.

When we notice an inclination to deflect, distract, or evade in response to another's communication, it's useful to examine and identify for ourselves the discomfort we're seeking to avoid, at the expense of connection. It may simply be an inconvenient moment, or there may be a substantive, significant personal issue involved, or there may be an appropriate need for a protective boundary that preserves privacy from the speaker's intrusion.

In most situations, rather than responding with one of these disconnectors, a connective response of transparency or an I-message would be possible, such as "Sorry, but there's something I'm really occupied with right now" or "I really don't know how to respond to that" or "Actually, that's not an area that I want to open for discussion."

The disconnector **deflecting, distracting, or evading** is illustrated in the following story:

Story 31: Linda

Minimizing or trivializing

A listener who minimizes or trivializes the speaker's topic or feelings is dismissing them as being far less important than they feel to the speaker. For example, you've told your mother that you're worried about the upcoming test in school tomorrow, and she answers with "It's just a little quiz. No need to be nervous."

Listeners may minimize or trivialize the speaker's message because it is their true view of the situation, and they intend to be helpful and reassuring without realizing the negative effect. (See also the disconnector "reassuring inappropriately" on page 183.) Or it may be that the listener is avoiding engaging with the speaker's topic or feelings for reasons that the listener may or may not consciously recognize. Either way, such responses function as disconnectors, and the speaker is likely to feel not only unhelped and left alone with the problem, but also characterized as over-reacting or overly sensitive, especially by comments such as, "You're making a big deal over nothing. Where's the big problem?" and "That's not really so bad; other people have it worse." Invalidating someone's feelings is always a disconnector. The most strongly disconnecting comments imply that the speaker's feelings have no validity whatsoever, such as, "You're so cute when you get angry" or "My poor little wife is feeling insulted."

To free oneself of the tendency to minimize or trivialize, it can be helpful to try the thought experiment of reversing the roles. How would it feel to be quite distressed about something and be told, in essence, that you're wrong and foolish to feel what you're feeling? Does that message lead to feeling heard, taken seriously, helped, and respected? Compare that to receiving this response: "I see how troubled you're feeling about this situation. What can you tell me about what's making this situation feel this troubling, and about what would help?"

The disconnector **minimizing or trivializing** is illustrated in the following stories:

Story 10: Christopher
Story 11: Deborah
Story 33: Magda

Not registering or responding to what was just said

Sometimes one person is talking to another, and the other appears not to have registered what has just been said. It's as if something totally different had been said, or even as if nothing at all had been said (see also the disconnector "not listening, literally" on page 174).

Example: Two people are sitting at breakfast. One says, "I woke up with such a headache today. No idea where that came from …." The other doesn't respond immediately, and then says, "I think I'll weed the garden after breakfast."

The speaker is left with a sense of overt disconnection – more so than with many other, more subtle types of disconnector. The effect can be so strong that the speaker may experience a desolate feeling of existing in a completely different reality from that of the (non-)listener.

There's a world of possible reasons for a person giving no response or recognition at all to what someone else has said, just as with other non-listening types of disconnectors. What gets in the way of listening and registering the content can be specific to the relationship, as when the listener feels bored or overburdened by what the speaker has said, or the listener may merely be heavily preoccupied with other issues or distracted by something unexpected.

While it may be difficult to catch oneself enacting this disconnector of non-responding, it can be quickly repaired by taking seriously any sort of objection that the other person makes in response, such as, "No, that's not at all what I'm talking about!" or "I'm wondering if you even heard what I just said!" A simple, sincere, three-second apology is usually all that's needed.

The disconnector **not registering or responding to what was just said** is illustrated in the following stories:

Story 3: Glenn
Story 32: James

Disconnection due to trying to fix the other person's problem

Giving unsolicited advice or giving advice prematurely

It's so tempting to offer advice, thinking we could help solve another person's problem or that we simply know better how to fix the problem. Advice-giving is well intentioned, as a rule, but the actual effects of advice-giving on the owner of the problem are not very likely to fulfill that good intention.

Usually what's most wanted and needed when someone begins to talk about a problem of any significance is some degree of sympathetic understanding of how it feels to *have* the problem or distress – not a solution for how to get *out* of it. Providing a bit of accompaniment for the person right there in that emotional experience, by simply trying to understand the experience, is what will be connective and comforting, whereas attempts to guide the person out of the experience mainly send the message that you don't want to hear about the difficulty of it, and that feels disconnective.

So, it's important to be sure that advice is actually wanted before offering it. It's easy to find out by being transparent and asking explicitly: "Is this a time when you'd like me to mainly listen and understand – or would you welcome a suggestion that might be helpful?" If advice is not wanted, then the respectful thing to do is not to give any.

If we are yearning to give advice, but the other person has not indicated interest or openness to that, then a neutral way to show our supportiveness can be, "Is there any way that I can help you with this?" or "If you'd like my support, just let me know."

If advice has been clearly welcomed, then a respectful way to offer it will leave the other person the room to make his or her own decision anyway, such as by saying, "I might handle it this way ..." or "In my experience, it has worked to do this ..." (rather than "You should do this ...").

The disconnector **giving unsolicited advice or giving advice prematurely** is illustrated in the following stories:

Story 9: Tiffany
Story 16: Jim
Story 23: Carl
Story 29: Nancy
Story 39: Jeffrey
Story 42: Grace
Story 43: Francine
Story 50: Amber

Praising, presented as fact

You may be surprised that in some instances, listening and responding by praising can be a disconnector. Praising is usually considered to be fundamentally positive – which it does appear to be, at first glance. In looking more deeply at what happens for the person receiving the praise, it becomes apparent how it sometimes creates disconnection.

Praise is often articulated as something objective and factual, as in "You look great today!" or "You're such a kind and generous person." Comments such as those can function well as connectors if the recipient of the praise happens to believe that the praise is warranted. Often, though, that isn't the case. Then the praise is a disconnector.

When we listen and respond with praise for someone's achievement with statements about an absolute value, such as "Yours is the best interpretation of that song on the market" or "Of course you got an A+, you're the smartest one in the class," we're implying that we are in an all-knowing position to judge the situation and the value of the achievement. The recipient knows that the presumed all-knowing position isn't true, and therefore also knows that the praise is an empty and false gesture, which is why such praise degrades rather than enhances the interpersonal connection. In addition, such all-knowing praise puts the praise-giver above the receiver in knowledge and wisdom, and the condescension felt in such praise is itself a disconnector.

There's also a danger, especially with children, that praise will be experienced as a reward. Children may then choose behaviors based on the likelihood of getting that reward rather than what feels intrinsically natural and right to them. This can contribute to the child developing an inauthentic personality designed for attracting external rewards.

We can follow our generous impulse to respond with praise without any of those pitfalls by using I-messages: "I really admire how you're handling such a demanding situation" or "I just want to acknowledge the great kindness I sense in what you've done for those people." Then we're expressing only our own subjective experience of the other person's qualities, rather than stating a seemingly objective evaluation of those qualities. It's that deeply personal note that makes responding with this form of praise such a meaningful and effective connector.

The disconnector **praising, presented as fact** is illustrated in the following story:

Story 21: Bethany

Reassuring inappropriately

In response to listening to someone about a troubling or anxiety-producing situation that the person is facing, expressing reassurance may seem to be an entirely positive and kind thing to do, and there certainly are situations in which reassurance is what a person really needs, yet it can be a disconnector in many instances.

Reassuring is most reliably useful when a listener responds with factual information that the speaker doesn't have and that could alleviate concern to some degree – for example, "That official process typically takes about a month, so it's not surprising you haven't received notification yet" or "There's poor mobile phone reception in that area, and that may be why your mom isn't reachable right now" or "That's a common side effect of the medication, but it's not generally considered dangerous."

On the other hand, when reassurance merely encourages positive thinking or optimism without also providing a sound, believable, factual basis for expecting things to go well, little or no actual reassurance or reduction of worry results. An example is a pregnant woman who just learned that she was exposed to an infectious disease and is worried about its possible influence on the fetus. She tells a friend how worried she is about that, and the friend tries to reassure her by saying, "Now, don't you worry. Nature has a way of doing the right thing." The pregnant woman does not feel taken seriously regarding her worries, and may even feel more chillingly alone with those worries than before the conversation. The attempted reassurance has landed as a disconnector, and to some degree that friendship might even be lastingly diminished by the friend's disappointing and somewhat alienating lack of empathy.

In addition, the friend's blindly optimistic reassurance contains an implication that the pregnant woman's feelings of vulnerability and worry are foolish and immature, in contrast with the friend's greater wisdom. Both that demeaning implication and the condescension inherent in such reassurances are other toxic ingredients of this disconnector.

Blindly optimistic reassuring is an attempt to fix (get rid of) the other's distress by inducing positive thinking. It can be useful to ask oneself, "What is *my* need for doing that?" Is it because I expect to be regarded as worthless if I'm helpless to make it better? Is it because I expect emotional collapse or chaos to develop if distress isn't quelled quickly? Finding the underlying driver might have liberating effects.

The disconnector **reassuring inappropriately** is illustrated in the following stories:

Story 40: Jamal
Story 47: Nicola

Asking leading questions

Much has been written about the virtues of asking questions as part of being a good listener. Questions can function as connectors when they foster others' greater clarity about their needs, purposes, difficulties, and methods of pursuing those. We greatly enjoy how the writer James Thurber put it: "All people should try to learn, before they die, what they are running from, and to, and why." Questions that elicit greater clarity of that kind are deeply helpful.

On the other hand, questions can be disconnectors if they are manipulative – that is, designed to influence the other person to fulfill the agenda of the person asking the question. Examples of such *leading questions* are: "Don't you think your unwillingness for us to buy a bigger house is something you should bring up in your next therapy session?" or "Why aren't you looking at the situation from a patriotic viewpoint?" These types of questions indicate that we're not actually listening entirely with helpful intent, but rather that we have our own agenda and are trying to steer the person in a particular direction. We're trying to convince the person of something and have packaged our own agenda as a question.

In short, leading questions are self-serving, in contrast to questions intended to help others find their own true path and go wherever their unique process leads. Instead of leading questions, we can ask, "What do you wish you were really free to do about this?" or "What's really at stake in this for you?" or simply muse out loud, saying something like "Hmm … I wonder what options there might be that you haven't considered yet …."

The disconnector **asking leading questions** is illustrated in the following stories:

Story 26: Destiny
Story 29: Nancy

Undermining the other person's autonomy or agency

Within a personal relationship, true listening is inseparable from respecting the other person's agency. Having agency in life can be described as having control and choice over one's own decisions, life path, solutions, body, thoughts, activities, and behavior.

Whenever someone imposes external limitations or constraints on another person, that person's agency is being restricted. A common example is expecting one's couple partner to share all of one's own beliefs and opinions and not differ with any of them, or else pressuring the partner into agreeing by jabs of criticism, stings of ridicule, or moody disapproval. Someone who needs to impose such restrictions is not interested in, and not even trying for, true listening, which would be fully respectful of the other's agency and supportive of that person's individuality. This wall of non-listening is a potent disconnector.

We live in a society and a country with laws, and it's normal to accept such restrictions in some areas of our lives. We accept that we're not allowed to create extreme noise at times when most others are sleeping, and we're not allowed to use physical violence against others simply because we find them annoying or offensive.

In interpersonal relationships, however, putting restrictions on each other rules out listening to each other. Saying or implying "I know better than you what you should do" restricts the other's autonomy over his or her own solutions and also implicitly means "so I'm not interested in listening to you about what you want or need to do." For example, saying or implying "Don't push me away when I try to touch you" is an attempt to deprive the other of agency over his or her body. Saying or implying "I'll give you the money, but only if you use it for paying tuition in law school" is an attempt to deprive the other of agency over his or her life path decisions.

Even children, who of course need guidance and limit-setting, also need the listening that communicates respect for their personhood and agency, giving them as much room as possible to find their own solutions, have control over their own bodies, think freely their own thoughts, and try out many behaviors.

The disconnector **undermining the other person's autonomy or agency** is illustrated in the following stories:

Story 19: Courtney (part 1)
Story 33: Magda
Story 38: Henry
Story 42: Grace

Disconnection due to making the other person's problem be about oneself

Making assumptions that disconnect

We describe certain assumptions as disconnectors between people because they tend to have negative effects that make the involved individuals feel less close psychologically and emotionally. Such assumptions include presuming to know what others are experiencing, thinking, feeling, or needing, as in "You shouldn't waste your time reading novels when there are books full of information about the real world" or "Not accepting a promotion to a management position is always a big mistake." These types of assumptions act as filters through which we perceive other people, limiting our ability to observe clearly and take in what people are really telling and showing us about themselves.

There are common, unquestioned, unrecognized assumptions that function as *disconnectors* because they lead us to respond in ways that push others away and leave them feeling not understood. For example:

- People who disagree with my views and feelings about a particular topic are wrong, and I'm justified in telling them so.
- I'm better able to know how you should solve your problem than you are.
- My needs in a given situation are intrinsically more important than your needs.
- You should be able to read my mind and know what I think and feel. I shouldn't have to tell you in words.

As a rule, disconnecting assumptions operate from outside of our awareness, so we also remain unaware of how limiting and disconnecting they can be. Our unquestioned assumptions – often learned early in life – seem to us to be the obvious truth of *how people are* or *how this world is* or *how I need to be*. Skillful listening can reveal our own implicit assumptions, making them explicit and available for revision, fostering connection instead of disconnection. We examine this area in more detail in Part 3.

The disconnector **making assumptions that disconnect** is illustrated in the following stories:

Story 13: Jonathan
Story 28: Ina
Story 40: Jamal
Story 44: Clint
Story 45: Suyin
Story 50: Amber

Telling rather than asking

The comments here extend and complement those given earlier in Part 2 about the connector "asking rather than telling" on page 161. *Telling* another person about him- or herself, rather than *asking* interestedly, sends the message, "Showing you that I *already know* all about you is my agenda, not listening to you and learning about you from you."

Examples of telling rather than asking are "You must be nervous about your upcoming interview" and "Haven't seen you in a while – but of course you've been living the good life, as always. Isn't it sad about Darlene's illness?" The recipient of these rigid caricatures feels an immediate rupture of connection, keenly feels the absence of receptive listening, and faces the uncomfortable choice of whether or not to correct the other's assumptions, which likely would be a somewhat strained interaction. A more inviting and open approach in these two conversations, free from assumptions about the other person, would be "How are you feeling about your upcoming interview?" and "Haven't seen you in a while. How has life been treating you?" Those overtures communicate an openness to actual listening.

Asking other people about themselves and their inner lives functions as a connector because it sends the message, "I'm interested to know more about you and I'm ready to listen," while also respectfully acknowledging, "You know best what's true for you."

Interaction patterns among family members in childhood are almost always the original cause of people having, as adults, the unquestioned assumption that they can (and should) know what others are feeling, thinking, and experiencing without asking them. That may seem an odd delusion to people who weren't inducted into that assumption in childhood, and who plainly see the impossibility of such mind-reading, but it is a fairly common piece of emotional learning. It can be unlearned, but unlearning it entails tolerating not-knowing regarding what's going on inside others. This initially may feel disorienting and induce a sense of vulnerability. It may take some time, practice, help, and introspection to arrive at feeling comfortable with asking about and listening to, rather than already knowing, the experience of others.

The disconnector **telling rather than asking** is illustrated in the following stories:

Story 13: Jonathan
Story 22: Sem

Interrupting

Interrupting – in addition to being considered by most people to be rude – sends certain negative messages to the person being interrupted, including "What I have to say is more important than what you have to say," "I'm not interested enough in what you're saying to keep listening until you finish talking," and "I won't be responding to what you're saying, because I've already decided what I want to say next."

There are many reasons people in the listening role may feel the impulse or the emotional or practical need to interrupt the person speaking, including: a positive, connection-seeking reason; a desire to get one's own message communicated; a desire to show off knowledge; discomfort with being in a less central and less influential role; discomfort or other strong emotions about the speaker's topic or views; impatience or time pressure; a well-meant belief in being able to offer a quick solution or correct some inaccuracy; and more.

Many people are so accustomed to interrupting, and perhaps grew up in a family or a culture where interrupting was the norm, that they actually don't notice that they are doing it. Interrupting, though, precludes listening – which makes it an interpersonal disconnector.

Avoiding interrupting can require a conscious decision to practice waiting until there's a natural pause in the flow of conversation before responding. If this proves to be difficult, either in general or in specific relationships, then it's beneficial to find and address the internal driver(s) of this particular behavior, such as the ones listed above.

Of course, we all know people who keep talking literally without end, creating a valid need to interrupt if being a completely passive, captive audience is not acceptable. In such cases, transparency is useful for maintaining a respectful exchange: "I know I'm interrupting, because I'd really like to say something in reply. Can you pause and listen for a minute?"

The disconnector **interrupting** is illustrated in the following stories:

Story 2: Manuela
Story 3: Glenn
Story 37: Jennifer

Saying "yes, but"

The phrase "yes, but" is very interesting to consider, because it's a standard part of the way many people communicate. This particular phrase runs the gamut from being a major disconnector – more often than is generally recognized – to being harmless or even, occasionally, useful.

Good listening necessitates the "yes" part. This is particularly true if the topic at hand is a serious or problematic one. When a person is sharing something important with us, and we respond with "yes," we are offering an important connector: "Yes, I hear you and want to understand you and what you're experiencing. You matter to me."

However, the "but" portion can instantly negate the "yes" portion, so that any positive messages of listening and understanding are effectively undone by that single syllable. The word "but" in this context generally has the effect of invalidating and dismissing what the other person has just tried to communicate. It implicitly conveys the potent message: "My understanding of this is truer and more complete than yours, so I'm not sympathetic to the mistaken way that you're experiencing this matter." The "but" part typically involves some sort of arguing, contradicting, or convincing, which are all disconnectors because they are adversarial and competitive, and they abruptly yank the focus of the conversation away from what the other person was trying to communicate and onto one's own superior views – quite the opposite of giving the gift of respectfully understanding the other's experience of the matters under consideration.

When people have a comfortable relationship with one another and are in an emotionally resilient state, and when the subject matter being discussed is factual or relatively lightweight, then it can be perfectly alright to disagree by using the phrase "yes, but." A conscious awareness of the potentially negative effects of this phrase is helpful in deciding whether it's appropriate to the situation.

Imagine you're late for an important appointment and desperately searching for a parking place in a crowded public garage. You spot someone walking purposefully, keys in hand, and ask him hopefully if he's about to drive out. He says, "Yes, but there are lots of empty spaces two levels up." That's an example of "yes, but" being helpful and not at all objectionable. You feel a momentary warmth of connection with this stranger who has gladly helped you in a moment of need. Now let's imagine that you've just been stood up by a fellow you're really interested in getting to know better. You call your best friend for some commiseration about how hurt, disrespected, and lonely you're feeling, and she says, "Yes, but if he does something like that he's not the kind of guy you should be going after." Rather than tuning in to you emotionally, she has too quickly responded according to her own feelings and her own view of the situation. Her intention to dispel your distress is entirely positive, of course, but her "yes, but" response is a disconnector that gives no comfort, and is a sizable disappointment over the missing empathy.

You may ask, "What if I disagree with what the other person is saying?" You're certainly entitled to disagree with other people's views and to convey yours. Choosing *when* and *how* to convey them is what determines the resulting effects. Communication that enhances connection is often a matter of timing. Have you listened and offered the "yes, I understand" message long enough, specifically enough, and sincerely enough for the other person to feel heard and understood? If so, then that person may now be receptive to your "but I have a different view to offer" message.

In that way, with patience it *is* possible to express disagreement without negating the other person's views and experience. In effect, you're turning the "yes, but" phrase into a "yes, *and*" phrase. You're respectfully taking *both* of you into consideration.

Are you able to stay with "yes," postponing the "but" until the speaker feels heard and understood? If you find that the patience and generosity needed for that elude you – whether with one particular person or more broadly in your interactions – it might prove quite valuable to begin examining the issue(s) driving that impatience and urgency.

Another reason people sometimes feel inclined to say "yes, but" is in order to object to a listener who has responded with a disconnector. Let's imagine you've just told a friend that you're concerned about the sleep problems you've been having lately, and she immediately starts talking about how she solved *her own* sleep problems instead of staying with your experience and your concern. If there was more you needed to say about the particulars of your problem and you fully expected to receive the time and space needed for that, but were cut off by the other person's self-involved response, you may well want to say, "Yes, but it's different for me." That way of objecting is appropriate, though a more ideal way of stating that might be a "yes, *and*" statement: "Yes, I understand how it went for you, *and* the trouble I'm having is quite different in some ways. Specifically ...."

The disconnector **saying "yes, but"** is illustrated in the following story:

Story 7: Paul

Interpreting

Interpreting the meaning or the cause of someone's actions, attitudes, or emotional responses is a normal, understandable response when we're trying to understand that person. We all have the basic need to make sense out of our world and the people who inhabit it. And when the needed explanations aren't forthcoming, we do the best with what we have by making sense of other people with our own interpretations. That is, we tend to apply whatever explanatory notions that we can conjure.

These responses become potent disconnectors, though, when we assert them to another person to explain his or her behavior. Doing that presupposes that we know more about that person from the outside than he or she does from the inside, and it forfeits the opportunity to connect more deeply by inquiring – rather than interpreting – and learning something about that person's world of meaning.

If a person says, "Gee, I'm feeling anxious today and I'm not sure why …," and the other responds, "That's because you're insecure about what your colleague said" or "You must be worrying about your upcoming trip," those responses create disconnection if they aren't accurate – and they probably aren't. Instead of showing interest and support, the listener is further complicating and straining the situation by saying, in essence, "You don't know why you're feeling anxious, but I do!"

As with other disconnectors, the first step toward decommissioning this one is to notice when we're on the verge of using it. That allows us to recognize and accept that the other person's behavior or experience feels like something of a mystery, bringing some uncertainty and a natural need for more understanding. And then we can notice whether that mystery feels workable and tolerable. Perhaps it induces an uncomfortable feeling of frustration, anxiety, or loss of control, which we've previously avoided by quickly locking onto some simplistic interpretation.

But now, instead of interpreting, there is the option to utilize the many ways described in this book to express curiosity, caring interest, and support, such as the examples listed here:

- "I see, you're not sure where that feeling is coming from …"
- "I'd love to hear more about that if you'd like to tell me …"
- "I wonder if this anxiety feels connected in some way to either your upcoming trip or what your colleague said the other day."

The disconnector **interpreting** is illustrated in the following story:

Story 37: Jennifer

Interrogating

As a form of interpersonal communication, interrogation means questioning in a somewhat heavy-handed, demanding, and invasive manner, similar to the way a police officer might interrogate a suspect. A person being questioned in this manner usually feels backed up against a wall, because the interrogator is demanding that questions be answered. Under that kind of pressure, people don't tend to remain emotionally open and communicative. Being subjected to interrogation is a significant disconnector because one's right to decide for oneself what information to share isn't being respected. The presumption of the interrogator to force the revealing of information is not only intrusive but also deeply offensive.

For example, a person opens up and shares the thought, "I should have told my brother how I felt. I actually wanted to, but somehow I didn't manage to open my mouth." If the listener responds in an even slightly demanding tone with, "So if that's what you wanted to do, why didn't you tell him?" that's interrogating and will feel unwelcome and jarring.

Instead, a non-interrogating response would be, for instance, "Hmm ... interesting ... I wonder what's behind that. If you want to tell me more, I'd love to understand what's going on for you." That way, the person has the choice about telling more – or not – without further information being demanded. There's no pressure. People don't usually have readily available answers to such "why" questions, and that difficulty alone creates additional strain and pressure when a response is demanded.

In general, avoiding "why" and "how come" questions about other people's actions or reactions goes a long way toward avoiding interrogating others and, instead, respectfully giving them the space to make their own choices about what to share.

The disconnector **interrogating** is illustrated in the following story:

Story 33: Magda

Diagnosing or labeling

As a response to someone describing emotional or behavioral difficulties, the use of terms designating a psychological disorder has many potential pitfalls and tends to be a strong disconnector. Examples are "That's obsessive-compulsive," "You're being paranoid," and "You're a workaholic."

Diagnosing sends a message of defectiveness that can evoke both anxiety and shame. Being the recipient of a diagnosis or label can lead to a person feeling narrowly and negatively categorized, and can diminish the individual's self-concept and life choices. For example, if you grew up believing that your thinking is fundamentally flawed and illogical because you were told that regularly, you may habitually avoid situations and opportunities that involve making your thinking known to others. Even a seemingly positive label can limit a person's view of him- or herself. A child who hears almost daily that she is the most careful one of all the children in the family has learned that her worth depends on maintaining that superior behavior, and she may avoid activities or situations in which she might be unable to do so.

Possibly the most effective way to rid oneself of any diagnosing or labeling tendency is by imagining how diminishing and undermining it feels to be the recipient of such a message. Even if the intention is to be helpful, imparting such messages is harmful to the person and to the relationship.

Rather than looking for a label that proves there is something significantly wrong with the person, our helpful intention as a listener is far more likely to be effective through expressing a combination of empathy and curiosity about the coherent emotional sense of whatever disturbance the person is experiencing. That type of support helps others move into a better position for making the kinds of shifts they need.

The disconnector **diagnosing or labeling** is illustrated in the following story:

Story 12: Veronica

Shifting the focus onto oneself

A listener might prematurely take away the focus of attention from the speaker and put it on him- or herself due to a number of different types of reaction. That can happen, for instance, when the listener has a strong personal reaction, whether positive or negative, to what the speaker is experiencing or relating. It's natural at that moment for the listener's attention to become focused internally on that strong response. At that point, though, the speaker is likely to feel the loss of real listening.

In another type of attention-shifting reaction, the listener may resonate strongly with aspects of the speaker's experience that feel very similar to his or her own experiences. Then it can be tempting to steer the conversation away from the speaker's experience and onto one's own, perhaps with the helpful intention of supportively showing how well the listener can understand the speaker's experience. That can work well if the listener is mindful enough to be quite brief and to clearly invite the speaker to resume. Then that brief sharing functions well as a connector, but it can turn into a disconnector if the listener becomes absorbed in a prolonged sharing and never passes the microphone back to the speaker.

Let's consider a woman whose business hasn't been prospering recently, and she's telling her friend about her large business expenses and small income. She's weighing her options and comparing what the consequences might be if she keeps the business running versus closing it down. The friend, who has himself had some desperate struggles with finances throughout his adult life, becomes visibly agitated hearing about this set of challenges and tells her, "What you're dealing with really touches a nerve for me, and my anxiety is ramping up as I think about what you *could* be doing with all that rent money and the other expenses you're paying for!" His emotional reaction has abruptly redirected the focus of the conversation to himself and how her problem is problematic for *him*. She immediately sees that no more discussion of her problem is possible, and even if she feels sympathetic toward his distress, she may now feel disconnected from her friend, as well as disappointed and frustrated by his sudden lack of capacity to provide the helpful listening that she needs.

He could have largely avoided those negative effects and maintain connection with her if, with transparency, he had said, "I wish I could help you with your problem, but I'm getting really agitated just listening, because I have so many money problems of my own! I'm really sorry to cut you off from telling me more about it. I hope we can resume some other time soon." His honest explanation and his apology are effective connectors that preserve their rapport even if she is disappointed.

The disconnector **shifting the focus onto oneself** is illustrated in the following stories:

Story 1: Olivia
Story 33: Magda

Talking instead of ever listening

"Talking instead of ever listening" describes a behavior in which one person makes him- or herself so uninterruptible that others feel bored, put upon, impatient, or annoyed much of the time when together. That kind of non-stop, output-only talking is a big disconnector!

Here's an example of how someone talks without ever listening: "Yeah … so what happened was really upsetting … um … in just a minute I want to ask how you are … mm … let me just tell you how it was … um … and it reminded me so much of when I had a similar experience with that other person, remember? … Hmm … yeah, really similar …." And 20 minutes later, there still has been no break in the monologue. Then it gets wrapped up with something like "I guess I'll let you go now …" or even "You probably need to get back to what you were doing …."

Of course, there are times in most relationships when one person or the other needs to be in "output-only" mode, for example when he or she has an urgent, intensely preoccupying problem. In that case there's usually an agreement (whether tacit or actually spoken) that *that* person legitimately needs the full conversational attention. That's a non-issue if, across time, there's been a fair balance in that regard, so that both people's need to talk and be heard and understood is usually satisfied – assuming it's a relationship, for example a friendship, in which such a balance is inherently assumed and expected.

Extreme, habitual non-stop talking can have many causes or coherent reasons, including staving off anxiety, compensating for inner insecurities, and trying to make up for an extreme lack of attention in the past or present (or both). When we, in turn, as *listeners* to that person, can empathize with the emotional coherence of such behavior (even without knowing which version of coherence is involved), then we might gently and transparently call attention to the conversational imbalance by saying, for example, "Today I've learned a lot about what's going on with you. I can catch you up on my life the next time we talk."

A further possibility is to address transparently the meta-level of the communication by commenting, for instance, "I notice that I'm having difficulty finding a chance to jump in and share my own thoughts with you."

The disconnector **talking instead of ever listening** is illustrated in the following story:

Story 5: Emily

Disconnection due to making the other person wrong

Moralizing

Moralizing refers to value judgments that are expressed with an air of self-righteousness or superiority, typically for the purpose of criticizing some person or category of persons. Examples of moralizing are "That was a selfish thing to do; you should be more generous to others" or "Just exercise some self-discipline. It can't be that hard!"

Such messages are strong disconnectors that induce an array of reactions in the recipient – ranging from annoyance to shame to self-doubt to guilt to estrangement and more. The person on the receiving end of moralizing is likely to feel defensive and become even more committed to his or her original reactions and behaviors.

Most of us have thoughts from time to time that another person "should" or "shouldn't" do or view things a certain way because we consider that the right or wrong way to act or to be. For one's own growth of self-honesty and self-awareness, it's beneficial to bring these thoughts into awareness and use them as a signal to examine what's motivating them (perhaps some unresolved personal issues) and choose a response that would not be a disconnector. Recognizing that moralizing is entirely self-serving, at the other person's and the relationship's expense, helps with keeping one's judgmental views and feelings to oneself and finding at least a neutral response that expresses listening, such as, "I can see that for you it felt okay to give him the help he was asking you for. I think I probably would have responded differently."

It helps also to remember the general principle of inner coherence: There *must be* something in that person's unique world of meaning and unique emotional memory that is generating what we're viewing from outside as a moral lapse or inadequacy. One of our favorite versions of this deep principle is from poet Henry Wadsworth Longfellow, who wrote, "If we could read the secret history of our enemies, we should find in each man's life sorrow and suffering enough to disarm all hostility."

The disconnector **moralizing** is illustrated in the following stories:

Story 30: Freddy
Story 42: Grace

Counteracting others' feelings, views, or actions

Counteracting is such a natural tactic when faced with difficulties or suffering of any type that it seems to be almost a reflex that everyone has. When someone we care about is struggling with a problem, or we ourselves are struggling, of course we want to put an end to that difficulty and distress. Counteracting consists of trying to instill in that person a behavior or state of mind that would occur in place of the problematic one. As a rule, that tactic is usually soon ineffective because it doesn't address – and therefore doesn't reliably prevail over – the real source and substance of the problem. But most people believe counteracting should work, so the return of the problem then appears to be a personal failing of the person trying to apply the counteractive tactic effectively, when the true reason is that *counteracting doesn't usually work*. In that way, counteracting can inadvertently make a struggling person feel even worse.

Counteracting takes many different forms, and includes any attempts to disregard, negate, or override a person's distressed feelings or thoughts, including the use of logic in an attempt to quell someone's distressed emotional state. Some common counteractive responses are:

- Try to calm down.
- It's not as bad as you think.
- Don't worry about it. Everything will be okay.
- You're too sensitive.
- The evidence doesn't support what you're feeling.
- Your reaction is not normal.
- You shouldn't see it so negatively.
- You're looking at it the wrong way.

With an understanding of emotional coherence, it becomes clear that counteracting cannot work to help a person become free of what's *really* going on inside and causing distress. (As we've mentioned before, there are urgent situations for which immediate counteracting in some form is necessary and right for relief or safety, but overall they are few and far between.)

With time and practice it will begin to feel more natural to simply *be with* what's happening for a distressed person and give understanding and accompaniment, rather than fighting *against* feelings, thoughts, or behaviors.

Ironically, it may be helpful initially to counteract one's *own* urge to counteract until gaining enough experience of how effective it can be to refrain from counteracting.

The disconnector **counteracting others' feelings, views, or actions** is illustrated in the following stories:

Story 7: Paul
Story 18: Manny

Implying "you shouldn't feel how you feel"

Feelings aren't right or wrong. Feelings *exist*, and there are always coherent reasons that particular feelings have arisen – whether or not those reasons are apparent.

Pathologizing or squelching feelings tends to make any related problems feel even worse – and doesn't get rid of the feelings, so they may as well be recognized and acknowledged. Telling people they shouldn't feel a certain way not only communicates a negative judgment about those feelings, but also tells them that their mind is defective. That message is both harmful and incorrect, and it only adds to the person's distress, as well as being a disconnector in the relationship.

When we witness another person in emotional pain or feeling angry, for example, it might seem as though it's our responsibility to try to assuage those feelings and calm the person down, so we try to talk the person out of feeling so upset. But actually, that isn't our responsibility as a caring friend or relative or colleague – and besides, it usually doesn't work. It is each person's own responsibility to find how to manage his or her emotional life. We certainly can be caringly helpful to others for that, and this book is largely about doing exactly that, but such helpfulness is distinct from *feeling responsible* for dispelling the other's distress. The more we try to shift people out of their difficult feelings, the more difficult we make their job of better understanding themselves and their feelings as well as better meeting and navigating life's challenges.

For a caring, empathetic listener it can be distressing to witness someone having strongly uncomfortable emotions. Some listeners can absorb and feel the other person's feelings almost as strongly as if they were their own, or feel anxious or tense over the vulnerability and uncertainty in the other's situation, or feel accused of something that led to the other person's feelings, or are too vividly reminded of previously feeling similar strong emotions or a similar dilemma that didn't go well, or have some other distressing response. In such moments, the urge may be strong to respond in some way that sends the message, "you shouldn't feel how you feel" in an attempt to put out the fire that's feeling too hot to be so near. It may be difficult to allow other people their feelings and to take responsibility for our own, even if only by reflecting on our own reactions later, when our conversation partner no longer needs us to be in listening mode.

Our job as a caring human being, should we choose to accept it, is to listen well and reflect back what we believe we've heard, so that the person feels seen, heard and understood. To give such a response of understanding doesn't necessarily mean that we *agree* with or share the other's views and feelings, but rather that we deeply respect and honor the sovereignty of that individual's personhood and unique experience of life. In that way we can give others a little bit of the fundamental experience that everyone hungers for, the experience of being met right where we are, with no agenda to impose change.

The disconnector **implying "you shouldn't feel how you feel"** is illustrated in the following stories:

Story 21: Bethany
Story 23: Carl
Story 27: Matt
Story 29: Nancy
Story 30: Freddy
Story 31: Linda
Story 33: Magda
Story 39: Jeffrey
Story 40: Jamal
Story 44: Clint
Story 47: Nicola

Implying "you shouldn't need what you need"

There are times when an individual's needs may strike us as extreme, rigid, or unreasonable – such as a person needing certain things to be done precisely according to his or her own wishes without consideration of the impact on others, or a family member feeling the need to be completely exempted from helping in the household. Even when such needs seem unacceptable to us, the quality of our listening and responding will determine whether the ensuing process is largely harmonious or largely adversarial and tumultuous.

To preserve harmony, the listener needs to hold on to the assumption of emotional coherence – in other words, to assume that the other's needs are emotionally necessary to have and are "right" for that person, however objectionable they may be to others. Then it's appropriate to say, for example, "I understand that's how you need things to be, and that that's important to you. We're different people, however, and for me that doesn't work, so we need to find a way to work things out."

In that way, one can listen and respond self-assertively but without pathologizing or criticizing the other's needs, which would be likely to create a sense of defectiveness, defensiveness, and distress for that person.

The disconnector **implying "you shouldn't need what you need"** is illustrated in the following stories:

Story 4: Annie
Story 23: Carl
Story 27: Matt
Story 43: Francine
Story 49: Judith

Using logic to dispel feelings

Using intellectual logic or rational argumentation to help someone work through a problem may seem perfectly sensible and universally appropriate, but doing so becomes a disconnector when the problem is largely emotional in nature. *Emotional* logic is a different matter entirely, so trying to fix an emotional problem with intellectual logic almost never works. In fact, that approach usually creates additional problems, because the owner of the problem either feels not seen or heard or understood in his or her emotional experience, or believes that logic *should* prevail, and therefore feels shame in failing at that.

Examples of pitting intellectual logic against the emotional nature of someone's dilemma are "Does it make any sense to miss him, when he was mean to you so much of the time?" or "Just figure out what steps you need to take next instead of letting your emotions get in the way" or "Yes, but it happened so many years ago, just let go of it."

Embracing the assumption of emotional coherence – whether we are privy to the specifics of a given problem situation or not – includes an understanding of the uselessness (and possible damage) of using logical arguments in an attempt to make an emotional problem stop being a problem.

Whenever we begin thinking that a person's actions or reactions don't make sense, that very thought can serve as a signal to remember, with humility, that there *is* a hidden sense – a coherent logic – we don't yet know. That's a very safe assumption, and it applies even when the person is oneself. Each person's life experiences have formed many coherent emotional learnings that are outside of awareness, so the behaviors and states of mind they generate are mystifying to our conscious awareness. We may be unaware of the hidden sense in our own and others' emotional learnings, but we can trust that it's there to be found and is findable – if the individual seeks honest self-awareness.

The disconnector **using logic to dispel feelings** is illustrated in the following story:

Story 40: Jamal

Lecturing or admonishing

A listener who responds with lecturing or admonishing is expressing an attitude of disapproval of the speaker's actions, feelings, or thoughts. The message sent is that the speaker is wrong or bad, and the individual doing the lecturing or admonishing knows better about what is right and good.

Contemplating the synonyms of these two terms – such as reprimand, rebuke, scold, chastise, berate, and criticize – can give us a good sense of how they might feel to the recipient. Examples are questions and comments such as, "Why didn't you …?", "How could you have …?", "That was wrong of you; you should have …," "Any normal person would have …," or "Why on earth would you …?" Compare those to the responses from a listener who says, "It's troubling to me that you did that, so I really need to understand your thoughts and feelings behind that choice." That communicates the respectful assumption of emotional coherence and therefore functions as a connector, and is free of the denigrating and shaming that lecturing and admonishing tend to deliver, making them function as disconnectors with harmful effects.

For a listener, there's a crucial distinction to make between how one's personal values are inwardly rating the speaker and what one outwardly communicates in response. Even if what the speaker has expressed is definitely very bad or very wrong according to one's own values, one still has a choice about what to say, and ideally it will be free of toxic disconnectors and, as in the example in the previous paragraph, will be useful in inviting honest self-examination on the part of the speaker.

If we're in the role of teacher, parent, or boss, and we feel in a given circumstance that it's our job to guide a subordinate person to become aware of and change some problematic pattern, both we and the other person will benefit from first taking the time to listen to and understand each other regarding the problem pattern. That way we'll find empathy and gather useful understanding for successfully designing the needed change.

The disconnector **lecturing or admonishing** is illustrated in the following stories:

Story 12: Veronica
Story 16: Jim
Story 51: Liam

Demanding or ordering

Ordering someone to do something and demanding certain behaviors are forceful disconnectors because they imply a hierarchical power structure. The person who makes the demand is exercising power over the other and presuming to control or manipulate the other. Giving orders implies having the right to deny that person the freedom to make his or her own choices. The recipient of an order or a demand may feel uncomfortable about this but find it difficult to push back or assert clear boundaries due to the nature and history of the relationship. This is a painful, diminishing, and potentially damaging situation to be in. (In contrast, see the connector "supporting others' agency and autonomy in their lives" on page 166).

Consider the difference between the respectful request "I'd really appreciate your using a chopping board when you're cutting vegetables, so the counter doesn't get scratched up. Agreed?" and the order "Use a chopping board when you're doing that!" Making respectful requests using I-messages to communicate our needs is itself a connector, even if further negotiating or problem-solving proves necessary.

In inherently hierarchical relationships, such as parent–child or teacher–student relationships, it can be tempting to use a demanding and ordering approach, and it may even seem appropriate to do so, yet even there the quality of the relationship is optimized by simply beginning the order with "please," as in "Please take out the trash in the next five minutes so that there will be enough room in the bin as I prepare our dinner." That simple technique packages the order to sound and feel like a respectful request, sparing the other person the offensiveness and humiliation of being ordered around and preserving harmonious connection as much as possible.

The disconnector **demanding or ordering** is illustrated in the following stories:

Story 6: Emma
Story 33: Magda
Story 39: Jeffrey
Story 43: Francine

Criticizing, judging, shaming, or blaming

This category overlaps with others already considered. It refers to comments that people make, usually unthinkingly – instead of offering genuine, caring listening – such as these: "You're too sensitive. Stop overreacting." "That was a dumb thing to do." "Hey, chubby – stop eating so much!" "That wasn't a good decision." "What's wrong with you? Why would you do such a thing?" "Aren't you embarrassed about that?"

Especially when a person approaches another by sharing something personal or emotionally sensitive and hoping to be heard and understood, such comments are strong disconnectors. They're frequently made offhand and without awareness that – in addition to disconnecting – they can stay with a person strongly enough to influence that person's fundamental view of him- or herself. The result can be an enduring sense of not being good enough in general or being defective in some specific way, lasting long after the initial spasm of hurt and shame in hearing the words.

If criticizing, judging negatively, shaming, or blaming is a habit, shedding it might require looking into what lies beneath it. Perhaps it's a way of interacting learned in one's family of origin and never questioned, making its toxicity invisible. Perhaps putting someone else down is needed as a way of pumping oneself up. There are many possible forms of the underlying coherence of this behavior.

The disconnector **criticizing, judging, shaming, or blaming** is illustrated in the following stories:

Story 6: Emma
Story 12: Veronica
Story 15: George
Story 37: Jennifer
Story 38: Henry
Story 49: Judith
Story 51: Liam

Believing and asserting stereotypes

Judging the value of a person or a person's behavior or expecting a person to act a certain way based on a single characteristic (gender, age, ethnicity, religion, size, sexual orientation, level of education, etc.) is believing and asserting a stereotype: A single identifying feature defines a class of people who are all characterized in the same way.

This mindset rules out the true listening that seeks to discover who the individual uniquely is. Stereotypes are powerful disconnectors.

Stereotypes can have seemingly positive content, as in "Older people are simply wiser." And yet any such overgeneralized characterization cannot possibly be true of all individuals in that group, though it may be true of some individual members. Another common example of a well-meant but discriminating gesture is that of a customer in a restaurant complimenting the waiter on his excellent language skills because the waiter looks ethnically different from the majority of residents in that area. It then emerges that the waiter was born and raised in that area and speaks the language natively. Here the customer is making an erroneous assumption based entirely on external physical characteristics of the waiter.

Negative stereotypes come out into expression more strongly at times of stress, when the ability to regard others respectfully as individuals may be diminished. For instance, a car driver on the highway has just been dangerously cut off by another driver and peers into the other car, sees someone with certain physical characteristics, and complains "Of course it's a(n) ____!" (substitute "woman," "foreigner," "old geezer," or any other group), as if it's clear that a person belonging to that demographic group inherently behaves badly in that way.

In a relationship, any negative regard based on stereotyped assumptions creates disconnection, as well as potentially having damaging effects on the recipient. Skilled, empathic listening to a friend, partner, colleague, coworker, or employee is thoroughly precluded by assumptions about the other person's assumed limitations due to belonging to a stereotyped group. For example, a pregnant woman sits down with her boss to plan out the next few months in the team, given her upcoming 12-week maternity absence, and says, "Of course the time I'll have with the new baby is very important to me, but I'm still really looking forward to getting back and then moving into that next level of leadership we've been talking about." The boss replies, "You realize, of course, that I won't be able to promote you to team leader as we had discussed. A mother with small children is never going to manage that kind of responsibility." His stereotype has completely foreclosed the listening she needed from him regarding her capacity to function fully well in both domains. Even his recognition of the possibility of *asking* her about her capacity as a unique individual was blocked by his belief in the stereotype. Where stereotypes rule, listening is ruled out.

Most of us have been "infected" by stereotypes of one kind or another, often by growing up in a family or cultural milieu that contained them. Usually acquired in that way is racism, one of the more virulent forms of stereotyping. Shedding our own stereotypes begins with recognizing their presence in our beliefs, attitudes, and behaviors. That requires tolerating the discomfort of realizing our own participation in the persecution that stereotypes of any kind inflict. Then it's possible to cultivate the disconfirmation and dissolution of those stereotyping beliefs.

The disconnector **believing and asserting stereotypes** is illustrated in the following stories:

Story 3: Glenn
Story 32: James

Saying "always" or "never"

Imagine a man arriving home from work and telling his wife he's upset because he and his project manager had a hefty difference of opinion and they hadn't yet managed to come to an agreement about how to move ahead with their current project. His wife replies, "You're *always* having problems with her! And you *never* seem to be in a good mood when you come home!" This type of response is a strong disconnector because the person who seeks sympathetic, supportive listening and understanding for the specific, difficult situation he's in is, instead, being blamed and criticized very unsympathetically with a rigid black-and-white characterization that allows no escape.

On a purely pragmatic level, it's a reliable guiding principle that a discussion of difficulties is much more likely to be constructive if the listener's replies focus on the current situation rather than on all the times something similar may have happened in the past. Instead of the always-or-never responses above, one can say, for example, "Mm … your work day ended with that unsolved, stressful problem. I see why that's on your mind and still bothering you. I know she can be very difficult. How do you feel about how you handled your side of it?" That's concrete and situation-specific, as well as respectful of the person's ongoing process of developing interpersonal skill, rather than a commentary on him overall, so it's much more likely to result in constructive, cooperative communication and harmonious connection.

Simply remaining aware of sometimes using the two words "always" and "never" is a good start. Then it's possible to consider filtering them out, depending on the specifics of the situation. If the other person is in a distressing situation, then it will probably be more connecting to avoid using those words. If not, those same words can send a powerful connecting message, as in "You've always done your best to help when I've asked for support" and "Never have you treated me disrespectfully."

The disconnector **saying "always" or "never"** is illustrated in the following story:

Story 23: Carl

Asking closed (yes or no) questions

"Closed" questions are those that force an answer of "yes" or "no" in an evaluative manner, rather than inviting open exploration of the topic being addressed. Examples are: "Are there any grades below an A on your report card?", "Did you stay out past midnight again last night?", "Do you want to get into better shape, or not?", and "Was that even helpful to your coworkers?" Such questions are another type of disconnector that communicates little or no interest in the substance of the other's experience and emotional coherence, whereas the use of open questions invites the other to share such material, creating deeper connection, such as "How do you feel about your grades?" or "Is there much helpfulness between you and your coworkers?"

Closed questions can also be a thinly veiled form of *telling* rather than asking, as in "You'll talk to your teacher about that, won't you?" or "You realize, don't you, that you can stop procrastinating any time you decide to, right?" Such pseudo-questions sound like questions, but are designed to make a point that puts the receiver in the unpleasant position of either agreeing obediently or being seen as bad.

The extent to which a listener asks open questions is based largely on the extent to which he or she is, in fact, respectful of and open to the other person's possible responses. Sometimes it's a stretch to stay open-minded toward another person's inner world. If we catch ourselves having posed a closed question when an open question would have been more appropriate or desirable, all is not lost! It's easy to follow up on the other person's answer by saying, "Interesting; tell me more about that, if you like" or "I see – how did you arrive at that?" There's almost always an opportunity to "open the door" a little wider by expressing some interest and caring.

The disconnector **asking closed (yes or no) questions** is illustrated in the following stories:

Story 12: Veronica
Story 26: Destiny

Disparaging

Questions such as "Don't you know that?" or "You mean you've never …?" convey a judgmental message of surprise that the other person could be so ignorant, inexperienced, limited, or disappointing. Such questions are pseudo-questions. They do not arise from the intention to listen and learn about the other person. Rather, they are disparaging statements disguised as questions, and the receiver feels that disparagement, causing disconnection and a self-protective withdrawal from any further open communication (though that reaction is likely to be well hidden behind an unchanged outer demeanor).

For each of those pseudo-questions, a non-disparaging, interested, genuine question is possible instead, communicating an intention to listen, such as "Are you familiar with …?" or "I wonder if you have ever …?" However, being able to inquire cleanly in those ways may be possible only after becoming aware of and facing the judgmental attitude behind the disparaging version and doing the inner work of deeply relinquishing it.

Several other disconnectors described here in Part 2 are also often expressed in disparaging ways, for example, "Don't you ever again use my things!" (demanding or ordering) or "You shouldn't be so upset about it" (implying "you shouldn't feel how you feel") or "Why didn't you think of that before?" (lecturing or admonishing).

Choosing words that don't imply any failing on the other person's part or any judgment leaves the door open to a safe space of kindness and authentic connection.

The disconnector **disparaging** is illustrated in the following story:

Story 51: Liam

Part 3

The path to profound change

DOI: 10.4324/9781003288589-3

People's stories continue

Some of the personal accounts in Part 1 of the book are continued here in Part 3, showing how high-quality listening and understanding can result in deep, lasting enhancements of well-being through the brain's innate mechanism of memory reconsolidation.

The initial portions of these stories from Part 1 are reproduced here, with the further adventures starting where you see the marker "~ ~ ~ ~ ~." Along the way, what's happening below the surface is revealed in italics. Additional in-depth comments follow each story, explaining the process that unfolded. (To protect the anonymity of each person, these extended stories are composites of true accounts.)

Nate's story (24)

Hi, people. My name is Nate, and I'm 42 years old. I grew up as the middle of three brothers, and I kind of got lost in the shuffle a lot of the time. My older brother was the achiever who brought home the honors, so he got a lot of attention, not leaving much room for me. My younger brother was the athlete of the family and outgrew me by the time he was 10.

> *Under those conditions, any child is very likely to form core, unquestioned beliefs of being unworthy and unlovable, which tend to generate accompanying feelings of anxious insecurity, shame, and depression.*

He had a ravenous appetite and grabbed half the food on the table for himself as a matter of course. The message I grew up with was: There's not enough to go around, there's not enough for me, so I'd better hoard and protect what I can get. And there's certainly not enough attention available for me, so I'd better not have any expectations of getting any or I'll feel painfully disappointed and neglected.

> *Nate learned at a young age that in his family, his needs for attention and for food were not going to be met and were not even regarded as important to meet. He also learned ways of limiting the suffering that those adversities would cause him: saving and protecting what little food he could get, and not expecting any attention or interest from anyone, which required cutting himself off from his feelings of needing any such attention. These solutions were his best, adaptive attempt to subsist on very thin rations and feel as little emotional distress as possible.*

In my adult years I've lived alone, surrounding myself with books and old LPs and technological gadgets that no one can take away from me, and I haven't dated much. I don't expect much interest from other people.

Nate is showing how tenacious the emotional learnings formed in childhood tend to be, persisting across the decades of adult life. These life-shaping and world-shaping core beliefs, expectations, and self-protective tactics do not fade over time.

When I don't feel like heating up a meal, I step out to the pizzeria across the street. They know me there, since I've been going at least once a week for years.

Last Monday evening I was there at the pizzeria, and business was slow. Sandy, the waitress, sat down at my table, something she hadn't done before.

Based on Nate's "knowing" that people won't give any personal attention to him, he certainly had no expectation of Sandy joining him at his table. He's not saying so, but he must have been quite surprised and possibly couldn't even make sense of what was happening, because her choosing to join him wasn't even a possibility in the world as he knew it to be.

This is how it went between Sandy and me:

Sandy: Hey, it's nice that you came in on a slow night. Now I have someone to talk to. Mondays are usually so boring.
Me (Nate): Oh! Glad to be able to help.

It doesn't appear to occur to Nate that Sandy has joined him because she views him as good company. His comment seems to mean he thinks he's merely doing her a favor.

Sandy: Yeah, I felt like talking to you some other times, but there was always too much going on.
Me (Nate): Really?

Notice Nate's surprise at hearing Sandy now making it clear that she has felt interested in him. This differs sharply from his lifetime of perceiving others as having no interest and offering no attention toward him.

Sandy *(smiling)*: Really!
Me (Nate): *(looking at Sandy, speechless)*

What might be going through Nate's mind at this moment? His unquestioned assumption was that Sandy wouldn't want to pay any particular attention to him. Why should she be any different from anyone else? Yet now he has just experienced something quite different from that lifelong expectation. We can sense Nate's mind being unsettled by this odd

> *departure from reality as he knows it, creating an experience of his unquestioned belief,*
> *"No one pays attention to me," side-by-side with the unmistakable, contradictory experi-*
> *ence of "Sandy wants to pay attention to me!" Both of those feel real and true, and yet*
> *they cannot possibly both be true, so their sudden juxtaposition feels strange and puzzling.*

Sandy *(jumping up)*: The cook made too much tiramisu today. I'll go get you a nice, big portion. Be right back.

I'm really disoriented! I *know* that people don't pay attention to me, and here's Sandy not only paying attention to me but also admitting that she's been paying attention to me and interested in connecting with me for a while. And then her impulse to bring me tiramisu took me totally by surprise. I even caught myself half-expecting her not to return from the kitchen. She's giving me not only attention, but also food?! In my experience, food isn't something that gets shared so easily. I'm suddenly full of stirred-up, unhappy childhood memories, and it's hard to sort out what's really going on.

Sandy's whole manner was so open and direct that the genuineness of her wanting to visit with me got across to me. I could see that she was actually happy to see me. To put it mildly, I'm not used to that! It seemed so simple for her to answer "Really!" as if she heard and understood my surprise.

> *This true story is a lovely example of how life sometimes arranges exactly the condi-*
> *tions that activate the brain's innate process of memory reconsolidation for unlearning and*
> *updating tenacious, lifelong emotional learnings such as Nate's. That can take place if,*
> *while a specific emotional learning is reactivated, simultaneously an experience occurs that*
> *sharply contradicts what the person knows and expects according to that learning. The*
> *brain quickly responds to that expectation violation (memory researchers call it* prediction
> error) *by actually destabilizing the original learning's neural encoding, which allows a*
> *fundamental revision and "rewriting" of that learning, at a neurological level, by the new,*
> *contradictory knowledge.*

> *Sandy's behaviors of giving Nate interest, attention, and food were such a sharp challenge*
> *to his core beliefs and expectations that those core beliefs were engaged and reactivated,*
> *bringing them into felt awareness to some degree, right alongside the clear contradiction of*
> *them by Sandy's behavior. In response to that* juxtaposition experience *(as it's called*
> *in Coherence Therapy), how Nate's brain responded is approximated in words as, "Hey,*
> *wait a minute! I've been assuming that all people would be the same as my family and*
> *view me as unimportant and uninteresting, but maybe not all people are that way after*
> *all." In other words, the brain notices that the world is not behaving as expected according*
> *to past learning. That is the moment when the memory reconsolidation process is launched*

and a fundamental change can occur. Let's see what then happened as Nate now continues his story.

~ ~ ~ ~ ~

For the next several days, I just couldn't get this experience with Sandy out of my head. It's not exactly that I was fixated on *her*; it's just that the whole experience kind of unsettled me in a really peculiar way – a *good* way, but still …

On Friday night I got together with Arnie, my friend since childhood. I was still perplexed by the Monday pizzeria experience, so I told him what happened. That's the thing with Arnie – we have a good balance of give-and-take. He's a good listener when I need it – like on Friday night – and next time, he might be the one who needs *me* to listen. We're pretty much always there for each other. He really got what was so surprising to me, since he knows how it was in my family and that I tend to steer clear of risking disappointments. We ended up talking for a good couple of hours, mainly about my stuff.

You know, as I'm telling you about this, something big is just now hitting me: *Arnie* pays attention to me! I mean, I've always known this on some level, of course, but I'm just now realizing that *he* doesn't fit the mold I learned as a kid – and that means the experience with Sandy wasn't a "first" or a one-off in my life! It grabbed my attention for whatever reasons, but now I realize that Arnie's been doing that for years! My brain is whirling around right now. And suddenly now I'm remembering a few *other* people who've been there for me in life – like my neighbor who's a plumber and generously helped me out when I had a leaky faucet a couple of years ago. And I'm remembering the heart-to-heart talks I had with a female colleague at my last job. Wow. How come I never put all this together before? How come I never noticed that people exist who *aren't* like my family? I was going through life assuming I'm in a world where no such people exist!

Sure, I need to be careful and sensible and get to know someone before I know what to expect. But I don't have to assume that there's *never* going to be enough of what I need – like attention or even food. I can see now that I made that assumption a long time ago, without ever questioning it. I guess that's what kids naturally do. They assume that what they experience in their little pocket of the world is how the whole world is. I just lumped everyone in with how my family was.

What a shame it is that it took me so long to realize these things and get to this point. I could get pretty sad about what I missed out on all along because of assuming everyone's going to be the same as my parents. I guess what haunts me most is spending so much time alone over the years, when I now see I could have had some satisfying relationships and felt generally better about myself. I'm surprised to hear myself say that! It's so new, and it feels good.

In Nate's fascinating account we get a glimpse of the subjective, internal experience of the brain's special process that can deeply transform a lifelong, ingrained emotional learning. It just so happened — on that Monday night in the pizzeria — that someone's sincere friendliness toward him differed so clearly from what he had been assuming was possible for him that it yanked those background assumptions into the foreground, while at the same time plainly disconfirming them. With that juxtaposition, Nate's lifelong core beliefs were opened to fundamental change, including a neurological re-encoding. The cascade of effects continued as his mind spontaneously retrieved memories of several similar adult experiences that also contradicted those beliefs formed in childhood. These other experiences had never before become consciously juxtaposed with his unquestioned assumptions. It may have been that fast piling up of evidence that prevented Nate from dismissing Sandy's behavior as a weird, meaningless fluke. The potentially liberating juxtapositions that life generates are often inadvertently blocked by people in that way. But Nate let it sink in, and he recognized, for the first time in his life, that this world has people who are ready, willing, and glad to give him their kind, caring attention — and even food!

Sage's story (46)

Hello, readers!

I'd like to tell you about an interaction with a dear friend who simply listens to what I share and accepts me as I am.

My name is Sage. I suspect I'm not the only person who feels ashamed of having a messy apartment, but my feeling of shame might be more intense than most people's. I had a lot of pressure from my mother when I was growing up about how a "proper" young lady conducts and presents herself. Having a disorderly household was a huge no–no.

> *It's clear that Sage learned deeply from her mother's heavy messages that her worth depends completely on maintaining all the "proper" external appearances. Her shame when her home is messy is her feeling of being exposed as being utterly unworthy.*

Every so often I do a major cleanup, and then I feel good about it for a short while. But then I get busy with life and work and friends, and my place goes back to wrack and ruin, and stays that way most of the time.

For that reason, I like to meet friends at a nearby coffee shop, especially if it's a spontaneous get-together. No muss, no fuss, as they say. My sister is the only person I don't feel embarrassed in front of when the apartment is a mess, so she's allowed to drop by unannounced, but nobody else, please!

My friend Miriam lives nearby and likes to ring my doorbell on her way back from doing errands.

Me (Sage): Hello?
Miriam: Hey, it's me. Wanna hang out? You have time now?
Me (Sage): The place is a mess, as usual. I'll come down. Be there in three minutes.
Miriam: Okay, I'll be at the coffee shop at our usual table.
(a few minutes later …)
Me (Sage): Nice to see you! Sorry I didn't invite you in.
Miriam: That's okay. I know you don't like me showing up when you're not expecting me.

> *With this relaxed acceptance and understanding from Miriam, Sage feels safe to reveal more about inviting people in (or not), because she's not feeling the need to hide or defend herself.*

Me (Sage) *(responding in kind to Miriam's relaxed openness)*: Yeah, thanks, but it's not just you. In fact, it's not about you at all!

Miriam: No? Good! I've been wondering … so I'm glad to hear that.

Me (Sage): Yeah. It's my embarrassment with *anyone* seeing my messy place. I always had such heavy pressure from my mother. She still expects me to keep my apartment neat, the same way she always made me clean up my room at home.

Miriam: Ah, so your mother has a kind of primal authority on what a household should look like.

> *Miriam is well attuned to Sage and is simply tracking and mirroring what Sage is revealing – which is what allows the next important piece of Sage's "knowings" to emerge.*

Me (Sage): She sure does! I wish I could shake it off. I'm the most loyal customer at this coffee shop thanks to my mother. She's the reason I meet people here instead of at home.

> *Sage now realizes consciously that her fear of her mother's negative judgments is just as strong as it ever was, even though Sage is an adult who lives in her own apartment – and her mother isn't even physically present when Sage decides whether her place is cleaned up enough to let Miriam come in.*

Miriam: That's interesting.

Me (Sage): It is, actually, now that I think about it. Every time I come here, it's because I'm deferring to my mother's standards on housekeeping. I'm going to remember that from now on, every time I walk through the door of this café.

Miriam: You mean, remember that you're doing it *her* way and not *your* way?

Me (Sage): Yeah, that I'm always making the decision in this automatic way, based on what's not acceptable to *her*, and that I'm not even asking myself what's okay with *me*.

> *In the most natural and relaxed way, Miriam's listening, interest, and curiosity have been so welcoming and understanding that in response, Sage reached an important new aware-ness of persisting in her childhood obedience to her mother's standards and of forfeiting her adult autonomy. Next, we'll see what developed from having this new awareness.*

~ ~ ~ ~ ~

Starting with that get-together with Miriam, it felt as though a fog had cleared in this area of my mind. That didn't change my feelings of shame about having a messy place, but I was now very aware that my mother was the one deciding whether my way of keeping house was acceptable. And my logic told me that *I* should be the one deciding that, given that it's my place and I live by myself!

People so often say, "It just doesn't make logical sense that I feel (or do, or believe) that!" But our deep emotional learnings are a lot more powerful than our rational logic, and that's what determines how we feel and act much of the time.

Miriam and I talked some more about this from time to time (at the coffee shop, of course!) and she kind of wondered out loud if I could imagine being free of my mother's rules and regulations about household orderliness. She was curious about what was keeping me in the grip of her rules, even now. Good question!

Miriam was expressing curiosity about Sage's inner world without any agenda of her own to get Sage to change. This is a crucially important factor that allows emotional truths to emerge freely. Sometimes called "coherence empathy," it's really just an expression of the listener's intention to understand how the other's inner world of meaning works, just as it is. Any smallest hint of judgment or disapproval on the listener's part will quickly close down the flow of emotional truths into conscious awareness.

Over time I realized more about how my mother's housekeeping standards affected me as I was growing up. She gave it so much importance that as a girl I believed everything was at stake – for example, "She'll love me and approve of me only if I fulfill her standards" and "Maybe there's something *wrong with me* that she's dissatisfied with me so often" and "I'd better not let anyone see how inadequate I am at being the proper young lady Mom wants me to be – and maybe I'm inadequate altogether." It was really surprising to see that I had such weighty negative beliefs based on housekeeping!

I really have Miriam to thank for sticking with me through all this. She never felt the need to give advice or suggest positive thinking or fix me. (We sometimes joke that she's actually the "sage" in our relationship!) I uncovered so much about myself just in the process of having her listen to me in her simple, caring way. I keep my whole string of housekeeping-related beliefs in mind, especially in circumstances that trigger them. I don't pressure myself to change; I just observe myself.

Miriam came by once when I was kind of ill and didn't feel like going to the coffee shop, so I made an exception and invited her up. She didn't even seem to notice the state of my apartment! That was an eye-opener for me when I stopped to think about it later. How could I possibly have had such a relaxed good time with someone visiting my place when it was so messy? It was as if something impossible had actually happened!

> *By living with awareness of her emotional learnings from childhood, Sage gives life a chance to disconfirm and dissolve them. Miriam's visit did exactly that, and Sage's description captures the curious quality of the juxtaposition experience that occurred: Something that can't possibly be happening (according to one's unquestioned beliefs) is happening! Sage's appreciation of how she has been helped by Miriam's gentle yet potent ways of listening is a beautiful thing in itself.*

Sometimes I even got gutsy and tried out saying things to my mother, like "Oh Mom, it's a good thing you're not coming over this weekend. I really need to clean up around here!" just to see what would happen. That turned out to be a good experiment. After a few of those, I realized that whatever she said, she still loves me just as much, whether I'm a fastidious housekeeper or not. Yes, she disapproves of messiness, but that doesn't make her love go away, the way I thought it did as a girl. The time that stands out most for me was when we were on a video call together and I commented on the mess that I knew she could see in the background. "Oh, my little girl!" she said wistfully. "I guess that's just how it has to be sometimes when you lead such a busy life …."

> *By revisiting and probing the very area that had been so distressing, Sage even more actively gave life a chance to create a disconfirmation. In her mother's responses she could now see a distinction that was impossible for her to see as a little girl: It became clear to her that Mom's dislike of messiness had nothing to do with how much she loved Sage – and, in fact, never did! That clear recognition dissolved her core troubling belief that her messiness makes her unlovable to her mother.*

I can't say I've become fully relaxed about inviting people into my place on the spur of the moment, because my housekeeping habits haven't changed much. But Miriam and two other close friends have now joined the ranks of my sister in that regard. They like and love me for myself, regardless of my housekeeping, and having them visit me is a real pleasure. With Mom, though, I think I'll keep on cleaning up before she comes over – but only because it's just easier on me if I know she's in her comfort zone. I no longer have any feeling that I'm at risk of losing her love. In fact it now seems almost absurd that I could have ever really believed that – but I did!

As Sage has indicated, after a core belief has been successfully disconfirmed, it loses all of its previous potent realness. That's a fundamentally different effect than is achieved through trying to build up positive beliefs, as a rule. Now that a messy home no longer means she is unlovable, Sage is no longer plagued by the feelings of shame that she described at the outset, and household neatness has become a pragmatic matter – no more and no less.

Philip's story (41)

My name is Philip, and I'm 43 years old. I left home at 16, and then kept my parents at arm's length ever since. I couldn't really tell you why if you'd asked me before recently. I also never thought about how that was for my parents. I just always knew that I was more comfortable living in a different city and seeing them only occasionally.

> *Philip wasn't born feeling the need to avoid contact with his parents, but in the course of growing up with them, in some way he learned that close proximity to them was not in the best interests of his well-being. Staying away from parents for one's entire adult life is a big thing, yet Philip also avoided giving any conscious attention to how and why staying away was so necessary for him.*

For Christmas two years ago, my wife and kids and I spent two days at my parents' house, and it just sort of happened that my mother and I were the last ones still up at night after everyone else had gone to sleep, and somehow we slipped into an honest kind of conversation, the kind that happens more easily when you're tired and your defenses are down. It was just a couple of minutes that went like this:

Mom: I can't tell you how wonderful it is to have you all here. I've been looking forward to this for months!
Me (Philip): Yeah, it's nice. Once or twice a year.
Mom: Aha … not too often …
Me (Philip): Right.
Mom: I have to admit, I've wondered about that over the years.
Me (Philip): About what?
Mom: About not too often. And about you living so far away.
Me (Philip): Hmm. Like … you wonder if there's a reason?
Mom: I'm sure you have your reasons. I guess people always have their reasons.
Me (Philip): What if I give a reason and that's upsetting for you?

> *Mom wonders out loud, without asking Philip pointed questions or pressuring him to reveal anything. She has expressed her interest in his reasons for keeping his distance and has an attitude of respecting that his reasons make sense to him, even before she knows what they are. In other words, she assumes emotional coherence in Philip's views and choices. This has created enough safety for Philip to move ever so slightly toward revealing them to her.*

Mom: Well … I'm your mother. I want to understand you and know what's going on in your life. Whatever you want to tell me, I'm here to listen. And I'm no stranger to hearing things in our family that are upsetting, okay?

Me (Philip): It's strange – if it were only you, I'd probably come to visit more often. I think it's Dad I'm allergic to in large dosages. Huh. I didn't realize that until now.

> *The further safety of knowing that Mom won't be judgmental has allowed Philip to pay attention to – and recognize – his own emotional truths more than before.*

Mom: Mmm. That's an important realization.

Me (Philip): Yeah. Somehow I always have the feeling he's judging me, and there's no way I can ever live up to his expectations.

Mom: I can certainly see how you might want to avoid large doses of that.

Me (Philip): For sure. But it wasn't even clear to me until just now when I said it to you.

> *Suddenly Philip is seeing the deep sense in his previously compelling but mysterious need to avoid visiting his parents. There is a moment of inner self-awareness when people are surprised to recognize that a behavior pattern they thought meant they were bad, defective, weak, or irrational doesn't mean any of that at all, because they see that the actual inner cause is valid and coherent.*

I've been feeling some relief from having this new understanding about why I keep my distance from my parents. I think somewhere deep down I've regretted not bringing my kids and my parents together more often. In fact I'm realizing I've felt a little judgmental toward myself about that, so it's a relief to know that I've had a good reason all along. That doesn't solve the problem, of course, but at least now I know what the problem really is, and it gives me a new way to think about it.

> *Philip's new opening up to self-awareness in this area has also allowed him to recognize the costs of his self-protective tactic of staying away from his father: It also keeps him away from his mother and it keeps his children away from their grandparents, and he is now allowing himself to feel his regret about that. Those costs were present all along, which illustrates how our emotional brain chooses the lesser suffering (those costs) in order to avoid the greater suffering (receiving his father's negative judgments).*

It surprised me when my mother said, "I have to admit, I've wondered about that over the years." In our family, no one ever talked openly like that about how we're really feeling or what's really going on. So that was a new move by Mom, and I really appreciate it. It let me realize something important and it brought us closer together than we've been in a long, long time.

When I thought about that conversation the next day, I realized that Mom must have had her own needs and feelings about family visits. I'm sure she wants to see her grandchildren more often. Yet she put her own feelings aside in order to give me a chance to come out with something I've been keeping buried inside for a long time.

~ ~ ~ ~ ~

Speaking of suppressing things … that's always been a difference between my wife and me. She feels really okay talking about her feelings, and in a certain way I've envied her on that score. Sort of. But there was always something that seemed unmanly about admitting to having certain feelings. Women have it easier that way, I guess.

> *Philip's expansion of awareness has begun to reveal to him the coherence of avoiding his own feelings. Perhaps having certain feelings was "unmanly" according to his father's judgments.*

When my wife fell into quite a depression after the birth of our second child, she went and got help, as if that were the most natural thing to do. And in fact, the therapist she found helped her enormously. So, after the talk with my mother and how good it felt to get more awareness of what was going on inside me, I actually started to wonder whether seeing a therapist could be a good thing for me, too. I eventually tried it out, and now that I'm through it and out the other end, I have to say that it was so helpful that I feel it was one of the best decisions I've made in a long time.

So, here's a summary of how it went in therapy. As I'd said to my mother, I always had the feeling Dad was judging me, and that there was no way I could live up to his expectations. So that was the "issue" I explained to the therapist, an older man. He then asked me what I'd like to change. What I most wanted, actually, was to change Dad into a father who loved and accepted me without any conditions attached and without being so judgmental. And I wanted to change him retroactively, right back to the beginning of my life!

Believe it or not, it took a while for me to come to terms with both of those wishes being unrealistic, beyond my control, and not a useful focus of therapy. In fact, it was even worse than that: I realized at some point that even though I could talk to Mom about this stuff to an extent, it would *never* be possible to talk to Dad about how he is – totally aside from the question of whether he'd ever change. He absolutely cannot listen without getting defensive and trying to prove me wrong. Same old problem.

At this point in Philip's account of therapy, we can see an important progression developing: He is realizing the impossibility of the breakthrough he's been hoping for: a fundamental change in Dad that would end the unhappy status quo. That sets the stage for Philip to look for and identify a different way of getting free of the longstanding pattern of avoiding his parents.

That led me to see that, given all the givens, the best outcome for me would be to feel okay enough about myself that Dad's criticisms would no longer affect me so strongly that I need to stay away. My goal for therapy became being able to spend some time around him without going into feeling that not fulfilling his expectations of me means I'm an unworthy and unlovable person.

As a direct result of arriving sadly at acceptance of his father as he is, with severe and unchangeable limitations, Philip's focus shifted toward identifying possible new solutions that are within his own sphere of influence.

Over the course of therapy, I discovered a number of beliefs and assumptions I'd been carrying my whole life without even knowing they were there. At first it was even difficult to see that these things *were* just beliefs and assumptions, because they completely felt like the reality of how the world is. Here's a list of them:

- The only way to get Dad to love me is to be the person he expects me to be.
- If I can't do that, it means I'm unworthy and he's right to not love me.
- Dad is the one who determines whether I'm worthy and acceptable or not.
- All people will judge me the same way as Dad does.
- Boys and men who show feelings are weak and defective, so I'd better hide how I feel.
- I'm better off staying away from Dad than letting him see any more of how flawed I am.

So my next task was to stay in touch with those assumptions as they surfaced. They felt like objective reality to me, though over time I experienced them as "simply" my own *subjective* reality that I'd constructed in my mind without realizing it. But I'm jumping the gun a bit. As I became aware of having those beliefs and assumptions, next I had to notice whenever one or more of them became energized and had me in its spell.

I shared some of the therapy stuff with my wife from time to time. She seemed very interested. One particular conversation sticks in my mind especially, the time when I confided my truth about "Boys and men who show feelings are weak and defective, so I'd better hide them." Her reaction floored me! She said, "Wow. Well, I know your dad, so I shouldn't be too surprised, but as far as I'm concerned, it's just the opposite! It's a great strength of character for a man to show his softer, more vulnerable feelings. I'll take more of that any day!" To say this was shocking news to me is an understatement.

> *Suddenly, the familiar meaning that it's a shameful weakness for a man to have vulnerable feelings was side-by-side with the new, contradictory meaning that it's a very desirable strength of character. This was a surprising juxtaposition experience for Philip, and exactly what allows the brain to unlearn the old and replace it with the new.*

Over time I became more aware of my feelings, such as feeling sad or feeling hurt, and sometimes I'd even voice them with a small, select number of people that I could trust: my wife, my kids, my best buddy, and occasionally my mother. Their reactions were never judgmental – surprisingly. My therapist encouraged me to hold these very real experiences of not being judged for having feelings right next to my expectation that I *would* be judged negatively as a man having vulnerable feelings.

> *Those were further juxtapositions of what Philip expected compared to what he was actually experiencing, deliberately prompted by the therapist as a core process of change.*

It took a while, but I was increasingly able to embrace these new experiences of the people closest to me as being real, and my older, black-and-white notions just didn't hold up as truths anymore. In fact, I could see that they *weren't* the truth. And it was fascinating to me that big things that I was sure I *knew* about people, or life, could turn out to be not the whole truth at all! Sure, there *are* people who react in those ways, but my old beliefs didn't feel like "truths about all people" anymore.

Unfortunately, though, Dad *is* one of those people, and I didn't have a solution for that big dilemma yet. Seeing myself as okay – *with* my feelings – just made Dad and any satisfying relationship with him feel even more unreachable for me. After all, what would still connect us if we no longer shared that old view of me being defective? This remained a hurdle for some time, at least for me inwardly.

> *In the past, Philip had not been aware that having the same negative view of himself as Dad apparently had was a major portion of what constituted his sense of connection with his dad. In other words, believing his dad's view of him made him feel seen by his dad, even though it was a negative view that they shared. An unavoidable result of Philip forming his own, different view of himself is the loss of that major area of shared reality and connection. That's a keenly felt discomfort, as Philip is describing. For some people in*

therapy, the specter of losing that connection – as unsatisfactory as such a connection may be – can be a temporary stumbling block in the process. Here again we see how the emotional brain chooses the lesser suffering: As distressing as it is to believe oneself unworthy and unlovable, losing that connection is a rupture that initially can feel even worse, and therefore has to be avoided by maintaining the shared negative judgments. Normally the emotional brain weighs those alternatives and carries out those protective tactics completely outside of awareness. Philip, however, was making good progress bringing conscious attention to all of that in order to free himself.

What started getting me over that particular hurdle was this: Once I realized I was starting to feel good about myself, including whatever emotions I happened to have at the moment, I tried out being around Dad and just keeping my new realizations and feelings to myself. First I did this in my imagination, as a rehearsal guided by my therapist, and then at the next family event I did it for real. So once again I was experiencing two different realities – one in which *I* was the judge of whether I was alright or not, and the other reality (the one I had known all my life) telling me "Dad is the one who determines whether I'm alright or not." I wrestled with that for a while, especially when I was actually around him. I had conversations with myself about how it would feel to stick with what I'd come to believe about myself instead of some version of "father knows best."

That process was new, strange territory for me. While I was in the midst of it, I really had no idea how it would turn out. I just knew I had to stick with it. At some point – I can't pin down exactly when or how – I began to notice something that I couldn't be sure of at first because it had totally escaped me before. I began to notice that Dad's judgments of me and his fatherly love were two separate things. Yeah, I always basically knew he loved me, but so many times it just didn't *feel* that way. As an adult and as a father myself, I could understand that difference from my own experience, which was something I couldn't do as a kid. Back then, I freaked out at any sign that he was unhappy with me in some way, because I was assuming that meant he didn't love me. That felt like the end of the world! It just feels different now. He's not the one deciding if I'm alright, and I feel his love even though I don't fully fit his image of how his son should be. Finally I got free of beliefs that had shaped my whole life. It wasn't easy and the process took some soul-searching, but where I've come to feels so much better!

All of Philip's liberating changes resulted from his use of his own mind's inherent capabilities for focusing awareness on his own core beliefs, or emotional learnings, and on the full range of his own knowings and experiences alongside those beliefs. However, it was by no means automatic that he would successfully make effective use of those capabilities. One's original emotional learnings are remarkably tenacious and tend to rule one's state of mind and behavior across the decades of life, unless a deliberate, skillful, sustained effort is made to apply one's native capabilities to them. Philip fortunately found a therapist who could guide that inner work.

You could say that therapy led me to find a better solution to my problem with Dad than just staying away from him. When I'm around him now, I'm relaxed because I'm not trying for more than what's possible, and I keep certain things private. It's not that I want to keep secrets from him. It's just that once I realized he was very unlikely to change, I stopped hoping to get from him what he couldn't give, and I focused instead on enjoying the fathering that he *could* give. Along the way to that, it was a strange reversal when, instead of always feeling so vulnerable to him being disappointed in *me*, I had to admit to myself that I felt disappointed in *him* – for not being able to see more of who I am and connect with me in ways I wished I could experience from my dad. Looking back, I can see that allowing myself to feel my disappointment was a crucial part of accepting Dad as he is and then figuring out how to be comfortable around him. I never would have guessed that it would be possible for me to accept him *and* accept myself, and that feels really good. Maybe even more curious is how it all got rolling with just a few minutes of my mom drawing me out in her kitchen.

Listening in order to connect deeply

In reading the dozens of stories in Part 1, you'll have gotten a palpable sense of how meaningful and satisfying it is to experience connection and attunement in inter-personal interactions, especially as a result of skillful listening. Three of those stories were continued earlier here in Part 3, showing how optimal listening can set people up to make significant shifts in their inner worlds, freeing themselves from long-term, limiting patterns of thought, behavior, and emotion. Those accounts show the process of memory reconsolidation at work, creating such shifts.

What's coming next is a review and expansion of key aspects of the all-important principle of emotional coherence. Then we'll move on to explore the world of mem-ory reconsolidation that began to emerge in the three stories above.

How connection results from assuming emotional coherence

Connection between two adults means having a *shared understanding* of each other and of things that matter to each one. In order to have that shared understanding, each one has to actually *pay attention* to the other by listening well, which means taking in, considering, and then remembering what that person communicates about him- or herself through words and behavior.

Everything below applies not only to interpersonal relationships, but also to the relationship people have with themselves, through self-awareness. People who have a significant degree of honest clarity about their own thoughts, feelings, attitudes, and behaviors – enabling them to understand and help themselves – are in a good position to understand and interact constructively with others, creating authentic and helpful connections.

Yet it can be challenging to pay attention and really listen to others in ways that cre-ate accurate, empathic understanding and connection. One of the main obstacles is the widespread, conventional view that a person's emotional reactions or other problem-atic, stubbornly persistent patterns are either irrational or caused by brain irregularities. Viewing others in that way, there is little motivation to listen to others closely and deeply. Listening for deep understanding makes sense to try for only if you're assum-ing that there is deep sense to find underneath what initially may appear to have no coherent basis. This is the assumption of emotional coherence. Emotional coherence means that how people (oneself included) think, feel, and act does indeed make sense according to what they have learned about the world from their lifetime of unique personal experiences. People's thoughts, emotions, and actions are generated largely by their unquestioned, unrecognized, but coherent core beliefs and assumptions about the world, about themselves, and about other people. Most of those assumptions are outside of conscious awareness, because we are unaware of learning most of what we learn in life, largely in childhood, but after childhood as well.

When someone else's views, feelings, or behaviors not only differ from yours but don't even make sense according to your own maps of reality, do you assume emotional coherence anyway? Most people don't, and as beginners at this, people usually find it quite counterintuitive to do so. If reality clearly operates in a certain way in our own world, doesn't it automatically operate and look the same in someone else's world? Even people who are familiar with the principle of emotional coherence sometimes find it challenging to operate from within the assumption that a hidden sense underlies what initially seems *non*sensical.

For example, consider the man who chronically provoked annoyance in his wife, boss, and coworkers by engaging in negative behaviors that would have been easy to foresee and correct. How hard could it be to remember to phone his wife to tell her he'd be arriving home late from work? Yet he kept neglecting to phone her, vexing her deeply. His behavior seemed irrational from the conventional, external viewpoint. The deep sense of his behavior was inside, in what he had learned about the world implicitly – that is, without awareness of learning it – as a child in his large family where he was lost in the midst of eight siblings: *The only way to get any attention is by doing something bad.* That was the hidden coherence and the emotional truth of his seemingly irrational, provocative behaviors. He had no conscious awareness that his behavior was driven by that potent core belief, forged throughout his childhood by his family life – until it came into awareness and was put into words during a therapy session. Before then, it didn't exist in words or concepts at all, yet was a well-defined knowing anyway. Such learnings about the world form and operate quite independently of the conceptualizing and verbalizing activity of our conscious mind.

Learnings and knowings of that kind are *emotional* learnings, because they were formed in the presence of strong emotion, which gives them great power and long-term tenacity, as we now know from neuroscience research. They do not fade out over time. We form and use these knowings in an attempt to minimize our suffering and maximize our safety and well-being, *according to what was learned.* However, as noted, as a rule the learning occurred outside of awareness, and these emotional learnings operate from outside of awareness.

As we interact with other people, we don't normally know what emotional learnings they have that are generating their particular attitudes, feelings, and behaviors. What we need to realize, though, if we are to inhabit the assumption of emotional coherence, is that there *is* a deep sense that would be understandable to us if we were thoroughly familiar with the person's unique emotional learning history and inner world of meaning.

Assuming emotional coherence requires tolerating the state of "not knowing" – not knowing the landscapes of another person's world, landscapes with various dangers, invisible to us, that the individual is actively avoiding without awareness of doing so. Tolerating not-knowing can be a big challenge, since most of us have been rewarded all of our lives for what we *know* and made to feel inadequate, or worse, for *not knowing.*

The more one understands about the existence and operation of emotional learnings, the easier it is to assume emotional coherence and tolerate not-knowing. The brain forms many different types of memory. Emotional learnings are the stuff of a particular type of memory, termed *implicit emotional memory* by researchers, and consisting of perceived patterns in the world that were experienced and learned while feeling strong emotion. This is different from the memory of particular emotional experiences and events, which researchers term *episodic memory* or *autobiographical memory.* An example of implicit emotional memory is what the man described above had learned early in life: *The only way to get any attention is by doing something bad.* That unit of memory, which had been driving his provocative behaviors, can also be understood as a mental model or a schema depicting a particular pattern of the world that the individual subjectively perceived and took as a general reality of human life (not merely how his particular family happened to operate). Another example is a child who has been chronically neglected, unhelped, and unprotected, and has stored in implicit emotional memory the knowledge (here put into words), *I can be in danger or be harmed at any moment, and nobody will protect or rescue me. I'm alone, helpless, and defenseless in this world.* That unit of memory, carried along unconsciously into adult life, generates persistent generalized anxiety, occasional panic attacks, avoidance behaviors, a chronic ache of feeling alone, unloved, and outside of the human family, and a deep despair that is felt consciously as a formless depression. All of those behavioral and emotional manifestations could be deemed irrational from an external viewpoint and termed "disorders" according to conventional psychiatric diagnostic criteria, but they in fact have complete emotional coherence and are sensible responses to life as this person actually experienced it.

Consider a person who in childhood was regularly ridiculed with disgust for being overweight, and therefore now, in adulthood, unquestioningly assumes that everyone looks at him with disgust, even when that isn't actually what others are feeling toward him. Another person grew up in a culture in which "extra padding" is considered to be a sign of good health and affluence, and so she views her ample weight as desirable and assumes that other people's views of her, accordingly, are positive and approving.

A person's emotional learning and memory systems make sense of what's happening *now* based on what he or she learned about the world in the *past.* And only that one person has experienced that past, so that way of making sense resides solely in *that* person – irrespective of whether the person is consciously aware of the emotional learnings involved. Listening deeply for true understanding of a person requires us to assume unique emotional coherence and enter, in effect, that person's subjective world to the best of our capabilities.

Most of us have had the thought from time to time that another person's behavior is simply *wrong*, and that we know better what's *right*. A true understanding of another person, however, requires knowing that we *don't know* the meaning of the behavior until we know the specific emotional coherence that is actually operating in that person. Listening for emotional coherence necessitates discarding the right/wrong way of thinking about people. Right/wrong evaluations of others create divisions and polarizations and block empathy and compassion – disconnecting people from one another – whereas assuming emotional coherence fosters empathy, compassion, and connection.

For a person who was once hit by a car while walking across the street, for example, the unpredictable lethality of cars is now absolutely real, so *any* vehicle within a certain distance and traveling at a certain speed is now perceived as a source of imminent, life-threatening danger. If we understand and empathize with that person's subjective perception and experience, the inappropriateness of right/wrong evaluation is obvious even though our own perceptions and experiences are very different.

Assuming emotional coherence makes it apparent that helpfulness consists of aiding others to find solutions or paths forward that actually fit into their inner and outer life patterns, rather than supplying solutions that are foreign matter and therefore unworkable. When we assume emotional coherence and are therefore open to discovering the unquestioned assumptions and emotional learnings that people – including ourselves – carry with them, a new level of connection and a new depth of interpersonal interaction open up to us.

What happens when connection is missing

It's a moving experience when psychotherapy clients tell us how they've gone through life hardly ever feeling truly heard or understood by family or friends. Such foreignness of attuned personal connection makes it very challenging to connect on a deep level in any personal relationships. Disconnection and aloneness, felt even in the presence of other people, then seem to be the normal quality of life, producing a state of despair and desolation, even without conscious recognition of what's missing or what can be done about it.

In looking to understand patterns of interaction among people, we've found the knowledge we've distilled from our therapy work on people's emotional wounds to be very helpful. In the population at large we see harmful patterns of interaction very similar to those that contributed to producing our clients' long-lasting emotional wounds. These harmful interactions have tenacious, wide-spreading effects, so any reduction in such interactions greatly helps reduce the emotional woundedness in the world.

Our main focus in this book, as you know, is on bringing about warm, harmonious connection, and to that end, it's useful to understand the long-term harm that can result when people's needs for caring understanding and emotional attunement are *not* met.

Most people aim to be kind, sensitive, and caring toward others, particularly those closest to them. At the same time, many people – for whatever complex but coherent reasons – are at times unable to interact with others in ways that foster enriching connection. One such example is a person who never received any listening or attunement from his or her parents and, in fact, had to provide *them* with listening and attunement. That person now perceives anyone's request for listening as more tyranny and therefore is unable or unwilling to give it.

Let's look briefly at some of the more extreme examples of what can happen when emotionally destructive interactions take place, because the more extreme cases can illuminate and alert us to the less obvious forms of damaging interactions in everyday life. In particular, we'll look at difficult interpersonal experiences that many children have, because the early, formative years lay the groundwork for a lifetime of assumptions and expectations about the larger world of people.

Some children are exposed to overt ridicule, criticism, anger, and blame, resulting in a pervasive sense of low self-worth that they carry forever after. When children are told by someone they trust and believe that they're dumb, ugly, disgusting, unlikable, unlovable, "too much," an embarrassment, a burden, shameful, different from everyone else, abnormal, defective, too sensitive, too emotional … they usually internalize those devaluing messages as the truth about themselves, without questioning the validity of such messages. These children develop deeply ingrained expectations and protective behaviors based on those notions of themselves, such as this one, if it were to be spelled out explicitly in words: "I have to hide my needs, desires, and most everything about me to protect myself from shame, ridicule, and disappointment." Such beliefs and behaviors are usually not consciously thought or recognized, though they are heavily life-organizing.

Other children may not be explicitly denigrated, but their basic needs for consistent physical care and protection aren't met. When babies or small children are left alone in times of dire need, they are likely to develop a pervasive, frightening sense of abandonment and aloneness, as well as a fundamental lack of trust in any human relationships.

Children can also suffer from *emotional* neglect even when their basic custodial, physical needs are being met. Children experience feelings and emotions very strongly, but sometimes parents aren't capable of recognizing and responding sensitively to a child's feelings and needs. Such children grow up with unquestioned (and largely out-of-awareness) assumptions such as, "My feelings and needs aren't important and won't be seen or met. I don't even have the right to *have* needs. Others' needs and wishes are always more important than mine." That tends to be accompanied by, "I'm alone in this world, in this life, with no possibility of deep connection with any person" and "I mustn't let myself even feel what I really want or need, because then I'd feel and know that I fundamentally and forever don't matter, and that would be devastating." A deep feeling of aloneness and lack of connection to other people is probably one of the most common sources of the growing incidence of depression in many demographics.

What do all these extreme – though not uncommon – scenarios have to do with how people conduct themselves on an everyday basis? These examples begin to give us an idea of how damaging it can be when our needs for understanding and human connection consistently aren't met in our everyday interactions. Naturally, children are most vulnerable and therefore most influenced by such conditions, but failures of connection often keep occurring into adulthood and throughout life, because many people aren't consciously aware of not listening, not understanding, and not connecting to those around them.

The stories in Part 1 show many of the ways in which people fail to listen well and create genuine connection in ordinary, everyday interactions, even though it isn't their *intention* to cut off meaningful communication. As we've seen, some of the most common habits are:

- simply not listening
- interrupting
- giving unsolicited advice or solutions
- assuming to know what the other person really means
- counteracting the other person's feelings or point of view
- viewing the other's feelings, views, or behaviors as irrational or incorrect
- criticizing the other person
- not showing empathy when needed

As we take notice of these habits, it becomes clear just how widespread they are.

We hope you've also begun to have an inkling of what can go *right* and the universe of fulfilling possibilities that opens up when people *do* listen well and, as a result, communicate and connect meaningfully with one another.

Discovering and understanding our emotional coherence: the how-to of high-quality listening

Assume that quality listening is needed

In everyday life, normally people don't openly and explicitly express their need for listening. In fact, many people who are emotionally starving for good listening are enduring that ache with no conscious awareness of carrying that deep need. (We have found that to be the case with a sizable fraction of our therapy clients.) So, as we interact with others, as a rule it is safe to assume, at least tentatively, that any high-quality listening we can give, even in an interaction lasting only a few seconds, provides a precious and sustaining bit of connection, of mattering, of understanding, of humanity. Sometimes there are fairly clear signals that listening is probably needed, such as when a person is having noticeable reactions, whether positive or negative, about something. However, an unexpressive, quiet person is just as likely to be "running on empty" regarding the need for listening.

The simple act of making oneself available to listen (opening the "listening door" and really giving full attention to what someone is expressing in words and behavior) delivers caring, respect, and acceptance. Implicitly, we're telling that person, "To me you matter as a member of the human family. I care about your well-being and I know that what you are now experiencing is important and meaningful in your life." Those are powerful messages! And those messages, delivered through quality listening, help to alleviate the aloneness a person may be feeling in facing challenges in life.

An important ripple effect is that people who feel listened to and understood are in a better position to "pay it forward" by being more of a listener in their other relationships. With their own needs met to some degree, they have more emotional capacity available, and the human world becomes a slightly more connected realm.

We benefit, too, by understanding another person. We discover whole new subjective realities to ponder. What we ourselves assume unquestioningly to be "givens" in life may not at all be what that other person takes to be a given or a truth. Expanding our own horizons in this way often turns out to be a rewarding, illuminating, even nourishing endeavor. That is particularly true in the authors' experience as psychotherapists. Therapists are often asked, "How can you spend all day listening to people's problems!?" Well, not all therapists approach the work from the same stance, but from our stance, we engage in our therapy sessions as anthropologists, aiming to discover and understand the inner world that exists within each person. With such an understanding as a foundation, we can then most effectively guide the desired processes of change. But it isn't necessary to be professionally trained in order to enjoy interpersonal anthropology through listening. Anyone can apply his or her natural listening abilities to be a budding anthropologist of emotional learnings and discover other people's inner, subjective, coherent worlds.

Of course, it isn't only *others* who have a fundamental need to receive listening. It's also oneself. And it often isn't recognized that not only is it *possible* to give yourself some of the listening you need, but also it's important and healthy to do so. On one level, such listening-to-oneself consists of paying attention to feelings, knowings, and needs that have not been allowed to register in conscious awareness, but are trying to do so and would show up if *allowed and received*. On another, even deeper level, such listening pays attention to the subtler knowings and guidings that the very core of one's being is trying to communicate to one's conscious personality. All such inner listenings have potentially life-changing substance and value, and an entire book could easily be devoted to them. In addition, clarity about our own inner world greatly enhances both our understanding of what we are hearing as we listen to others and our ability to communicate meaningfully about ourselves to others.

Transparently reflect what's being communicated

Thomas Paine wrote in *Rights of Man* in 1791, "such is the irresistible nature of truth, that all it asks, and all it wants, is the liberty of appearing." All we need to do is notice and acknowledge a person's "truth." The idea is straightforward: Just say what we're hearing or noticing or sensing from the other person, without judging it in any way, so that the other feels seen and heard.

We can't ever understand and connect with *all* of what's going on inside other people, since we're not inside their minds with them. As jazz musician Miles Davis said, "If you understood everything I said, you'd be me." Nevertheless, any amount we *can* and *do* understand is valuable.

As touched upon previously, having a stance of "not knowing" is of fundamental importance for the listening that creates inner connection. That means recognizing, as a good anthropologist does, that one in fact doesn't actually know *anything* about what the other person thinks, means, or feels – and must learn it from that person.

Transparently reflecting what's been heard through such listening can be done in the form of a simple *overt statement* such as, "Yes … it's been a rough day for you." Overt statements can sometimes seem almost trivial or obvious, yet they are very effective for giving the gift of making the other feel caringly seen and heard. It's a simple comment consisting of what we're noticing or what we think we're understanding from the other person, whether or not it was communicated explicitly in words.

Overt statements are a way of being *transparent* about what it is we're understanding about the other person – be it behaviors we're observing, feelings we notice, or views that have been expressed. Such a response, communicating a personal understanding of what the other is experiencing, is also called *active empathic listening*.

As noted above, one listens from a position of not knowing, and our emerging understanding of the other's experience is always approximate and susceptible to inaccuracy. As a rule, then, it's best to include some words that respectfully acknowledge that. Some examples are:

- "I have the impression that ..."
- "I think I'm noticing that ..."
- "You seem to be ..."
- "I understand you to be saying that ..."
- "It looks to me as if ..."

Those ways of beginning an overt statement invite the other person to provide some correction if anything we've reflected is inaccurate in some way – and going through *that* process together is itself a "listening success story" and a deepening of connection. It's fascinating how often something seems clear or even obvious to us, and yet it turns out that the other person's experience is very different from what we've assumed. For example, a woman was sure her boyfriend would be angry at her for cancelling a coffee date, when in fact he became caringly worried about what might be going on in her life that made it necessary to cancel the date, and he had no feelings of anger at all, only concern.

In any particular situation, what a person experiences and how he or she responds to that situation is generated by the individual's *subjective meanings and assumptions* about the situation, not by the circumstances themselves. An unanswered text message, for instance, can mean to the sender simply that the other person must be busy and will answer later; or it could be interpreted by the sender to mean that the other person must be uninterested and is purposely and rudely leaving the message unanswered. The two interpretations will generate very different emotional and behavioral responses, tempered by how strongly the individual believes that his or her interpretation is the truth of the matter. There are vast individual differences not only in the particular meanings and assumptions that people apply in order to "make sense" of situations, but also in their degree of mindful awareness that they are making an interpretation that could be wrong.

In addition to the words we use to show the speaker that we're really listening, our non-verbal communication (facial expressions, body language, vocal tone, speed, decibel level, etc.) speaks volumes. We might nod to show understanding of what we're hearing, or lean toward the speaker in rapt attention. When we use an overt statement to reflect what we're understanding, our tone of voice should naturally match the mood and meanings of the speaker – for example, an almost whisper-like voice level for commenting on a sharing about a current, troubling vulnerability, or a lively tone for commenting on a promising new development.

Another way of showing real listening is by encouraging further communication with an open-ended invitation, such as these:

- "I'd really like to hear more about that."
- "I appreciate your telling me about that."
- "I'm curious about …"
- "If there's more you want to share about that, please do."

Such invitations respectfully leave it to the other person to choose whether he or she wishes to communicate more. Direct, specific, substantive questions, on the other hand, can pose a dilemma for a person who doesn't wish to disclose more or doesn't have an answer but feels pressure to respond, for example:

- Why did you choose to do *that*?
- Why do you feel *that* way about what happened?
- How did you *expect* her to respond to your saying that?

We aren't suggesting that such questions should be rigidly avoided, but for a harmonious interaction, they should be asked with a soft tone of voice that indicates caring concern and a recognition of vulnerability.

Reflect what we're noticing or sensing in ourselves

As noted earlier, one's own need for high-quality listening can to a meaningful degree be met by applying listening skills to oneself. Doing that consists firstly of simply paying attention to what is present in your own subjective experiencing, and then naming what you notice, which directly increases self-awareness. Just as in reflecting to another person what you're hearing and noticing in that individual's communication, you can say what you're noticing or sensing in yourself. This, too, is a type of overt statement and can be viewed as the *self*-reflecting or self-listening counterpart of active empathic listening. In Part 1, each storyteller's statement of "what I needed" was possible to make only after first paying attention internally to his or her own subjective experience of feelings, experiences, and needs at that moment.

There are myriad possibilities for how to put this type of self-reflection into words, whether we're doing it silently or sharing it with someone. Some examples are:

- "I notice that something is bothering me."
- "I'm confused about …"
- "I have mixed feelings about …"
- "I'm sensing that I'm feeling …"
- "When … happens, I tend to …"
- "When … happens, what it means to me is …"
- "I'm feeling sadness but don't know what it's about yet."
- "What I need right now is …"
- "I'm really at a loss for words just now."

It's natural that at times what we're experiencing inside remains outside of our awareness and unnamable, even though we're paying attention to the experience as well as we can. With persistence, usually some aspect finally becomes at least vaguely namable, and then with continuing persistence that aspect comes into sharper focus. It's something of an intriguing adventure, actually, to bring into awareness in that way what's in play in your own mind and heart by listening closely to what's inside. If paying attention to your inner experience and naming what you notice is very new for you, it might be very helpful, as well as illuminating and fascinating, to look through a list of "feeling words" (which can be found online).

Opening the way for transforming troublesome emotional learnings: memory reconsolidation in action

Throughout this book, a central theme has been that when we combine skillful listening with assuming emotional coherence, we foster rich connection with others as well as with ourselves. Now let's go a step further and consider how familiarity with the brain's process of memory reconsolidation can open up the prospect of actively supporting and promoting deep, lasting change.

Earlier in this book we considered how emotional learnings acquired earlier in life tend to persist far longer than the situations in which those learnings were accurate and helpful. For example, a child learns to never say anything at all about what she knows or feels because her drunk father would predictably respond by roaring denigrations and shaming at her, and sometimes physically hitting her. Decades later in her marriage, she always feels strangely unable to voice her feelings, needs, or views in any direct, clear manner, which in turn causes a range of chronic problems and conflicts. Here we see an emotional learning that was originally vital for maintaining emotional and physical safety, continuing to drive the same protective pattern in a later, very different phase of life, seriously impairing the person's functioning, harmony, and happiness.

That "prisoners of childhood" phenomenon affects most people to some degree. The unfading persistence of emotional learnings across decades of life is their inherent nature, not a dysfunction. The emotional learning and memory systems evolved to have that feature, so it must have been favorable for survival.

What can we do about such emotional learnings that were originally fully relevant and adaptive but now only cause difficulties? This is where the fascinating process of *memory reconsolidation* comes into play. It's the brain's built-in process for deeply unlearning and getting free of the grip of emotional learnings that no longer are accurate about the current circumstances.

At the beginning of Part 3, the continued stories show that when a particular emotional learning has been reactivated and energized and, at the same time, the person has an experience that's distinctly *contrary* to what that learning knows and expects about how the world functions, a unique type of puzzled surprise is felt from suddenly finding that the world is behaving differently from what was expected according to unquestioned knowings, assumptions, expectations, or beliefs. Neuroscience research has shown that in response to that unsettling violation of expectations, the brain immediately does something remarkable: the neural memory circuits that are the encoding of those assumptions or beliefs undergo a rapid biochemical transition that makes them directly revisable by current experiences that differ from the original assumptions. True unlearning happens through that process when new experiences fully contradict the old assumptions and rewrite their neural encoding accordingly. Then the old assumptions or beliefs no longer exist in memory and no longer feel real or have compelling power. The unlocked, changeable state of the neural encoding automatically reverts to a locked, stable state after five hours, which is the *reconsolidation* of the memory, though researchers also refer to the whole process, starting with the initial transition in response to a violation of expectations, as the *memory reconsolidation* process.

Let's revisit the woman described above – her name is Julia – who still carries the implicit emotional learning that she formed in childhood – specifically, the knowing that it's urgent to never directly, openly express her views or feelings, because she expects to be harshly assaulted emotionally and even physically for doing so by the man she lives with (originally her father, now her husband). The "implicit" status of that knowing means it doesn't show up in her conscious thinking or awareness, so she is often mystified by the strange blockage or force field that she feels holding her back from voicing her views, feelings, or needs to her husband.

One evening, Julia and her husband, Van, were watching a movie about a fictional but psychologically astute portrayal of a family's relationship patterns across three generations. Some of the patterns shown were similar to those in her own family that produced her emotional learnings – similar enough that while sitting there next to her husband, she experienced a deep, lucid awareness that the mysterious force field that paralyzes her self-expression is actually her own urgent self-protective tactic learned under the violent tyranny of her alcohol-addicted father. Her blocked self-expression suddenly was no longer a mystery, and it now made sense to her completely. She had found the emotional coherence of her behavioral paralysis.

At first Julia was almost dazed by the magnitude of this realization as she continued viewing the movie next to Van. So much of her life was suddenly making sense after decades of bewilderment about herself. Soon her thoughts pivoted and focused on how this realization would affect her life going forward. This quickly led to the thought, "Oh! Now I won't be in the grip of that force field anymore! I'll finally be able to have a voice and take up space as an equal in my marriage." And she felt thrilled by that happy expectation.

But in the following days, Julia became dismayed by finding that the force field was persisting despite her clear, accurate understanding of its meaning and origins. She remained unable to come out with her views, feelings, or needs in her interactions with Van. Seeing that such lucid, deep awareness wasn't able to unlock and dispel the old blockage, her situation now seemed even more hopeless than before her awakening. She went through the days now in a mood of despair – which she kept well hidden, of course.

239

Some weeks later, Julia had lunch with a close friend, Diana, a woman she'd met many years ago at her first job, and she told Diana all about her realization and her despair that it didn't free her. Diana was a very skilled listener, and what she was hearing brought to mind what she had learned in recent months from reading about memory reconsolidation. She knew that *awareness* of an emotional learning is necessary *but not sufficient* for unlearning and nullifying it – exactly as Julia had described. She also knew what else is needed, and this knowledge now guided her replies to her dear friend.

Diana said, "I can really see why you're feeling so deeply discouraged by the continuation of the old pattern, after feeling so wonderfully hopeful at first. You didn't just have an intellectual, theoretical insight into the blockage, you experienced a real illumination of the deep emotional learning that all along has been maintaining that blockage from below awareness. Well, that's a major achievement in itself, and *of course* you'd naturally expect that to put an end to it. But it didn't." She took a sip of coffee, then continued, "If I'm understanding you correctly, this emotional learning that plagues you is essentially the gut-level expectation that if you express anything of your own feelings or views to Van, all manner of abuse is likely to come at you. And up in your head you know that's not true about Van, and yet your whole body believes that expectation, which you first learned as a girl with your dad. Correct? Okay … Keeping all of that in mind, there's something I'm feeling really curious about: Can you remember, in all your years of being married to Van, any time when some direct expression of your feelings or needs spontaneously came out of you, and was *not* followed by any mistreatment from Van?"

That question was met at first by a blank gaze from Julia, followed after several seconds by her eyes darting around as she searched her memory for such instances. Then Julia said, "How weird: The image of our big plasma TV is what's coming up. Oh! I see why! We bought it several years ago after I spontaneously told Van how much I'd *love* for us to watch movies together at home on a big screen! And Van liked the idea. I never thought about that again, until now, but I guess that's an example of what you asked about."

"It sure is," said Diana. "It's a *good* example. And how would your *dad* respond to your saying what you want with strong feelings, in that same way?"

"He'd ridicule me for wanting whatever I said I wanted, as if it's utterly foolish to want that. Or he'd say angrily, 'Who do you think we are, the Rockefellers?'"

Hearing that from Julia, Diana knew that this was the opportunity for launching the memory reconsolidation process, and she said, "So, in looking back at that moment of spontaneously telling Van you'd *love* to have a big-screen TV, just notice that *that clear statement of what you want is what should bring on the abuse*, but what actually happens is Van's supportive response – the very opposite of what your emotional learning expects from a man if you express yourself."

Those suggestions put Julia in touch with *both* her expectation of abuse and, concurrently, her perception that what came was not abuse but good-natured support and cooperation. That juxtaposition is the subjectively felt violation of expectation that initiates the memory reconsolidation process. In response, Julia gazed at Diana, blinking, as her surprised brain was grappling with that initially puzzling juxtaposition. Her neural encoding was unlocking. Diana knew that the first juxtaposition does the unlocking and that a few more are needed to drive the unlearning and the rewriting of the encoding, so she now continued the process by saying, "The big-screen TV is the first memory to surface. What comes next as another instance of Van not responding negatively even though you directly expressed what you were needing or feeling?"

Julia's blinking continued for several seconds, and then she said, "The time he told me he wanted to go sky-diving with a few of his co-workers. That terrified me as soon as he told me, but for a few days my fear and my objection stayed bottled up inside me as usual. My feelings got stronger day by day, until one night they finally burst out of me. I was a sloppy mess of tears, fear, and anger, too, as I told him that this was literally unbearable for me and how could he do this to me. I really expected he'd be absolutely disgusted with me and want a divorce, but I just couldn't hold it in any longer. He seemed stunned to hear that come out of me. Well, we both were. Then we became quiet and just went to bed without talking about it. In the morning, I was in the kitchen when he came in and walked over to stand right alongside me and he said quietly, 'I don't want to do anything that makes you feel so terrible. Going sky-diving isn't so important that it's worth that. Okay?' I turned to him and hugged him and whispered, 'Thank you.' We never talked about it again."

Diana put that incident into the same juxtaposition template as the first one by simply reflecting empathetically back to Julia, "You came out strongly with sharply negative feelings against what he wanted, and you really expected he'd be disgusted with you and even want to divorce you … but what actually happened, again, was a very supportive, caring response from him."

Hearing that from Diana, some tears spilled down Julia's face and in a whispery voice she said, "That's right." Clearly she was touched deeply to realize in this way how different Van's reaction was from the hostile negativity she had been expecting from him. This was an indication that Julia was actually unlearning that expectation. But Diana didn't stop yet. She said, "Can you find one more?"

Almost without delay, Julia said, "Our cat, Lola. The vet said surgery for her cancer could probably make her cancer-free, but the cost would be $1,500. We drove home in silence, and that night Van said it just didn't make sense to him to spend that kind of money on a pet. As usual, I bottled up my feelings for as long as I could. I really, really love our cat as a unique living being. To me she isn't just 'a pet.' I guess this was like the sky-diving episode, but in this I didn't have any big eruption. I had a quiet eruption. At dinner one evening I had no appetite because of this and I was in a pretty dark place, and spontaneously I said, quietly, 'To me, Lola is a family member, not a pet. If we just let her die when we could have saved her, I don't know how I could recover from that.' Van put his fork down and stared at his food for a while, and then said quietly, 'I see. So, go ahead and schedule the surgery.' I said quietly, 'Thank you, Van.' He nodded, and resumed eating, and I went and sat on the couch with Lola."

Diana asked, "And no harsh negative reaction from Van, only that supportive response, in reaction to you saying clearly how you felt, against his wishes?"

"That's right," Julia confirmed, and again a tear rolled down each cheek.

Four months later, at their next lunch together, Diana asked Julia how it had been for her in struggling with the force field. Julia explained, "I've been really looking forward to telling you: Ever since we talked, it's just so clear to me that Van isn't my dad. And now I really can't imagine how I had them as the same. The grip of that emotional learning was like a spell that I couldn't snap out of by my own efforts, but you got me out of it! Now I *know* Van is safe, not just intellectually, so I can say what I need to say to him, and I'm feeling much closer with him. You helped me profoundly, Diana, and I'm grateful."

The process that Diana guided for Julia was simple, but it was exactly the process that the brain requires for recognizing that one of its emotional learnings no longer applies, and unlearning it decisively. It's the same process that happens in the most effective therapy sessions, but as the example of Julia and Diana shows, there is no reason for it to happen only in therapy sessions, because it can happen very naturally in the course of personal conversations. Notice that Julia never felt "therapized" by Diana.

Some other aspects are also worth noticing. Diana did no counteracting of Julia's problematic behavior or emotional learnings, and made no attempt to oppose, prevent, or correct them or to build up preferred behaviors or beliefs. There was no "yes, but" as in, "Yes, but don't you see – Van really isn't like your father!" Instead, Diana focused on setting up the crucial juxtaposition experience, in which Julia had her own direct, lucid encounter with both her existing emotional learning and her own past experiences that contradicted and disconfirmed that emotional learning. It may at first seem counterintuitive not to counteract anything as we're trying to help someone with a problematic pattern. Counteracting in the face of suffering is a deeply habitual and caring human reaction. When someone is having difficulty, we want to get rid of the problem and the suffering, and the most obvious way to do that appears to be through counteracting. However, when we recognize how much more effective the juxtaposition experience is than any type of counteracting, *that in itself is a juxtaposition experience for us as listeners*, and we unlearn and dissolve the automatic tendency to respond with counteractive tactics. The shortest route to alleviating suffering deeply and lastingly is to first acknowledge and empathize with the difficulty, then to listen well enough to understand the coherent emotional learning at the root of the problem, and then to set up juxtaposition experiences, as Diana did for Julia.

Lastly, notice also that not once did Diana tell Julia what she should believe, feel, or do. All Diana did was to prompt Julia's mind and brain to use the process and the knowings already there inside herself. There is a deep satisfaction to be found in being a catalyst for others to use their inherent capabilities for changing and freeing themselves, a satisfaction that further encourages us to be the best listeners we are capable of being.

Don't just take our word for it ...

If we can share our story with someone who responds with empathy and understanding, shame can't survive.

> Brené Brown, *Daring Greatly: How the Courage to Be Vulnerable Transforms the Way We Live, Love, Parent, and Lead*

Too often we underestimate the power of a touch, a smile, a kind word, a listening ear, an honest compliment, or the smallest act of caring, all of which have the potential to turn a life around.

> Leo Buscaglia, *Love: A Warm and Wonderful Book about the Largest Experience in Life*

Emma felt that she could not now show greater kindness than in listening.

> Jane Austen, *Pride and Prejudice*

Listening is about being present, not just about being quiet.

> Krista Tippett, *Becoming Wise: An Inquiry into the Mystery and the Art of Living*

Listening is a magnetic and strange thing, a creative force. The friends who listen to us are the ones we move toward. When we are listened to, it creates us, makes us unfold and expand.

> Karl A. Menninger, *Love Against Hate*

Most people do not listen with the intent to understand; they listen with the intent to reply.

> Stephen R. Covey, *The 7 Habits of Highly Effective People: Powerful Lessons in Personal Change*

You cannot truly listen to anyone and do anything else at the same time.
M. Scott Peck, *The Road Less Traveled: A New Psychology of Love, Traditional Values and Spiritual Growth*

We can't see or understand someone in the moments that we are trying to control what they are saying or trying to impress them with what we are saying. There's no space for that person to just unfold and be who they are. Listening and unconditionally receiving what another expresses, is an expression of love. The bottom line is when we are listened to, we feel connected. When we're not listened to, we feel separate.
Tara Brach, *The Sacred Art of Listening*

The first duty of love is to listen.
Paul Tillich, *Love, Power, and Justice: Ontological Analyses and Ethical Applications*

The most basic of all human needs is to understand and be understood. The best way to understand people is to listen to them.
Ralph Nichols, *Are You Listening? The Science of Improving Your Listening Ability for a Better Understanding of People*

When people talk, listen completely. Most people never listen.
Ernest Hemingway, *Across the River and into the Trees*

So when you are listening to somebody, completely, attentively, then you are listening not only to the words, but also to the feeling of what is being conveyed, to the whole of it, not part of it.
Jiddu Krishnamurti, *The Book of Life: Daily Meditations with Krishnamurti*

Deep listening is the kind of listening that can help relieve the suffering of another person. You can call it compassionate listening.
Tich Nhat Hanh, interview on *Super Soul Sunday* with Oprah Winfrey, June 24, 2012

Welcome friend, come inside, you've come to me …
Maybe there's something sacred that you need,
like someone to listen.

Tori Olds, song lyric "Near to Life"

246

Appendix

Simple first steps to take: exercises to try out with a partner

In Part 2 we shared suggestions for how and when to implement each connector and how to become more aware of any tendency to use disconnectors. Please consider those suggestions as a kind of invitation to practice your new skills, as exercises you can do at any time, alone or with others, to further your experience in connecting more deeply in your relationships.

The exercises described in this appendix are intended for two (or more) people who wish to practice together in an intentional way. They are for increasing awareness and consciousness about your communication habits and the role they play in connecting with or disconnecting from other people.

It's very effective to have a partner to practice with, especially when your partner is as curious and open as you are toward trying out new ways and observing what happens.

The process of lifting old patterns from the unconscious into everyday awareness requires focus, attention, time, openness, and guidance. These partner exercises offer that guidance.

How long to practice each exercise

Plan your practice sessions to be approximately 30 minutes (longer if you're more than two people working together), so that each person has multiple opportunities to practice the described listening behavior.

Even a few minutes of practice on a regular basis add up over time to increased skill. Some exercises may seem easier than others. You may experience nice surprises in everyday life while implementing these new patterns.

How the exercises are organized

The exercises start out quite simply with the listener inviting the speaker to share something, and then listening. That's it. Each additional exercise adds skill and awareness by building on the skills practiced in the previous exercise. It's a natural progression. If the first few exercises are more elementary than your current skill level, you could skip ahead and enter the series at the point where the exercises are becoming useful for you.

Some of the short scripts used in the exercises may sound somewhat formal or exaggerated to you on first reading or first speaking, not at all typical of the way you would normally speak. Try them anyway. The scripts were designed with the explicit goal of giving you the opportunity to try out new ways of communicating and connecting, in order to maximize your experiential learning. For them to feel unfamiliar at first is normal. Once you're fully comfortable with a given exercise, please feel free to repeat it using your own words to express your own emotional truths.

In a few exercises, we ask you to try things out in a *disconnecting* way before then having you repeat the exercise in a *connecting* way. At first glance this may appear to be paradoxical. Why on earth would you want to practice communicating in a disconnecting way? Here's why: to create a distinct *contrast*, which is highly effective for best learning and retention. Often we appreciate an experience in a particularly conscious way when we've just experienced the opposite. Imagine you've been sitting in a freezing cold room for the last hour without a jacket, and now you step out into the warm sunshine ... It's likely you'll have a particularly conscious, vivid experience of the warmth and the well-being it gives you. The same principle is the background behind trying out *disconnecting* from your practice partner before focusing on *connecting*.

Getting the most out of the exercises

We'd like to stress that *reading* the exercises in this appendix is very different from – and not nearly as effective as – *doing* the exercises with someone, and that *most* effective is actually responding with your new patterns in real life and real relationships, and *experiencing* your own feelings and others' reactions on an emotional level when living these patterns and principles.

What if you don't like a particular exercise or don't want to listen to your partner?

When you are in the listener role, if you don't feel that you can honestly speak the proposed script in the exercise with authentic feeling, then it's probably not the right thing for you to be doing right now. There is no shame in this. Simply notice what you are experiencing and be transparent about it. Try reversing the roles and, after being invited in by your practice partner, talk about what's going on for you that's making it unworkable for you to inhabit the listener role.

Structure of a typical practice session

In general, the practice session runs this way:

1. **Person A (speaker) shares** some information or story or experience or memory or goal or dream or vision or … anything real, true, personal, or important, for an agreed-upon number of minutes (between 3 and 10).
2. **Person B (listener) responds** in the way described in the particular exercise.
3. **Persons A and B spend 5 minutes "debriefing"** – sharing with each other what they experienced, noticed, thought, and felt during the exercise.

   Note: When person A is sharing his or her experiences with the exercise, person B only listens, without commenting. When person B is sharing his or her experiences with the exercise, person A only listens, without commenting.
4. **Persons A and B reverse roles** and carry out steps 1–3.

Exercise #1 – Opening your "listening door" and inviting the other person in

In this exercise, you're practicing an open, inviting, and nonjudgmental stance that helps other people feel at home, welcome, safe, and trusting. To that end, you'll be saying specific things that you might not necessarily say out loud in everyday life, although you might actually choose to say them sometimes and with some people.

~ ~ Beginning of exercise ~ ~

Listener: Hi. I'm really looking forward to listening to anything you'd like to tell me. I will listen to you speak, uninterrupted, and I'm curious about your world of feelings and thoughts and experiences.

Speaker: *(speaks about anything at all for 3–10 minutes)*

Listener: *(only listens interestedly, does not comment or interrupt or pose questions)*

~ ~ End of exercise ~ ~

Exercise #2 – Expressing ongoing interest

This exercise builds on the previous exercise of "opening the door" and adds the skill of showing the speaker your ongoing interest in listening to him or her.

When you are in the listener role, you'll start again by inviting the speaker to share something meaningful with you. Then you'll take the opportunities the speaker offers you to remind the speaker of your ongoing interest in listening.

When you are in the speaker role, you'll build some pauses into your speech, so that the listener has a chance to respond with ongoing interest.

~ ~ Beginning of exercise ~ ~

Listener: Hi. I'd like to listen to anything you'd like to tell me and learn more about you. I'm curious about your world.

Speaker: *(speaks about anything at all for 3–10 minutes, allowing frequent pauses to give the listener space to express his or her ongoing interest)*

Listener: Mm–hm ... I see ... *(said with genuine openness in each pause in which the speaker appears to want connection and confirmation of listener's interest)*

~ ~ End of exercise ~ ~

Exercise #3 – Allowing time and space

This exercise builds on the previous exercises of "opening the door" and "showing ongoing interest." We now add the skill of allowing the speaker ample time and space to experience deeper feelings and find the best words to express his or her emotional truths. What a gift!

~ ~ Beginning of exercise ~ ~

Listener: Hi. I'd like to listen to anything you'd like to tell me and learn more about you. I'm curious about your world. And please feel free to take your time and find your own tempo for expressing what's inside. I'm here with you.

Speaker: *(speaks about anything at all for 3–10 minutes, with frequent, extended pauses to focus inwardly; feels free to stare off into space or close eyes to get in touch with inner experience)*

Listener: Mm-hmm … I see … *(said occasionally, with genuine openness, and then silence, allowing the speaker space and time.)*

~ ~ End of exercise ~ ~

Exercise #4 – Openly not knowing what the other person means

A listener doesn't always understand right away how the speaker's statements fit together and make sense. Often there are extended periods of *not knowing* what the speakers means. Sometimes clarity comes simply by listening a bit longer – but not always. This exercise consists of dispelling confusion by asking the speaker what he or she means by a particular word or phrase.

Here's an example of how this might go:

Speaker: People who behave that way don't have any respect for my rights as a citizen of this country!

Listener: Mm-hm … I see … I don't want to assume I know what you mean. I'd like to understand better what you mean by "respect for your rights" …

> When you are in the speaker role, try talking about something that you have strong feelings about. Build in pauses to give the listener a chance to pick out interesting words or phrases to be curious about.
>
> When you are in the listener role, you'll invite the speaker to share, you'll listen openly, and you'll ready your ears for noticing intensely meaningful or

emotional words or phrases. When you find yourself genuinely curious what the speaker actually means by a particular word or phrase, then ask (nonjudgmentally) for more insight on that.

~ ~ Beginning of exercise ~ ~

Listener: *(expresses openness and interest, as in the previous exercises)*

Speaker: *(speaks about a "hot" or personal or intense topic for 3–10 minutes, allowing frequent pauses to focus inwardly and choose what to express next.)*

Listener: *(listens for interesting or "hot" words or phrases, uses speaker's pauses to "not know" and to ask for more insight)* Mm-hm … I see … I don't want to assume I know what you mean. I'd like to understand better what you mean by "[*insert speaker's phrase here*]"

Speaker: *(shares more about that phrase and its meaning to speaker, if this feels welcome.)*

~ ~ End of exercise ~ ~

Exercise #5 – Active listening, accurately and empathically reflected

Now the aim of the listener is to understand the essence of what the speaker has expressed and actively reflect back what has been understood – no more and no less than that.

Here's an example of how this might go:

Speaker: Uh-oh, the long holiday weekend is coming up and I'm not sure how to fit in all the shopping I need to do.

Listener: Sounds as if you're feeling concerned that some things might not get done. Is that right?

~ ~ Beginning of exercise ~ ~

Speaker: *(speaks about any topic briefly)*

Listener: *(listens actively to really "get" what the speaker is saying; then reflects back the message he or she has understood, followed by "Is that right?")*

~ ~ End of exercise ~ ~

Exercise #6 – Empathetic you-messages

You-messages can be empathic and effective for showing the speaker that we've heard and understood what has been said. This is sometimes called "active listening" and functions to reflect back what we've understood. The exercise begins, however, with experiencing the opposite, namely you-messages that disconnect, for example, by lecturing, correcting, admonishing, trivializing, moralizing, etc. This will illuminate the difference especially well.

The speaker's sentences are given below, and your job as listener is to think up, firstly, a disconnecting response using a you-message, and then an alternative connecting response that uses a you-message to show, in a respectful, caring way, that you've understood (as well as you're able to) what you're hearing.

Here are two examples of how this might go:

Example 1

=== *disconnecting response* ===

Speaker: We've managed to stay married for 18 years so far – amazing. If I met my husband now, I wonder whether I would be attracted to him.

Listener: *(answer #1 – disconnecting due to using an unempathic you-message)* Well, that's pretty selfish of you, after he's given you the best years of his life!

=== *connecting response* ===

Speaker: We've managed to stay married for 18 years so far – amazing. If I met my husband now, I wonder whether I would be attracted to him.

Listener: *(answer #2 – connecting by using an empathetic you-message)* You seem to feel as if something may have changed for you in the chemistry between the two of you.

Example 2

=== *disconnecting response* ===

Speaker: Hey, I'd really prefer that we get through a whole meal without being interrupted by cellphone activity.

Listener: *(answer #1 – disconnecting due to using an unempathetic you-message)* You always say that. You apparently think your rules are more important than mine.

=== *connecting response* ===

Speaker: Hey, I'd really prefer that we get through a whole meal without being interrupted by cellphone activity.

Listener: *(answer #2 – connecting by using an empathetic you-message)* Well, your wanting us fully focused on being together for the meal is totally understandable, and I'll try, but I have to admit it's something of a struggle for me to fully pry myself away from this thing.

~ ~ Beginning of exercise ~ ~

Exercise 6a

=== *disconnecting you-message* ===

Speaker: I've been thinking about what kind of an outing we can take on Sunday. I haven't been to the park across town in a long time. The flowers should be beautiful at this time of year. But we'd have to walk slowly due to my leg injury.

Listener: *(answer #1 – disconnecting due to using an unempathetic you-message)*

=== *connecting you-message* ===

Speaker: I've been thinking about what kind of an outing we can take on Sunday. I haven't been to the park across town in a long time. The flowers should be beautiful at this time of year. But we'd have to walk slowly due to my leg injury.

Listener: *(answer #2 – connecting by using an empathetic you-message)*

Exercise 6b

=== *disconnecting you-message* ===

Speaker: I can't go out to eat with you guys this weekend. I'm feeling nervous about money right now. My account's in minus, and it's been a slow month.

Listener: *(answer #1 – disconnecting due to using an unempathetic you-message)*

=== *connecting you-message* ===

Speaker: I can't go out to eat with you guys this weekend. I'm feeling nervous about money right now. My account's in minus, and it's been a slow month.

Listener: *(answer #2 – connecting by using an empathetic you-message)*

———————————

Exercise 6c

=== *disconnecting you-message* ===

Speaker: Hey, I was thinking … If I quit my job, we could start our own business. We have a basement full of stuff we could sell online.

Listener: *(answer #1 – disconnecting due to using an unempathetic you-message)*

=== *connecting you-message* ===

Speaker: Hey, I was thinking … If I quit my job, we could start our own business. We have a basement full of stuff we could sell online.

Listener: *(answer #2 – connecting by using an empathetic you-message)*

~ ~ End of exercise ~ ~

Exercise #7 – Staying focused on the speaker rather than shifting the focus to yourself

As in the previous exercise, this one is a two-part process that begins with a deliberate sampling of the disconnector – in this case, switching the focus to yourself – followed by the connector, staying focused on the speaker.

The speaker's sentences are presented in the three exercises below, and your job as listener is to think up, firstly, a *disconnecting* response that shifts the focus to yourself, and then an alternative *connecting* response that leaves the focus on the speaker. And you don't have to stop after the three exercises provided here; feel free to continue practicing with your own examples.

Here's an example of how this might go:

=== *disconnecting response* ===

Speaker: Oh man, I'm so tired. I really didn't sleep well last night.

Listener: *(answer #1 – disconnecting by shifting focus to him-/herself)* Same here. There was a lot of noise in my building and I couldn't sleep.

=== *connecting response* ===

Speaker: Oh man, I'm so tired. I really didn't sleep well last night.

Listener: *(answer #2 – connecting by keeping focus on speaker)* Hmm, do you know why? Was there some disturbance during the night?

~ ~ Beginning of exercise ~ ~

Exercise 7a

=== *disconnecting response* ===

Speaker: Ooh, I love this song! It reminds me of my childhood.

Listener: *(answer #1 – disconnecting by shifting focus to yourself)*

=== *connecting response* ===

Speaker: Ooh, I love this song! It reminds me of my childhood.

Listener: *(answer #2 – connecting by keeping focus on speaker)*

Exercise 7b

=== *disconnecting response* ===

Speaker: I can't wait for my 18th birthday! Mom and Dad promised me the money for a special trip.

Listener: *(answer #1 – disconnecting by shifting focus to yourself)*

=== *connecting response* ===

Speaker: I can't wait for my 18th birthday! Mom and Dad promised me the money for a special trip.

Listener: *(answer #2 – connecting by keeping focus on speaker)*

Exercise 7c

=== *disconnecting response* ===

Speaker: We live right across the street from a huge old-age home. Sometimes I feel sorry for the residents there.

Listener: *(answer #1 – disconnecting by shifting focus to yourself)*

=== *connecting response* ===

Speaker: We live right across the street from a huge old-age home. Sometimes I feel sorry for the residents there.

Listener: *(answer #2 – connecting by keeping focus on speaker)*

~ ~ End of exercise ~ ~

Exercise #8 – Not giving unsolicited advice

Here the aim is to sharpen awareness of any tendency as a listener to give advice, although the speaker has not actually requested our advice. As in the previous exercises, this is a two-part process that begins with a deliberate sampling of the disconnector – in this case, giving unrequested advice – followed by the connector, not giving unrequested advice.

The speaker's sentences are given below, and your job as listener is to think up, firstly, a disconnecting response that offers unsolicited advice, and then an alternative connecting response that leaves the focus on the speaker's material and assumes that the speaker will ultimately find his or her own solutions.

Here's an example of how this might go:

=== *disconnecting response* ===

Speaker: We've been having lively discussions with the kids about where to go on vacation this year.

Listener: *(answer #1 – disconnecting by giving unsolicited advice)* If I were you, I'd book one of those family-friendly hotel chains.

=== *connecting response* ===

Speaker: We've been having lively discussions with the kids about where to go on vacation this year.

Listener: *(answer #2 – connecting by refraining from giving advice and keeping focus on speaker's content)* Oh, is there a variety of opinions about where to go?

~ ~ Beginning of exercise ~ ~

Exercise 8a

=== *disconnecting response* ===

Speaker: I'm not sure how much longer I can survive this work pressure.

Listener: *(answer #1 – disconnecting due to giving unsolicited advice)*

=== *connecting response* ===

Speaker: I'm not sure how much longer I can survive this work pressure.

Listener: *(answer #2 – connecting by refraining from giving advice and keeping focus on speaker's own process)*

Exercise 8b

=== *disconnecting response* ===

Speaker: It's high time I get back to exercising regularly.

Listener: *(answer #1 – disconnecting due to giving unsolicited advice)*

=== *connecting response* ===

Speaker: It's high time I get back to exercising regularly.

Listener: *(answer #2 – connecting by refraining from giving advice and keeping focus on speaker's own process)*

Exercise 8c

=== *disconnecting response* ===

Speaker: You can't trust politicians these days. They're in it only for the power and the money.

Listener: *(answer #1 – disconnecting due to giving unsolicited advice)*

=== *connecting response* ===

Speaker: You can't trust politicians these days. They're in it only for the power and the money.

Listener: *(answer #2 – connecting by refraining from giving advice and keeping focus on speaker's own process)*

~ ~ **End of exercise** ~ ~

Exercise #9 – The contrast between empathic listening and counteracting

Sharpening awareness of the tendency to counteract (oppose or prevent) is the focus of this exercise. The absence of empathy in a seemingly helpful counteractive response is largely what makes it a disconnector, plus the implication of personal failing.

The speaker's sentences are given below, and your job as listener is to think up, firstly, a disconnecting response that counteracts the speaker's message, and then an alternative connecting response that leaves the focus on the speaker's content and expresses some degree of empathy for the speaker's message.

Here's an example of how this might go:

=== *disconnecting response* ===

Speaker: I'm really nervous about my presentation tomorrow. I've never spoken in front of so many people before.

Listener: *(answer #1 – disconnecting by counteracting)* Oh, come on – you of all people have nothing to be nervous about.

=== *connecting response* ===

Speaker: I'm really nervous about my presentation tomorrow. I've never spoken in front of so many people before.

Listener: *(answer #2 – connecting by remaining empathic)* Sounds as if the bigger audience changes something for you.

~ ~ **Beginning of exercise** ~ ~

Exercise 9a

=== *disconnecting response* ===

Speaker: OMG, this shirt used to fit me. I can't believe how much weight I've gained. I'm shocked!

Listener: *(answer #1 – disconnecting by counteracting)*

=== *connecting response* ===

Speaker: OMG, this shirt used to fit me. I can't believe how much weight I've gained. I'm shocked!

Listener: *(answer #2 – connecting by remaining empathic)*

––––––––––––

Exercise 9b

=== *disconnecting response* ===

Speaker: I've decided it's time to write my will, but it's not easy. I resent that the kids simply expect me to keep giving, giving, giving …

Listener: *(answer #1 – disconnecting by counteracting)*

=== *connecting response* ===

Speaker: I've decided it's time to write my will, but it's not easy. I resent that the kids simply expect me to keep giving, giving, giving…

Listener: *(answer #2 – connecting by remaining empathic)*

––––––––––––

Exercise 9c

=== *disconnecting response* ===

Speaker: My husband wants to move out to the country, but I feel nervous about leaving the city, where everything is so reachable … and all my friends are here. Somehow being in the city gives me a sense of security.

Listener: *(answer #1 – disconnecting by counteracting)*

=== *connecting response* ===

Speaker: My husband wants to move out to the country, but I feel nervous about leaving the city, where everything is so reachable … and all my friends are here. Somehow being in the city gives me a sense of security.

Listener: *(answer #2 – connecting by remaining empathic)*

~ ~ End of exercise ~ ~

Exercise #10 – Assuming the other person's emotional coherence, even without understanding it

This exercise helps build the capability of remembering that the other person's behaviors and feelings have a coherent inner basis, even when we don't understand what the coherence is. In fact, at those times when the other person's behaviors and feelings don't seem to make any sense, it's *especially* important to remind ourselves that they somehow do make sense within that person's unique life learnings.

The speaker in this exercise expresses something extreme, wild, passionate, or controversial that many people would view as unreasonable.

Here's an example of how this might go:

Listener: Hi, I'd like to listen to anything you'd like to tell me.

Speaker: Yeah, you won't believe this! I caught my daughter riding on a motorcycle with that loser she's been seeing. I'm thinking of forbidding her to see him again.

Listener: *(takes a few seconds to recognize own inner reactions)* I'm sure that feeling and responding in that way fully makes sense from your point of view, even if I don't yet understand. But I'd like to, if you'd want to tell me about that.

~ ~ Beginning of exercise ~ ~

Listener: Hi. I'd like to listen to anything you'd like to tell me.

Speaker: *(expresses feelings and behaviors that are extreme, wild, passionate, or controversial …)*

Listener: *(takes a few seconds to recognize own inner reactions)* I'm sure that feeling and responding in that way fully makes sense from your point of view, even if I don't yet understand. But I'd like to, if you'd want to tell me about that.

~ ~ End of exercise ~ ~

Exercise #11 – Repairing rifts

In this exercise we're trying out, as listeners, ways of rebuilding the connection when there has been a rift or conflict. Some ideas:

- Use active and empathic listening to let the other person know he or she has been heard.
- Apologize if something you've done/said/not done/not said has caused the other person distress.

- Express appreciation for the opportunity to communicate openly about the rift or conflict.
- Give a short explanation of what was going on inside you at the time of the problematic incident.
- Ask the other person what he or she would prefer in the future.
- Express what you would prefer in the future, while looking for common ground with the other person.

Here's an example of how this might go:

Speaker: I'm feeling alone with my problems right now, and really sad about that. I tried to tell you what was going on when we were in the living room together yesterday evening, but I got the impression that watching the movie was more important to you than listening to me. So I left. And that's why I've been avoiding you today.

Listener: *(listens actively and empathically)* Oh, I see, you were really trying to communicate something important to me yesterday, and I gave you the impression that you were less important than the movie. I'm truly sorry that I left you with that impression, because you're *very* important to me. And I'm glad you're telling me so honestly and directly, so that we can clear this up. I think I was just tired after a long day at work, and maybe I wasn't very receptive – definitely not as receptive as you needed me to be. Hmm, if something like that happens again, what do you think we could do differently? It's important to me that your feelings aren't hurt.

~ ~ Beginning of exercise ~ ~

Speaker: *(expresses feelings of hurt, disappointment, or anger toward the listener)*

Listener: *(uses many known connectors to repair the rift and restore emotional connection)*

~ ~ End of exercise ~ ~

Index

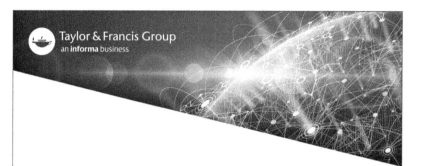

www.ingramcontent.com/pod-product-compliance
Ingram Content Group UK Ltd.
Pitfield, Milton Keynes, MK11 3LW, UK
UKHW010023280225
455677UK00024B/791